Governing Schools: Powers, Issues and Practice

Terry Mahoney

Tutor Organiser for the WEA in the
East Midlands with responsibility for
School Governor Training in Leicestershire

**MACMILLAN
EDUCATION**

First published 1988

Published by
MACMILLAN EDUCATION LTD
Houndmills, Basingstoke, Hampshire RG21 2XS
and London
Companies and representatives
throughout the world

Printed in Hong Kong

Mahoney, Terry
    Governing Schools: Powers, Issues and Practice
    1. School management and organisation —
    Great Britain   2. School boards — Great
    Britain
I. Title
379.1–531–0941   LB2901

ISBN 0–333–45102–3

Contents

Acknowledgements

Any book such as this is a jigsaw of various sources of information, ideas, and opinions, owing much to many people. Grateful thanks go to Russell Gent, District Secretary of the East Midlands District of the Workers' Educational Association who, on learning of my initial attempts to put pen to paper, gave me every encouragement. I am indebted to the District Committee of the WEA East Midlands District for granting me a short period of study leave to expedite my writing. Particular thanks go to: Colin Crane, Chairman of The Bosworth College Governing Body for his helpful comments on Chapter 3, especially his advice on the 1986 Education Act, and on sex education, and the 1987 Teachers' Pay and Conditions Act; Angela Thody of Leicester University School of Education for her helpful comments on Chapter 3 and her permission to use the Infants Cookery lesson excerpt on pages 89–90; Councillor Nick Harris, Chair of Policy Sub-Committee, Manchester Education Committee, for useful background information on the 'Obscene Graffiti' case in Chapter 9; John Izbicki, former education correspondent 'Daily Telegraph' for forwarding to me the 'Wreckers' Charter' on pages 228–30; staff of Leicester University School of Education Library who helped me locate appropriate material; officers of Leicestershire LEA who were always willing to answer my queries; my team of Governor trainers with whom I have shared much discussion on the issues covered in this book; the hundreds of Leicestershire school governors who have attended training courses since 1982 and have enthused me by their commitment and who have taught me more than I have taught them — especial thanks to those who have read draft chapters and commented on them; those heads and teachers with whom I have discussed the role of school governors; my wife, Angela, who read all draft chapters and whose advice and comments were particularly helpful, especially in Chapters 5 and 6; my family which gave me precious space at weekends for writing; my secretary, Wendy Martin, who is one of the few people who can read my handwriting and performed miracles with the untidiest manuscript which was constantly being revised in a vain attempt to keep up to date.

Needless to say, the author bears full responsibility for any inadequacies which remain in the text.

Terry Mahoney

The author and publishers wish to thank the following who have kindly given permission for the use of copyright material:

Advisory Centre for Education (ACE) Ltd. for an extract from 'Rethinking the Governor's Role', *Where,* March 1984: Birmingham Education Committee for an extract from 'Notes for Guidance of Governors and Managers', 1980: Berkshire Department of Education for an extract from 'A Handbook for Governors', 1982: The Bosworth College for an extract from their school prospectus: Bradford Education Committee for an extract from a 1982 policy statement: Cambridgeshire Education Department for an extract from Handbook for Governors: The Chartered Institute of Public Finance and Accountancy for statistical material: Equal Opportunities Commission for extracts from 'Equal Opportunities and the School Governor', EOC, 1985: Gateway Sixth Form College for an extract from their school prospectus: The Hall County Primary School for an extract from their 1982 school prospectus: Controller of Her Majesty's Stationery Office for Crown copyright material: Leicestershire Education Committee for extracts from reports of the Director of Education to Schools Committee: Mail Newspapers p.l.c. for an extract from the *Daily Mail,* 31.1.78: The Publishers Association for statistics concerning Capitation and Book Spending (Primary and Secondary) 1983/84: The Observer for an extract from 'Boys World of Computers' by A. Stevens, July 1983: Maureen O'Connor for extracts from 'How can we possibly cope?', *The Guardian,* 28.5.85 and 'X marks the black spots', *The Guardian,* 23.4.85: The Sherwood Press Ltd. for extracts from 'Multi-ethnic Intolerance', June 1983, 'Teacher and Social Worker – an inevitable conflict', Spring 1984, 'Education and Race – An Alternative View', Winter 1984 and 'The Right Education', January 1985 by Ray Honeyford from *The Salisbury Review:* Times Newspapers Ltd. for extracts from *The Times Educational Supplement,* 24.10.86, 19.11.82, 2.9.83 and 20.12.85: Wreake Valley College for material from their 1984/85 school prospectus.

Every effort has been made to trace all the copyright holders but if any have been inadvertently overlooked the publishers will be pleased to make the necessary arrangement at the first opportunity.

Introduction

There are some 300,000 school governors in England and Wales – no-one knows the exact number. This book is aimed at each and every one of them, whatever their length of experience of serving on a governing body, and whatever group – parent, teacher, LEA, foundation, co-opted – the governor represents. (Governors in Scotland and Northern Ireland will find that much of the content of the book is pertinent to their situation, although there are some slight differences in detail.)

It is assumed that most who read the book will be new governors; if they can supplement the reading of the book with a course of training, it is expected that their effectiveness will be significantly improved. Experience has shown that governors feel themselves to be isolated, unaware of their role and lacking in information. By reading this book the latter two points should be clarified. Of course, not all governors will want, or be able, to attend a course of training, so to assist the solitary reader there are at points throughout the text tasks or discussion points which it is hoped will stimulate you to consult with others. Governors are more effective when they do not feel isolated, when they act as body, and when they act confident in the knowledge that such action is soundly based. It is important to remember that it is only when governors act as a body that they have any real influence or power. Moreover, when governors are seen to be acting diligently and purposefully they will gain the respect they deserve.

Education is a fast-moving, ever-changing entity. However much we try, none of us can ever keep pace with all the changes in legislation, all the new research evidence, all the government reports, all the new books on the subject. This book, which is based on the author's experience of mounting training courses for hundreds of school governors, aims to provide a framework upon which governors can build. It is for this reason that this book is not a slim volume of handy tips for school governors; it is the writer's contention that governors should not be sold short in this way. Consequently, no apology is made for the occasional lengthy expositions in the text; where they are given, it is my experience that, for the new governor particularly, they are required. However, sensible readers will skim through, or omit, sections which they consider do not meet their situation currently, although it is hoped that such sections will eventually prove useful.

There is no doubt that by the time you have read this some of the facts and figures may be out-of-date, some of the research evidence may be questionable. Provided you take appropriate steps to inform yourself, and read the book in a questioning frame of mind, this should not be a problem; the basic framework is there to be built on; the reader is given advice on where to go for more information, and is encouraged to treat this book as merely an introduction, a stepping stone.

All schools should welcome supportive, informed governors. The headmaster whose school was destroyed by fire had a legitimate grievance when he announced that not one of his governors had phoned him or had offered to help clear up. No school wants or deserves such governors. Education is going through turbulent times at the moment, and in many ways it is fortuitous that governors have emerged as even more potentially strong allies than they have hitherto been considered.

The headmaster in the 1970s film 'If' complained that:

> 'Education is like a nubile Cinderella: scantily clothed and much interfered with.'

Governors will appreciate that a similar view may be shared by heads and teachers today when education seems to be under siege. There has rarely been a time when schools have thought themselves to be well resourced and well loved by the general public. Schools have usually felt themselves to be vulnerable to all kinds of outside pressures. Governors function best when their schools view them as partners and friends and can look to them for support. The very fact that you are reading this book is a step in the right direction.

This book is particularly aimed at governors in maintained LEA primary and secondary schools, although governors in special schools and voluntary schools will find that most of the book is also relevant to them. Teachers on management courses may also find the perspective of this book of interest. Governors in independent schools or colleges of further education will find the book of interest, but will need to supplement it with more pertinent information from elsewhere.

The book is arranged in three main sections: the legislative background to governors' powers; the major areas of governors' day-to-day responsibilities; and case studies illuminating the types of problems which can confront governing bodies if they are unlucky and/or careless.

The constant theme throughout the book is that the position of school governor is an important one, but one that needs to be worked at. Since governors are in regular contact with 'professional' teachers, they need to show that they have not only an interest in the pupils and the school, but also a desire to come to grips with wider educational issues, not only their rights as governors; this book seeks to set governors on the path to a fuller understanding of their role in our educational system. It is hoped that once you have read what follows, not only will you be more effective as a school governor, but also you will gain more satisfaction and pleasure from this most important voluntary contribution to the education of our children.

I Why have school governors?

If you have ever asked yourself this question, you may have fumbled around for an answer. Indeed, in one of your next governors' meetings, it might be informative for you to ask if time can be set aside for a discussion on this theme. If nothing else, it would show you the range of views held in your governing body, and the need for some of your colleagues to read this book!

The school governing body has a long and honourable history, having its roots in the old grammar schools of centuries ago. Before there was any state intervention in the provision of schooling, and this has only been in the past century and a half, schools were founded by various religious, charitable or other groups. They were obviously keen to secure value for money so a system of trustees or managers/governors arose, i.e. locally appointed lay people to oversee the running of the school. As the education system grew in the last century, the old model seemed to be a good one to follow. After all, public money was being used to finance schools, therefore members of the public should ensure that money raised by the taxpayer was wisely spent. In your area you are no doubt aware of the existence of Board Schools – schools with their roots in the Victorian age and looking like a cross between a church and a factory. It is probable that such a school was looked after by managers who were responsible for producing an annual report, inspecting premises and equipment, appointing staff, inspecting school records, dealing with complaints against teachers and overseeing such duties as arrangements for school meals, open days and school visits. Indeed, they may have had greater duties than you feel your own governing body has!

Just as today no two Local Education Authorities (LEAs) or governing bodies are the same, so too the history of board schools is not so straightforward as it seems. Our educational system has grown up in a haphazard, patchwork way. We have no state system, centrally administered (although some would argue that there has, recently, been an increasingly centralist feel about our educational system). Rather, we have a national system which imposes certain rules and regulations, such as the need for schooling to be provided at certain stages, the length of the school year, the rights of children with special educational needs, the powers of governors, and so on, but these are administered locally by the LEA; hence the enormous variety of our educational provision in this country. Furthermore, within an LEA district there may be a number of types of educational provision on offer, each reflecting the historical tradition prevalent in that area.

In England and Wales there are some 30,000 primary and secondary schools. For administrative reasons, those established and run by LEAs are know as *county* schools, in which religious education and worship must be non-denominational. Those maintained financially by the LEAs but established by other bodies are known as *voluntary* schools; they were generally established by religious bodies such as the Church of England, the Roman Catholic Church, or the Church in Wales, and are commonly known as church schools. Voluntary or church schools comprise roughly one third of all our schools; they consist of two main groups – aided and controlled, and a small residual group – special agreement.

Aided schools account for more than half the total of voluntary schools. The voluntary body appoints the majority of the governing body which is responsible for finding 15% of the costs of most structural alterations, external repairs, extensions and new buildings, for which grant aid is available from the Secretary of State for Education. The LEA pays for internal repairs and maintenance and other running costs. The LEA fixes the establishment of teachers and pays their salaries, although the governing body appoints the teachers to its service and controls both the secular curriculum and religious education, which must, generally, conform to the trust deed.

Controlled schools do not have a majority of governors appointed by the voluntary body. The governing body has no financial burden: the LEA meets all their costs. Teachers are appointed to the service of the LEA, although governors are consulted over the appointment of headteachers and teachers who give denominational religious education according to the trust deed; such teachers are known as 'reserved teachers'.

Special agreement schools are similar in most respects to aided schools. Some 150 such schools, all secondary, were established by special agreement under the 1944 Education Act. This group is not likely to increase since it is more financially advantageous for voluntary bodies to seek aided status.

In all such voluntary schools, governors appointed by the voluntary body to ensure that the school is run according to the trust deed are known as foundation governors.

On appointment every governor of whatever category is supposed to be issued with a set of 'Instruments and Articles'. These outline your constitution and your powers and should be studied very carefully. They probably have a sentence in them somewhere to the effect that: 'It must be stressed that the instruments and articles of Government are the main authority for the governors who should have them available at all times and should always consult them when in doubt as to their power and authority.'

Those of you who are governors of voluntary schools should study your Instruments and Articles very carefully. If in doubt, ask the chairman of your governing body, or your clerk, to give advice; you may find it interesting to dip into the school's trust deed which may outline some special, local condition that applies to your school.

Do you, as governor, feel welcome in your school, or do you feel a little uneasy? Do you feel you are in the way, or do you detect a little tension in the air sometimes when you deal with staff and the head? If you do, the cause of this unease and tension probably has its roots way back in the past, being a function of the uncertain status governing bodies have been afforded by their school and/or LEA. For example, it may well be that your school or individual members of the teaching staff have had a particularly unfortunate experience with a governor, or governing body; if so, these kinds of memories stick, and, understandably, subsequent relations with the governing body may be a little wary.

It may well be that your very title, 'governor', is one which erects barriers. One writer, admittedly writing on a different theme, put it this way:

'to be governed is to be watched over, inspected, spied on, directed, legislated over, regulated, docketed, indoctrinated, preached at, controlled, assessed, weighed, censored, ordered about by men who have neither right, nor knowledge, nor virtue.'

Perhaps you feel that this is a little too strong. But if you could find another label to apply to yourself, what would it be? Again, this would be a useful talking point with other governors. During my discussions with governors the following words have been suggested: adviser, supporter, watchdog, moderator, facilitator, guardian, manager, director, trustee. It can be argued that at times you are all of these, and more; for example, when financial matters loom large, trustee and director seem appropriate. But is any of these an adequate catch-all? Indeed, some governors may be very happy with the engineering analogy: a governor stops excessive speed and controls underrun.

Your title may not concern you, but have you ever stopped to wonder why you are a governor? Amazingly, some governors appear never to have given this any thought. 'I was just asked,' or 'It seemed like a good idea at the time,' are the kinds of comments sometimes heard when governors are asked the question. Quite clearly, your motives for being a governor will decisively affect the way you perform your duties. As one head put it when talking to a new governor, 'Are you serious in your intentions?'!

And remember, you are just one member of a very diverse group of people: some are there for political motives, others for professional, others religious, others educational, others social, others commercial, yet others parental. One group of governors may feel very suspicious about the others. For example, you may question the motives of the overtly political governor, or you may feel that the very presence of the professional governors (head, teachers) stifles debate or impedes progress. The very diversity of your governing body may be its strength – you have at your disposal many branches of expertise, many useful contacts – or its weakness – the 'chemistry' is wrong, the governing body does not pull together. It is only when you have a united governing body, which works harmoniously, enjoys meeting, knows its school and community, that you have any real chance of success. Any other kind of governing body will be hard to work with, but if you are prepared for the challenge, your efforts will be rewarded.

What qualities do you possess which will make you a good governor? What can you offer your school? Almost one hundred years ago, in 1888, a Royal Commission made an analysis of the work relating to 'school management', from which the following qualities were considered necessary for school 'managers':

'A general zeal for education ..., breadth of view, business habits, administrative ability and the power of working harmoniously with others ..., some amount of education, tact, interest in school work, a sympathy with the teachers and the scholars ..., residence in reasonable proximity to the school, together with leisure time during school hours.'

A better list of qualities would be hard to beat. As you work through the following chapters, you should keep the above list in your mind. Your school needs as much enthusiasm and commitment from its governors as you are able to muster. When you have finished the book, it is hoped your breadth of view will be widened, and your zeal for education will be increased, for you will appreciate more why a school needs its governors.

2 Towards an equal partnership

During the late 1960s and early 1970s there were growing demands for more accountability in the education system, and for more public participation in the running of schools. The 1967 Plowden Report, whose principal focus was on primary education, had highlighted the importance of parental involvement in children's education and looked to the LEAs to encourage more parents as managers. The Plowden Report gave voice to many of the criticisms which were in the air concerning school management: that it was too dominated by local politicians with no real interest in the particular school: that LEAs had abused their powers in grouping schools. Such points tended to get lost as the Report was mainly seen as one that gave a boost to a whole range of initiatives in primary methods. The 1960s, too, were a time when such pressure groups as the Pre-School Playgroups Association (PPA), the Advisory Centre for Education (ACE), and the Campaign for the Advancement of State Education (CASE) were established. In 1970, the National Association of Governors and Managers (NAGM), the governors' pressure group, was launched; local government was reorganised in the early 1970s; Jim Callaghan, Labour M.P., began a national education debate following his Oxford Speech. The 1970s were also the time when worker participation was a constant theme, and teachers wished to see this translated at the school level. And the Conservative party was concentrating on parents' rights. Moreover, during 1976, the William Tyndale Junior School in London was receiving wide, and bad, publicity in numerous articles and reports in the media. The complex issues cannot be dealt with here, but the role of the school managers in this affair – one faction of the managers alerted the press to their dissatisfaction with the school – came under public scrutiny.

Hence, education was increasingly in the limelight, and governing bodies gained more attention than ever before as the possible agents of change at school level, and the main result of this attention was to show just how ineffective and pathetic many governing bodies had become. Where they existed, they were merely rubber stamps and had delegated most of their powers to the heads; and it was clearly in the head's interest to allow such a situation to continue. Governorships were honorific positions to be allocated, they were not something for those who wished to get things done. If they were not reformed, there was the feeling that they might become extinct.

THE TAYLOR REPORT

In the light of the various pressures for reform, Mr Reg Prentice, the Labour Secretary of State for Education, established in 1975 a Committee under the chairmanship of Tom Taylor, to review the current state of governing bodies. Its exact terms of reference were:

> 'To review the arrangements for the management and government of maintained primary and secondary schools in England and Wales, including the composition and function of bodies of managers and governors, and their relationships with local education authorities, with head teachers and staffs of schools, with parents of pupils and with the local community at large; and to make recommendations.'

The Committee reported in 1977 under the title of 'A New Partnership for our Schools', more commonly known as the Taylor Report. If you read nothing else about school government, you are strongly recommended to read this report, especially if you are in the mood of despondency which many governors seem to encounter every so often. The Report is short and to the point, is full of common-sense advice for the school governor, and is perspicacious about the problems facing governing bodies. Many of its recommendations have found their way into subsequent legislation.

The Taylor Report argues strongly that governing bodies should be allowed to exercise their full authority as outlined in the 1944 Education Act, being allowed to determine the general conduct of the school. One of the reasons why governing bodies were so ineffectual was the general level of confusion about the distribution of power and responsibility between LEAs, governing bodies and head teachers. This is partly a product of the way the imprecise wording in the 1944

Education Act is interpreted. We will see that this can still be a problem when we examine Chapters 9 and 10 of this book.

Clearly there was a need for functions to be spelled out more clearly than hitherto, so Taylor proposed that no group on the governing body should be allowed to have a dominating presence; governing bodies should be a forum of all those with legitimate interests in the affairs of the school. The Report's claim to fame was to argue for a *partnership*, in equal proportions, of all the parties concerned for the school's success: the LEA, teachers, parents, community. All schools should have their own individual governing body to make decisions about the way a school operates because of 'the need to ensure that the school is run with as full an awareness as possible of the needs and wishes of the parents and the local community, and conversely, to ensure that these groups in their turn are better informed of the needs of the school and the policies and constraints within which the local education authority operates and the head and other teachers work'.

The Report restated the chain of command through which the 1944 Act had envisaged decisions would be made and information exchanged, i.e. from LEA, through the governors, to the schools, and vice versa. What had happened since 1944 was that the chain was between the LEA and schools, and vice versa, with the governors being effectively squeezed out, relegated.

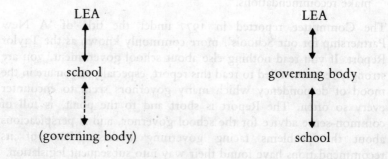

Fig. 1: *Chain of command*

This chain of command was spelt out thus:
The LEA has important statutory duties with regard to education in its area:
(a) the local education authority is responsible for the provision and efficient conduct of county schools and so

must be empowered to prescribe general policies and issue general directions, and must have, if it thinks fit, the final word on any matter affecting the exercise of its statutory duties for such schools;

(b) subject to the overriding functions of the local education authority, the governing body should be in a position to determine the lines on which the particular school is organised and run;

(c) many day-to-day decisions must in practice be made by the head and staff of the school.

Therefore, governing bodies should stand in direct line of responsibility between LEA and school.

According to the Taylor Report (p. 6, para 2.4), the responsibilities of governors cover all or some aspects of:

- the appointment and dismissal of teachers, and other staff
- admission of pupils
- internal organisation and curriculum
- finance
- care and upkeep of premises
- fixing of certain holidays.

Where these responsibilities were concerned, the Report asserted that there was 'no area of the school's activities in respect of which the governing body should have no responsibility, nor on which the head and the staff should be accountable only to themselves or to the local education authority.'

You will understand from this why the Report was received bitterly by the teachers' unions. The NUT called it a busybodies' charter and the NAS/UWT warned that it would give governors 'powers to participate on matters of discipline, the details of school organisation and teaching methods', adding that 'we must register our complete opposition to what is nothing less than an attempt to give lay people the right to dictate to professionally trained and experienced teachers how the teachers should carry out their tasks.'

We now turn to a review of the Report's main recommendations commenting on some of their implications for governors. One of its first recommendations was that the term 'manager(s)' should go and that 'governing body' should be applied to both primary and secondary school boards. In line with this recommendation, which became law in May 1980, we will only discuss governors and governing bodies throughout this account, although old habits die hard, and many teachers and governors still use the former nomenclature.

It is quite evident that the reformed governing bodies needed to have wider representation and that rules for membership needed to be spelt out; this was a direct criticism of the way the LEAs had allowed local political parties to dominate governing bodies. Many of the recommendations Taylor made about membership of the new governing bodies were taken up by the 1980 and 1986 Education Acts which are discussed in the next chapter. Suffice it to say that setting a limit to the number of governing bodies on which any one governor could sit was one of the most important means of ensuring that governors would be encouraged to develop a close interest in their school and more commitment to it. The various means by which the four partners in the governing body were to be elected/selected were discussed, e.g. the community governors should be chosen and co-opted by the other three interest groups. It is a measure of the Taylor Committee's forward-looking views that there is even discussion about possible ways of involving older school pupils in the work of the governing body. (Only a few LEAs experimented with pupil governors, a practice which is now banned since the 1986 Education Act prohibits the selection of governors under 18.)

If the newly constituted governing body were to be effective, there would need to be more efficient lines of communication, not only in the school itself, but between the school, its parents, and community. The governing body was to be truly a forum, where the views from any interested party – LEA, parents, staff, pupils, community – could receive a hearing. This would mean that parents and pupils would need encouragement to develop their own organisation, within the school, with school facilities at their disposal. Governors were even encouraged to produce a standard letter for prospective parents which would establish a working relationship between parents, governors and the school. If communication and co-operation were to mean what they said, and if governing bodies were to be in a position to determine the lines on which their schools were organised and run, then teachers, via their teacher governor, or individually, should have access to the governing body. Moreover, if a governing body is to be accountable to its community, then, subject to any confidential issues, the minutes of its proceedings and any other notices and agendas should be made available in the teachers' common room, and should be open to inspection by staff and parents; additionally 'non-members' or observers should be admitted to all meetings. This idea of accountability is taken even further in the relevant sections of the 1986 Education Act which deal with access to governors' papers, provision of written public statements concerning the curriculum and sex education, and the production of an annual report to be discussed at an annual parents' meeting – see next chapter for fuller details. (This chapter concludes with a short section on making meetings more effective, which is aimed at new members of the governing body who feel isolated and powerless at the termly governors meeting.)

The next controversial section of the report dealt with the curriculum. This was the area of governors' responsibilities which had been most neglected. The 1944 arrangements, which gave governors their legal powers in this area, were spelt out: it was the duty of the LEA to determine the general education of the school and its place in the local educational system, subject to which the governors have the *general direction of the conduct and curriculum of the school* (my emphasis), subject to which heads were to control the internal organisation, management and discipline of the school. Few governors realised the significance of this division of responsibilities. In a 1944 House of Commons debate, Mr R.A. Butler, President of the Board of Education, explained the intent of the legislation thus:

'The governing body would ... have the general direction of the curriculum as actually given from day to day within the school. The head teacher would have ... responsibilitiy for the internal organisation of the school, including the discipline that is necessary to keep the pupils applied to their study, and to *carry out the curriculum in the sense desired by the governing body*' (my emphasis).

Whilst in general the LEAs and teachers' unions tended to wish to keep the status quo, that is, no governors' interference in the curriculum, parents and community representatives tended to want some influence. It was the Taylor Committee's view that the school is not an end to itself; that it is vital that teachers had the support of people outside school in the increasingly difficult task of reaching its objectives in a much-changed world. Schools are vulnerable to public opinion, and rightly so, therefore teachers need informed support; the case for a partnership was made once again. However, a big duty was to be placed on governors: they should be given by the local education authority the responsibility for setting the aims of the school, for considering the means by which they are pursued, for keeping under review the school's progress towards them, and for deciding upon action to facilitate such progress. A number of steps were outlined to help governors: they should involve heads and teachers, make school visits, and invite the advice of local advisers and inspectors. To show that they had lived up to their expectations, they were to present a written appraisal of the school's progress within four years. Perhaps in order to sweeten the pill for the teachers, it was stated that 'the teachers should continue ... to be responsible for deciding how to teach the members of his own class in the light of his own capacities and any general teaching policies adopted generally in the school ... all decisions involving questions of consistency of approach and continuity of method are likely to be of sufficient importance to concern the governing body'.

The 1986 Education Act attempted to strengthen the governors' curriculum role as can be seen in the next chapter. For a fuller discussion of governors and the curriculum, see Chapter 4.

It was an intention of the 1944 Act that governing bodies should have a significant financial role, preparing estimates for their schools of their individual income and expenditure and submitting these estimates to the Local Education Authority. In reality, this rarely happened, partly because governing bodies were not given this opportunity by the LEA, and partly because of the complexities of LEA financing, much of which is subject to national controls (e.g. teachers' salaries, rate support grants), centralised budgeting and tight local authority financial timetables. However, there was, and still is, a view that only when governors have some responsibility for school finances – say to do with the particular requirements of their own school – would they have any real feeling of serving a useful purpose. Clearly, overall control must lie with the LEA which has a responsibility to balance the books county-wide, but the Taylor Committee recommended that LEAs involved their governing bodies in submitting estimates in the spirit of the 1944 legislation, and that governing bodies were given powers to incur their own school-based expenditure; it was recognised, however, that special studies would need to be made so that governors were given advice on good practice.

Because of the complexities of this issue, it is likely that your governing body has never had to submit its own estimates, or even to rubber stamp the authority's estimates for your school. But change is in the air: there are some pilot projects examining the way in which governing bodies can be given more financial powers in LEAs such as

Solihull, East Surrey and Cambridgeshire. For example, since 1982 Cambridgeshire LEA has had a pilot scheme involving six secondary schools and one primary school in the control of their finances. It was felt that this was one way of attracting good governors when the responsibilities of governing bodies were limited. With the head teacher, these governing bodies have financial discretion in relation to:

- allocating teacher staffing
- supplying cover for occasional teacher absence
- all non-teaching staff other than those in school meals and ground maintenance
- rent and rates
- fuel, light, water, cleaning materials, protective clothing and laundry
- furniture and fittings
- text books, library books, stationery and materials
- exam fees
- administration, educational and domestic equipment
- printing, office stationery, postage and telephones
- educational visits, staff travel and subsistence income

On top of this frightening list of added responsibility, there was even further scope for school-based community education, school meals, minor maintenance and repairs and Schools Library Service. At the end of its pilot stage this scheme was judged as successful, and although it is clear that enormous extra burdens were placed on LEA officers, heads and governing bodies, the scheme has been extended. Such local experiments are to be welcomed for the faith they show in the potential of governing bodies. Indeed, as a result of Section 29 of the 1986 Education Act which deals with finance, governors are to be given an increased financial role as envisaged in the 1944 Education Act – consult the following chapter for precise details. In future years your LEA may operate a scheme like Cambridgeshire's, in which case your governing body will be radically reformed. Your workload will increase dramatically, as will your responsibilities.

Of course governors already have a minor, though important, role over one source of income completely separate from LEA finances – the school fund, (sometimes known as the voluntary fund). This consists of monies coming into the school as a direct result of such school-based initiatives as photograph sessions, school trips, spelling bees and charity efforts. This fund can amount to only a few hundred pounds annually, or to tens of thousands of pounds in the larger secondary school. The day-to-day management of this fund is undertaken by the headteacher who has control of its security and banking. In some areas, governors have to give their approval before this money is spent, and in most authorities governors are required to receive an annual financial statement from the head and to approve the audited accounts; in other words, although governors have, generally, no say in how this fund is spent, they have a responsibility to ensure that everything is above board. It should be remembered that misappropriation of school funds is one of the most common disciplinary offences concerning staff.

The Taylor Report called for more governor involvement in all staff appointments. All the evidence suggested that governors were allowed very little scope in the appointments procedure, apart from in a few progressive LEAs. Taylor's hopes for increased involvement in this key area have been met by the 1986 Education Act which spells out in detail the governors' role in the appointment and dismissal of staff. The relevant sections are outlined in the following chapter, and Appendix C gives a fuller discussion of the appointments procedure and teachers' salary scales; the sensitive issue of staff dismissal is covered in Chapter 10 of this book.

Apart from these most important of functions, the Taylor Report had significant points to make about other neglected fields of governor responsibility: admissions, suspensions and expulsions, school premises (including care and maintenance, lettings) and holidays. Where admissions were concerned, the feeling was that appropriate arrangements should be made by the LEA, in consultation with the governors. There could be no excuse for excluding governors, who may well have special local knowledge and may want to try to influence LEA policy, say over proposed changes in catchment areas. Indeed, every so often such proposed changes are the subject of a great deal of heated local controversy. Of course, governors of aided and special agreement schools already have control over admissions, and, as a result of the 1986 Education Act (Section 33), all governors will at least be consulted by the LEA annually concerning admissions. Moreover, now that parental choice has been given more prominence as a result of the 1980 Education Act, parents being able to appeal if their choice of school is denied, it is quite clear that governors cannot be excluded from discussion about admissions.

Taylor felt that the area of suspensions and expulsions was yet another which needed to be tidied up, with more specific guidance as to the responsibilities and powers of governors, heads and LEAs. Suspensions were common, but procedures were unclear, and the child's best interests were not always protected. Consequently, the governing body, with its concern for the welfare of the school and the pupils, was seen to have an important role to play. The case of the suspended pupils in Poundswick, Manchester, focuses on this very sensitive area and is the subject of a chapter at the end of this book. This, too, was another area taken up by the 1986 Education Act; the relevant sections are outlined in the next chapter.

The governors' responsibility in relation to the condition and state of repair of premises is perhaps the one which they feel most confident about; it is, after all, an area of responsibility over which teachers have no real authority. Indeed, your governing body probably feels more comfortable discussing smelly toilets and broken windows than any other issues. Research shows that governing bodies spend their time discussing fabric maintenance, safety and other administrative details, rather than educational issues. The Taylor Report simply confirmed governors' responsibilities with regard to care and maintenance of school premises; you should be aware of the important Health and Safety Regulations which apply to your school, and be meticulous in reporting inadequacies to your LEA. Additionally, you should be aware that your school is an important community resource, and that you may be called upon to decide to what uses the school premises may be put out of school hours. Problems can arise from outside use, and governors, especially of large community colleges, may spend a considerable part of their meetings discussing such issues. Section 42 of the 1986 Education Act confirms governors' control of premises outside school time. Where holidays were concerned, it was the intention of the 1944 legislation that governors had powers to grant occasional holidays up to ten days in any one year. Because of the LEA problems of arranging transport, co-ordinating local industrial holidays and similar considerations, many LEAs took the occasional holidays to themselves, thus imposing standard practice throughout their area. However, Taylor considered that governors should be allowed to exercise their power to grant occasional holidays, in consultation with the LEA. As with many aspects of governors' roles, this is something where practice varies throughout the country.

The need for governors to receive training was the theme of one short section of the report; this will be dealt with fully in Chapter 11 of this book.

The Taylor Report was not empowered to make recommendations concerning the 9000 voluntary schools (1976 figures), but it did recommend that as far as possible governors of such schools be encouraged to adopt the practice of the reformed governing bodies of the county schools.

For those who are interested in reading about the historical development of governing bodies, the Report ended with a most informative historical retrospect.

It is the fate of many government reports that their impact is small, and they end up on library shelves gathering dust. For a time it appeared that this might be the case with the Taylor Report. However, subsequent legislation confirms that the good advice of Taylor did not go unheeded as the next chapter reveals.

MAKING THE MOST OF MEETINGS – A POSTSCRIPT FOR THE INEXPERIENCED GOVERNOR

Schools are best served by a united governing body which uses its termly meeting(s) efficiently and effectively. It is a sad fact that many people, especially parents, are discouraged from standing as school governors because they do not feel confident about taking their place on the 'board'; they are intimidated by the formal, business aspects of the governors' role which are played out in the governors' meetings. It is understandable, but regrettable, that many potentially excellent governors feel that they lack the experience and skills which, to be sure, are essential if they are to make the most of meetings. This short section aims to dispel some of these fears.

The governors' meeting is a committee meeting. All kinds of committees constitute the fabric of an organised society, and many people are likely, at some stage in their life, to become involved in a committee. Committees exist to advise and to get things done; this is their only purpose in life. The governing body is a committee which exists to advise the head and get things done for the school. Remember that your governing body is an important element in your local education authority structure. Your LEA is responsible, through its various committees, for administering many schools: it is responsible for an enormous budget and a small army of employees, as well as many buildings, and, of course, the education of many thousands of school children. This it cannot do by itself. Hence your governing body serves as an important link in the bureaucracy which is your LEA. As you read through this book, you will learn how many responsibilities and duties your governing body has as a legally constituted body; it can only fulfil its obligations by collectively meeting to discuss its business and proposing the best course of action (e.g. concerning appointing new staff members, making a case for resurfacing the playground, working out its sex education policy, deciding arrangements for the next governors' visit, or whatever) for your particular school in its particular community at a particular point in time.

Many of us feel uncomfortable in committees because we do not like to expose our ignorance of the procedures involved. Governors will find that they are given a good deal of support by the LEA, and more is available if governors ask. All governors are given copies of their Instruments and Articles on appointment. The Instrument of Government outlines the composition of the governing body, specifying who can be appointed to serve on a governing body, how they are appointed, and how they are to conduct their business. The Articles of Government outline your responsibilities, what you can do and are expected by law to do. The two documents together are generally known as your Instruments and Articles; they are legal documents which should be freely available to you. In other committees they would be known as 'the constitution', and your possession of them signifies that you are a member of a committee which is legally constituted and has a number of legal responsibilities. You should make it your business to read through these documents – often combined into one booklet – so that you are acquainted with them. You will probably also find that your LEA issues its governors with a handbook of guidance. Although this does not have the same legal status as the Instruments and Articles, it is nevertheless an important document and one which, like the Instruments and Articles, will repay careful reading. You should have these documents available at all times. If there are parts of your Instruments and Articles or handbook of guidance which you do not understand, then ask the clerk to the governing body, a fellow governor, the chairman, or the head for clarification. This will not be taken as a weakness on your part, rather as an expression of interest and an indication of your commitment to your governorship. You will also feel more prepared and knowledgeable if you have a good working knowledge of the relevant provisions of the 1980, 1981 and 1986 Education Acts as summarised in Chapter 3 and Chapter 7 of this book. This is not to say that an effective governor needs to be a legal expert. Far from it. But you need to have some understanding of the extent of your powers and responsibilities. The very fact that you are reading this book is a further indication that you are actively seeking the kind of information which will help you play a significant role in governors' meetings: it is much more rewarding participating in a meeting when you understand what is happening, and you feel you are able to contribute. If you can spare the time, there are books on committee procedures in your local library (the further reading section at the end of this chapter gives some details), and you may find an adult education class entirely devoted to committee effectiveness.

As governing bodies become more representative following the 1986 Education Act, and as the skilled politicians who know all the rules and regulations relinquish their places, governing bodies may become less formidable. If you still feel nervous about your ability to play a full and active role in your termly meeting(s), remember that attendance at these meetings, though vitally important, is only one aspect of your role, and that as you become more acquainted with the school and your duties, you will grow in confidence.

You are not alone if you feel 'inadequate'. One study found that parent governors were the least effective committee members, basically because they were unaware of the contributions they could make. But this does not make them any less important. It is not unknown for governors to ask questions such as:

'Am I allowed to put items on the agenda?' (asked by a chairman of six years' experience)

'What do I do if I'm unhappy with the minutes?' (asked by a G.P. parent governor)

'Should we have the headteacher's report sent to us in advance? We always receive it on the day.' (asked by an 'inexperienced' parent)

'What can we do if the discussion rambles on with the same points made again and again and no attempt by the chairman to sum up or draw the discussion to a conclusion?' (asked by an LEA nominee with four years' experience)

Such questions may reveal a basic lack of knowledge of committee procedures, but such knowledge can be gained, if not from books and courses, then from close observation of what goes on around you in the committee itself.

Some governors are worried that since they are new to the governing body, their views will not be listened to. This is the understandable worry of any person entering a formal group for the first time. Remind yourself that you are there because you were elected or selected, that you have a legitimate place as an *equal* member on the governing body. Your view should carry as much weight as any other governor's since you are a group of equals, an *equal partnership*. This important point notwithstanding, it may well be that you spend the first meeting or two as a silent, frustrated member. Turn this silence and frustration to advantage. Each governing body has a history of its own, a particular style of operation, peculiar characteristics (or characters). Spend your early meeting(s) *observing* the governing body. How does the chairman conduct business? Who seem to be the influential governors? How do successful governors make their points? How are decisions reached? Do like-minded governors sit together? Do you detect evidence of behind-the-scenes wheeler-dealering? If you wish to make the most of your time on this particular governing body, it makes sense to act according to your observations.

You will probably notice that the chairman is the most influential member of the governing body and is usually the person who sets the tone of the meeting. Now that governors elect their chairman annually, the chairmanship is more vulnerable, and it is likely that chairmen will work harder to impress, if reselection is desired. It is not unknown for governing bodies to change out of recognition after the appointment of a new chairman, even though the membership of the governing body is unchanged, so vital is the role. You may find that a separate, private meeting with the chairman early in your governorship will pay dividends. At this meeting you can discuss your concerns, interests and wishes. It would be an insensitive chairman who failed to make subsequent use of the expressed interests and expertise of a new fellow governor. A similar meeting with the headteacher would pay similar dividends. Similarly, between meetings you may find it useful to meet with one or more governors to discuss the work of the school and the role of the governing body. It cannot be emphasised too much that governors do not have the power to act as individuals, unless delegated to undertake special tasks on behalf of the governing body; this applies especially to the chairman. Your termly meetings are the only occasions in which the governors, acting corporately, can advance the interests of their school. Hence governors have a duty to prepare themselves in advance and to play a full and active part in meetings.

What happens at the governors' meeting? This is usually convened by the clerk to the governors (sometimes known as the correspondent) and you should receive, preferably at least a week in advance, various background papers concerning your meeting. You should do your best to read through these papers at least once before the meeting so that you have some idea of the nature of the business at hand and can plan the part you will play in the meeting (e.g. are there any questions you will ask, is there any information you can give, will you be proposing a resolution?) You may gain some confidence if you share this preparation with a fellow governor.

The *Agenda* sets the scene for the meeting; it provides the structure for your business. All committees have an agenda which, by custom, follows a set pattern. Where governing bodies are concerned, practice varies throughout the country. For some, especially primary schools, the agenda is arranged by the LEA and is the same for all schools; for others, the agenda is unique to the school. If you are not sure how your agenda is assembled, ask the chairman or clerk. It is especially important to know the procedure for putting items on to the agenda – it is, after all, the governors' meeting, not the LEA's or clerk's.

Now that it is a legal requirement for governing bodies to elect their chairman annually, you will probably find at your initial meeting that the first business conducted is the election of the chairman and vice-chairman for the ensuing year. If only one person is nominated and seconded, then that individual becomes the chairman or vice-chairman. If more than one person is nominated and seconded, a vote will be taken. You may use your vote, or decide to abstain since you do not know the candidates. There is nothing to stop you from nominating your own candidate, but you will need to have asked him/her if he/she is willing to stand, and it makes sense to have briefed a seconder. However, since this may be your first meeting, it is unlikely that you will be involved in nominating, or being nominated; this is something you may aspire to eventually. Votes for co-options may also be taken at this early stage, or at a subsequent meeting. It is normal practice for the chairman to welcome new governors to the meeting as a way of introduction; now is your big chance to make yourself known to the rest of the governing body, so acknowledge any welcome with a smile or make some short statement of thanks.

Agendas start with an *Apologies for absence* item. It is courteous to inform the clerk if you are unable to attend. You must remember that if you miss three consecutive meetings you are, under the 1981 regulations (see page 52), eligible for removal from the governing body. If you take your duties seriously, you will do all you can to attend every meeting, arranging your diary accordingly. You cannot be an effective governor if you fail to attend, for whatever reason, the majority of meetings. If you find attendance at meetings difficult, you should examine whether you ought to keep your place on the governing body. There may be others willing, and able, to take your place. No governing body wants, or can afford, to carry dead wood.

You will be asked to approve the *Minutes of the previous meeting*. If this is your first meeting, you will keep quiet at this point! The minutes, which are a record of the meeting, should be a correct record. If there are inaccuracies, now is the time to point this out; if others agree with you, propose an amendment to the minutes which you believe more accurately reflects the discussion and/or decision(s) of the previous meeting. Since up to four months may pass between meetings and people's memories fade, you may find it useful to take your own notes of a meeting, especially of the key decisions. The chairman will sign the minutes, once they are approved as a correct record.

The minutes now serve a number of functions: they must be available – along with the agenda – for public inspection at the school; copies will be kept by the local authority and will be read by staff in the education department (including the chief education officer) as a way of keeping their finger on the pulse of your school; they will form an important record of your governing body's deliberations and can be referred to in the months and years ahead (this may be useful if you need to prove a point); and, eventually, these minutes will be an historical record.

You will procede quickly to a *Matters arising* section which should be a brief interlude for discussing any issue from the previous meeting which is not covered in the agenda. Badly-run meetings spend too much time on this section at the expense of more important agenda items.

The Headteacher's report will constitute the major item of most meetings. Since you need time to digest the information contained in this report, it should be written and circulated at least a week in advance; verbal reports should no longer be acceptable. Feel free to question the headteacher about information contained in the report; the writer will be flattered that you have taken the trouble to read it and, since there is so much information that cannot be contained in such a report, most heads will be pleased that their reports stimulate debate. The head's report is not a news broadcast which must be received by a passive audience.

Visiting governors' reports feature as a prominent item on some agendas. Some take the form of a verbal account of the official governors' termly visit (such visits are organised in a variety of ways: in some governing bodies a rota system operates in which governors only have one opportunity every few years to make an official governors' visit. This is clearly not sufficient. Some schools arrange for two governors to visit every month. It is up to your governing body to arrange its own pattern of visiting governors which provides them with real opportunities to get to know the school during their governorship). Visiting governors' reports are best written and circulated in advance of the meeting for the same reasons as outlined in the previous paragraph. Your clerk should be able to help in the production and circulation of these reports. Now that governors have a duty under the 1986 Education Act to produce a brief annual report about their school and to present it at the parents' meeting, written visiting governors' reports (and headteachers' reports) may be drawn upon as source material.

Other agenda items, which may precede the visiting governors' report item, might include a report by the chairman on any action he has taken on the governing body's behalf, issues specifically raised by the chairman, a governor, the LEA or the voluntary body, e.g. details of a letter of complaint from local shopkeepers about unsupervised children in the local shopping arcade at lunchtime; discussion of a local authority policy statement on equal opportunities; receiving a report about some government legislation which affects the work of the governing body; approving the LEA financial statement, or whatever.

The agenda will conclude with the *Date of the next meeting*. For obvious reasons it is customary to plan meetings well ahead, usually for the year, and at times convenient to most governors.

It is standard committee practice to end an agenda with *Any other business (AOB)*. Such business is taken at the chairman's discretion and usually takes the form of short, non-controversial items which have come to light since the agenda was assembled (e.g. asking the clerk to send a letter of congratulations to a teacher whose work has gained the school some good publicity). In extreme cases some urgent item may be discussed here: say an allegation made only that day about a member of staff. However, since towards the end of a meeting members of the governing body may have reached the limit of their concentration, and since some governors may already have left the meeting (a practice which is not to be recommended), it is unfair to use this agenda slot for such items. It is because the AOB slot has been abused on some governing bodies (as on other committees) that some authorities prefer to exclude this item.

Such is the structure of a typical governors' meeting which may last little over one hour to a marathon five or more hours if some really controversial issue is at stake – see Chapters 9 and 10 for examples. Two hours is about as long as anyone can remain at ease and efficient in a business meeting before fatigue sets in. It used to be the case that governors busied themselves with trivial, non-educational business at such meetings, taking on the air of cosy social occasions at which tea and biscuits were taken. One small survey of governors' minutes concluded:

'Most ... governing bodies spend their time discussing accommodation, fabric maintenance, safety matters and other administrative details. They spend little time discussing educational aims in general, or the curriculum of their schools in general. Thus, although in theory these boards are seen as a means through which the professional educationalists are made accountable to a locally recruited lay body, in fact most ... governors are reluctant to discuss the curriculum or other major educational objectives, and seem content to busy themselves with time-consuming administrative matters.' (Bacon, 1978, p. 228–9)

The situation has changed dramatically since that study and it is hoped that the extract does not describe your meetings.

At the other extreme from the cosy social governing body is the overtly political board. Since governing bodies are part of an authority's political structure, since they compose a political element, (especially in LEA nominees, although it can be argued that anyone who puts him or herself forward for selection or election to such a group is a political animal), and since they involve making crucial decisions, governing bodies can attract people whose motive for membership is questionable. They know their Instruments and Articles inside out, are well versed in committee procedures, and seem to do their best to dominate and hijack most meetings. In some parts of the country they are known as 'wreckers' and an extreme, and it is to be hoped, isolated, case of their tactics is featured on pages 228–230 of this book.

Clearly, what every school deserves is a governing body which is effective because it is interested and concerned. This requires governors who know how to do their bit in meetings and know their way round the procedures. This is not to say that you need to know the A–Z of committee procedures so that you continually chip into meetings with 'points of order'; such meetings become tedious and fail, by and large, to transact the business on the agenda (indeed, this may be the motive behind the interruptions). However, it helps if you know how to get the governing body to reach a decision. In many instances the chairman will sense the mood of the meeting and sum up a discussion without a vote being necessary. Sometimes it will be necessary to put an issue to the vote. This will require a governor to propose a motion, suitably seconded by another governor. A motion is a device for moving business along. There is an art in framing motions, and they require careful construction. Generally they combine three main components:

● an identification of the sponsors of the motion
● an explanation of why the motion is necessary
● decisions about *who* should take *what* action, and *when*.

If you have a motion, your version will be read out, then discussed and put to the vote, the chairman asking for those in favour, those against, and abstentions. The clerk will normally count the votes so that the result can be recorded. For example, you may propose that:

'This governing body, while appreciating the many demands made on the clerk's time, calls for all papers connected with the governors' meeting to be sent by the clerk to governors at least 10 days in advance of any meeting'

or that:

'The governing body requests that the headteacher consult the staff and report on the place of competitive sports in the school curriculum at the next governors' meeting.'

If your motion does not have the support of the governing body, this may signify that it was badly framed or that you are a voice in the wilderness on this particular issue; you must be prepared for a disappointment. Before your motion is discussed it may be challenged by another committee member who wishes to propose some amendment to the wording. In this case, and providing a seconder is found, the amendment is discussed first. If this receives support, the amended motion is discussed and put before the meeting for the final vote.

Meetings can become bogged down with motions and amendments and a good chairman will ensure that the meeting does not deteriorate into a complicated web of procedural devices. However, if you wish to get things done, you have to ask someone to do them for you, and this is where the motion comes in. Once the motion has been moved, seconded and carried by a meeting it becomes a resolution, which must be acted upon. Even though you may have arrived at a resolution, you will still need to ensure that it is, eventually, followed through to the governing body's satisfaction.

Some governors are very good at manipulating the structure of meetings to their best advantage, but not in the destructive way of the 'wreckers'. They know that important business is best placed early in the agenda before participants become jaded. They appreciate the social psychology of meetings, sitting next to those whom they know share similar views, and opposite those they may be likely to take issue with. They are involved in every aspect of the meeting, because they have prepared themselves for it and they are keen for it to be a worth-while and fruitful meeting for the school. A meeting can only be as good as those who attend it. If none of you speak, there is no meeting. If you all approach a meeting positively, you will get things done: there is a saying that 'it is the squeaking hinge that gets most grease'.

As the occupant of a position on the governing body, you have been elected or selected as an individual in your own right. You are not a delegate, nor can you be delegated to act in a particular way. Occasionally you may find yourself in a difficult position since you may be under pressure from different factions each with a strong, and in their view, legitimate case to make. In such instances your role will be to weigh up the pros and cons, but to act according to your own beliefs.

The issue of confidentiality is one that concerns new governors. In a sense, everything you discuss at your meeting is confidential, especially where individuals are concerned (e.g. a pupil or staff disciplinary case). As a member of a legally constituted public body you are given qualified privilege which means that within your meeting you may speak, or give a written report, about any issue without fear of prosecution for defamation providing what you say or write is not malicious. Consequently, it would be improper if everything said or reported at a governors' meeting were open to public scrutiny. However, governing bodies are now more accountable: minutes and other relevant documents relating to your meetings are available for public inspection; annual parents' meetings are held at which the governors' annual report is discussed. Subsequently, the issue of confidentiality is changing so that many governing bodies now agree that, unless agreed by the governing body as a whole, the gist of what they discuss is no longer veiled in secrecy.

If you feel frustrated that your governors' meetings are too full of business, or that important issues are glossed over, remember that your termly meeting is a minimum requirement. Many governing bodies meet more frequently, some at least twice per term. As your responsibilities increase as a result of the 1986 Education Act, you may feel that more meetings are appropriate. This is an issue which can be raised at a governors' meeting (and may be settled by taking a vote on a suitably worded motion). In any case, under Section 4 of the 1980 Education Act, any three governors may request a special meeting. You may not prove popular if you exercise this right, but at times you need the courage of your convictions. It may emerge, of course, that such a meeting fails to reach its quorum (i.e. three governors, or one third of the governing body (rounded up to the nearest whole number), whichever is greater – this rule applies to *all* governors' meetings). If your fellow governors do not wish to exceed the burden of three meetings per year and object to special meetings, it may help if you suggest the formation of sub-committees (say to draft the annual report) and/or working parties (say on equal opportunities within the school) as devices to spread the load between meetings.

For those governors who still doubt their potential contribution to the governing body and who feel themselves to be little fish in a big unfriendly pond, it is worth mentioning the findings of Lewis Carroll, author of *Alice in Wonderland*, about committees: apparently, if in a committee of 21, a group of 4 agree, then there is an 83% chance that their point of view will be carried if everyone else votes randomly; this increases to a 98% chance of success if a group of 6 in the same committee votes one way, others voting randomly. So, even though you may regard your meetings as a Mad Hatter's Tea Party, you may find that if you make your case well you do have real power to influence your fellow governors and to play an important part for your school via your meetings.

FURTHER READING

Bacon W.	'Public accountability and the schooling system', *Harper and Row* 1978
Brooksbank K., Revell J., *et al.*	'County and Voluntary School', *Councils and Education Press* 1982
DES	'A New Partnership for our Schools' (commonly known as the *Taylor Report*), *HMSO* 1977
Janner G.	'On Committees', *Gower* 1986
Locke M.	'How to run committees and meetings', *Macmillan* 1980
Sallis J.	'School Managers and Governors: Taylor and After', *Ward Lock Educational* 1977

3 Getting in on the Act: the legal basis to governors' powers

The constant thread running through the history of education in Great Britain has been the partnership which has evolved between the churches, local and central government, governing bodies and parents; into this partnership has been woven a complex set of duties and responsibilities, which successive pieces of education legislation have sought to clarify and strengthen. This chapter highlights in particular the 1980 and 1986 Education Acts which are of especial importance to school governors, since they seek to clarify and strengthen the governor's role and power.

THE 1986 EDUCATION ACT

This Act, which extends to England and Wales almost exclusively, was described by the Secretary of State for Education as the largest and 'certainly one of the most significant pieces of legislation since the Butler Act of 1944'. Its main provisions relate to school government, including securing more parental participation; the composition of governing bodies and the allocation of functions between the governing body, the local education authority and the headteacher. The main other provision of this Act concerns the controversial issue of teacher appraisal, which was inextricably bound with the long-running teachers' dispute which had reached a temporary lull during this period.

The intention of this Act is to raise standards by improving the management of schools and improving teaching quality. A DES Press Release claimed that as a result of this Act 'the governing body of each of the 30,000 maintained primary and secondary schools in England and Wales will be re-established as the main focus for its school's life and purpose'. Where governing bodies are concerned, the Act contains no major surprises, its intentions having been publicly rehearsed and debated since the 1984 Green Paper, 'Parental influence at School', and the 1985 White Paper, 'Better Schools'; details of which can be found later in this chapter and in the Appendices.

Where the exact dates of implementation are known at the time of writing, the details are given in the text; for such sections this indicates practice nationwide. However, LEAs have a certain amount of discretion in respect of more than half the Act's various sections, many of which cannot be implemented until the governing body is reconstituted – see Sections 3 and 4 below – which must be by 1 September 1988 for county and maintained special schools, and by 1 September 1989 for voluntary schools. Therefore, since no standard practice for such sections can be given in a text such as this, governors will have to consult their clerks about the dates for implementaion of the sections marked ** in the text. (Fuller details can be read in the DES Circular 8/86, issued in December 1986.) All the provisions of the Act are applicable to *new* schools from 1 September 1987.

The 1986 Education Act's main provisions are:

INSTRUMENTS OF GOVERNMENT AND ARTICLES OF GOVERNMENT (SECTIONS 1 AND 2)**

The LEA, after consultation with the headteacher and governing body, to be responsible for making the instruments and articles of all maintained schools (previously those for secondary schools were subject to approval by the Secretary of State); the LEA to consider *any* governing body's proposal for the alteration of the provision made by the instruments and articles; governors of voluntary schools who find themselves in dispute with their LEA over their Instruments and Articles may refer the matter to the Secretary of State.

COMPOSITION OF GOVERNING BODY (SECTIONS 3 AND 4)

To be the same as proposed in the White Paper, as detailed in Table 1 below.

It should be noted that the level of LEA appointments is prescribed so that they cannot dominate a governing body: effectively this amounts to a considerable reduction; no pupils under 18 are to be allowed to serve (in some parts of the country such pupils had been allowed); neither are non-teaching staff. For aided and special

Size of School	Elected by and from parents	Appointed by LEA	Head Teacher	Elected by and from teachers	Co-opted or, for Controlled Schools: Foundation	Co-opted	Total
Fewer than 100 pupils	2	2	1	1	3		9
					2	1	
100–299 pupils	3	3	1	1	4		12
					3	1	
300–599 pupils	4	4	1	2	5		16
					4	1	
600 pupils or more	5	5	1	2	6		19
					4	2	

Table 1: *The composition of governing bodies for county, controlled and maintained special schools*

NB 1 The head teacher may choose not to be a governor. If choosing to be a governor, the head is treated for all purposes as ex officio.

2 All primary schools where there is a minor authority must have one governor from the minor authority.

3 An LEA can, if it chooses, treat a school of 600 pupils or more as though it were a school of between 300–599 pupils; this would mean it would have a smaller governing body – 16 instead of 19.

agreement schools, there would be:

- at least one governor appointed by the LEA
- at least one governor appointed by the minor authority in a primary school, where applicable

- foundation governors
- at least one parent governor
- at least one teacher – two if school contains 300 + pupils
- head, if he/she chooses

In other words, such governing bodies can in effect be whatever size they choose, provided that foundation governors constitute a majority of 2 in governing bodies of fewer than 18 people, or 3 in larger boards; even if a head chooses not to be a governor, he/she is still counted as one for the purposes of calculating the required numbers; additional governors can be included.

The reconstitution of the governing body must be completed by 1 September 1988 in the case of county and maintained special schools, and by 1 September 1989 for voluntary schools.

APPOINTMENT OF PARENT GOVERNORS BY GOVERNING BODY (SECTION 5)**

This provides for the appointment of parent governors by the governing body if elections are impracticable (say at a residential maintained special school) or if insufficient parents stand. Such appointments are preferably to be parents of children at the school, or at least parents with children of school age. The Act does not allow elected members of the LEA, co-opted members of any LEA education committee, or employees of the LEA or of the governing body of any aided school maintained by the LEA, to be appointed as parent governors.

CONNECTION WITH THE LOCAL BUSINESS COMMUNITY (SECTION 6)**

This places a duty on governors of all schools (other than aided) to strengthen links with the local business community by co-opting a representative from that community (otherwise than as a foundation governor) if they feel that the governing body as it stands is insufficiently represented.

APPOINTMENT OF REPRESENTATIVE GOVERNORS IN PLACE OF CO-OPTED GOVERNORS (SECTION 7)**

Provides for the appointment of a minor authority governor in primary schools where applicable (other than aided); for a governor to be nominated by the District Health Authority in a hospital maintained special school; and for one (or two if the school exceeds 100 pupils) appropriate voluntary organisation governors of special schools (not hospital schools), unless the LEA is satisfied that no appropriate voluntary organisation exists. For such appointments the instrument of government is to name the person(s) by whom the governor is to be nominated, and, in the case of a controlled school of fewer than 600 pupils, will not provide for a co-opted governor (see table on page 30 for clarification): in other cases the instrument is to provide for one (or two if applicable) fewer co-opted governors than permitted. References to co-opted governors in this section exclude co-opted foundation governors.

GOVERNORS' PROCEEDINGS AND TENURE OF OFFICE (SECTIONS 8–12)★★

Appointments are for a four-yearly term (other than ex officio governors) and governors can seek re-election; (there is no requirement for teacher or parent governors to sever their links with the governing body if they cease to have an involvement with the school); governors can resign, or be removed by those who appointed them (no guidance is given on the removal of elected or co-opted governors). Grouping to be allowed in special circumstances (see Section 9, and Schedule 1 (pages 67/68 of the Act) if applicable). Temporary governing bodies to be allowed for new schools: (Section 12). The Act contains a detailed schedule – Schedule 2: see pages 69/80 of the Act – applicable to such bodies. This came into force in April 1987. If a governing body is too large, adjustments in their number are to be made according to category, either by resignations, or by selection on the basis of seniority – the longest-serving governors to be the first to go, with lots drawn if governors have equal seniority (this procedure is not applicable to foundation governors, although there is provision for the instrument of government for every controlled school to adopt this procedure if a foundation governor is required to cease to hold office) – see Section 14 of the Act for details.

ELECTION OF PARENT AND TEACHER GOVERNORS (SECTION 15)★★

Outlines detailed procedures for this, among other items. As with all aspects of this Act, or any other, it is wise to consult the exact wording, but, briefly, it is the duty of the LEA, or governors of aided and special agreement schools, to take all reasonable steps to ensure that all parents of registered pupils are informed of parent governor vacancies and of their entitlement to stand as candidates and to vote. Provisions must be made for elections by secret ballot; in the case of parent governors this must include the opportunity to vote by post. No person under 18 is eligible for election (or appointment or co-option) as a governor.

GENERAL RESPONSIBILITY FOR CONDUCT OF COUNTY, VOLUNTARY AND MAINTAINED SECONDARY SCHOOLS (SECTION 16)**

This states that the articles of government of every county, voluntary and maintained secondary school 'shall provide for the conduct of the school to be under the direction of the governing body', subject to any specific provision in the articles, other provision of this or other Acts. Whilst recognising that in most cases the governing body will be consulted by the LEA or headteacher *before* a particular step is taken, this section also provides for the LEA or head to act in matters of urgency if the chairman or vice-chairman are not contactable.

SCHOOL CURRICULUM (SECTIONS 17, 18 and 19)

The relationships and responsibilities of the various partners regarding the school curriculum are specified.

The LEA has a duty:
'(a) to *determine*, and keep under review, their policy in relation to the secular curriculum for the county, voluntary and special schools maintained by them; (my emphasis)
(b) to make, and keep up to date, a written statement of that policy; and
(c) to furnish the governing body and headteacher of every such school with a copy of the statement and publish it in such a manner as the authority consider appropriate.'

The LEA has to have regard to the range and balance of the curriculum, and the headteacher has to make his copy of the LEA statement available to those who wish to inspect it.

As far as the *governing body* of every county, controlled and maintained special school is concerned, it has a duty *to consider* the LEA's secular curriculum policy and how, if at all, that policy (excluding sex education) should be modified in relation to their school. The governors are to state the aims of the school's secular curriculum and make and keep up to date a written statement of their conclusions.

Sex education is to be considered separately, and governors have a duty to decide whether sex education should form part of the curriculum, taking into account any LEA statement. The governors have a duty to make and keep up to date a separate written statement either of their policy as to content and organisation of sex education, or their reasons for excluding sex education from the curriculum.

NB This is supplemented by a further clause in the Act, as follows:

SEX EDUCATION (SECTION 46)

The LEA, governing body and headteacher of all schools are required to 'take such steps as are reasonably practicable to secure that where sex education is given to any registered pupils at the school it is given in such a manner as to encourage those pupils to have regard to moral considerations and the value of family life.' (For a fuller discussion of sex education and the governor's role, see pages 79–86.)

In considering their role in the curriculum, governors have a duty to consult with the headteacher and to have regard to the views of any member of the community, including 'any such representations which are made to them by the chief officer of police and which are connected with his responsibilities'. The governing body also has a duty to include the LEA in this consultation process *before* they make their own statement or vary any LEA statement. Any statement consequently written has to be given to the LEA and to the headteacher; this statement is to be made available for inspection by the headteacher at all reasonable times.

As far as the headteacher of these schools is concerned, the determination and organisation of the secular curriculum is her/his responsibility, and it is her/his 'duty to secure that the curriculum is followed within the school'. In discharging these duties, the head is to consider the LEA's and governing body's written statements and to have regard to community and chief officer of police representations. This must be done in a way which is compatible with the policy of the LEA, or, if incompatible with that policy, with the policy of the governing body. Where sex education is concerned the headteacher is to ensure that the governing body's policy is followed 'except where that policy is incompatible with any part of the syllabus for a course which forms part of that curriculum and leads to a public examination', and in particular that it is compatible with the law relating to children with special educational needs.

If a school materially changes, e.g. if it tranfers to a new site or suffers a reduction in numbers, then the governors have a duty to review their curriculum statements – or have the power to do so whenever they choose. Such a review having been completed, and a new written statement produced, it is the governing body's duty to supply the LEA and headteacher with a copy.

As far as the governing body of aided or special agreement schools is concerned, it has control over the content of the secular curriculum, having regard to the LEA's curriculum statement. The governing body is to allocate to the headteacher 'such functions as will, subject to the resources available, enable him to determine and organise the curriculum and secure that it is followed within the school'. No separate responsibility for considering sex education is placed on governors in such schools although they have a duty to have regard to community and chief officer of police representations concerning the curriculum and to supply a copy of their written statement to the headteacher – whose copy is to be available for public inspection.

NB The Act contains two further curriculum-related clauses on:

POLITICAL INDOCTRINATION (SECTIONS 44 and 45)

The LEA, governing body and headteacher of all schools must *forbid* 'the pursuit of partisan political activities by any of those registered pupils at the school who are junior pupils', and for all pupils 'the promotion of partisan political views in the teaching of any subject in the school', taking such steps 'as are reasonably practicable' to ensure that any political issues covered in school or during extra-mural activities present a balance of opposing views.

In connection with the above curriculum regulations, Section 20 of the Act provides for the Secretary of State to require all governing bodies to make available to parents of registered pupils 'in such form and manner and at such times as may be described' information regarding syllabuses and other educational provision available to the pupils.

The LEA's duty to state its policy (Section 17) and the sections relating to political education and sex education (Sections 44, 45 and 46) came into force on 7 January 1987.

Section 20 of the Act (on syllabus information for parents) came into force on 1 September 1987.

The governing body's duty to state its curriculum policies must come into effect by 1 September 1988 for county, controlled and maintained special schools, and by 1 September 1989 for aided and special agreement schools.

TERMS, SESSIONS AND HOLIDAYS (SECTION 21)★★

It is the LEA's duty to determine school session times and the dates of school terms and holidays for all schools other than aided and special agreement schools where the governing body carries this duty.

DISCIPLINE (SECTIONS 22–27)★★

These cover the various procedures and responsibilities concerning discipline, exclusion of pupils, their possible reinstatement and the appeals procedure.

The headteacher has the duty to determine appropriate discipline measures and the duty:

'(i) to act in accordance with any written statement of general principles provided for him by the governing body; and

(ii) to have regard to any guidance that they may offer in relation to particular matters.'

Both the head and governing body are to consult the LEA if any increased expenditure is likely to occur as a result of the discipline policy, or if any measure affects the responsibilities of the authority as an employer.

Only the headteacher has the power to exclude pupils 'by suspension, expulsion or otherwise', but she/he has to consult the LEA and governing body, without delay, giving details of the period of exclusion and reasons for it if public examinations are affected or if the exclusion amounts to more than five days in one term. The head also has a duty to inform parents (or pupils if they are over 18) of all the details of the exclusion, and their rights to make representations to the governing body and the LEA.

Sections 24 and 25 outline the complicated decision-making process for the reinstatement of excluded pupils. In all schools other than aided or special agreement, if the exclusion is permanent it is the LEA's duty:

(i) to consider after consulting the governing body whether

reinstatement should be immediate, by a particular date, or not at all;

(ii) if reinstatement is considered appropriate, to give directions to the head; and

(iii) where reinstatement is not an option, to inform the parents (or the pupil if over 18) of the decision.

(In other words, both the LEA and governing body can decide to reinstate.)

Where exclusions exceed five days (in aggregate) in one term or involve public examinations, it is the head's duty to reinstate if so directed by the LEA if the exclusion is for a fixed period, or if so directed by the governing body if the exclusion is for an indefinite period or is permanent. If the exclusion is indefinite, then the LEA has a duty to consult the governing body, and can direct immediate reinstatement or reinstatement within a certain period. For fixed periods of exclusion the LEA has a duty to consult the governing body if they propose to direct reinstatement. The headteacher has a duty to comply with the LEA's directions, but in situations where the head receives conflicting directions from the governing body and the LEA, 'to comply with that direction which will lead to the earlier reinstatement of the pupil'. Both the LEA and the governing body have a duty to inform each other, and the pupil's parents (or the pupil if over 18) of their directions.

A similar procedure for reinstatement of excluded pupils applies to the governing body of aided and special agreement schools, except that they, and not the LEA, decide whether to reinstate in cases of permanent exclusions, in exclusions of more than five days (in aggregate), or where public examinations are concerned: the LEA, after consulting the governing body, can give directions, if the governing body does not, in cases of fixed periods of exclusion. In all other cases, the respective functions of LEA, governing body, and headteacher are identical to those outlined in the previous paragraph.

APPEALS (SECTION 26 AND SCHEDULE 3, (PAGES 81–83) OF THE ACT)★★

The appeals procedure is outlined: every LEA, or the governing body of aided or special agreement schools, has to make arrangements for the parents (or pupil if over 18) to appeal against a decision not to reinstate following permanent exclusion. The governing body of county, controlled or maintained special schools can appeal against an

LEA's direction to reinstate a permanently excluded pupil. The appeals procedure is to follow that used in cases of school choice disputes, and the appeal committee decision is to be binding on all concerned.

Section 28 of the Act gives an LEA reserve powers to step into any maintained school, and to make representations to the governing body of aided or special agreement schools, if the LEA considers there to be a breakdown of discipline at a school (resulting from any action by pupils or parents), the governing body having been informed in writing. The LEA may consequently give directions to the governing body or headteacher. This section came into force on 1 September 1987.

FINANCE (SECTION 29)

The LEA has a duty to provide an annual financial statement 'with a view to assisting the governing body to judge whether expenditure in relation to their school represents the economic, efficient and effective use of resources'. This statement is to include the school's current expenditure – itemised if the LEA chooses – and its capital expenditure, if considered appropriate. To give the governing body a more definite role where finances are concerned, the LEA has a duty to make an annual sum available to the governing body which they can *spend at their discretion* on books, equipment and stationery; the LEA can also specify other heads of expenditure. The governors have to comply with any reasonable condition imposed by the LEA concerning the expenditure. The governors can delegate some, or all, of their LEA sum to the head, and they also have a duty not to spend this money on items which the head considers 'would be inappropriate to the curriculum of the school'.

(Before making any regulations, the Secretary of State will consult local authorities, especially those which have had pilot schemes giving governors more financial responsibilities, see pages 12–13.)

This section came into force from 1 September 1987.

GOVERNORS' ANNUAL REPORT TO PARENTS (SECTION 30)

This section came into force from 7 January 1987.

Governors of all schools will have a duty to prepare a *brief* annual report, 'the governors' report', containing 'a summary of the steps taken by the governing body in the discharge of their functions during the period since their last report' and action taken regarding any previous resolution. The report must include the following information:

- date, time, place of next annual parents' meeting, and its agenda, indicating that not only the governors' report will be discussed, but also the performance of the governing body, LEA and headteacher in discharging their functions in relation to the school.
- name and category of each governor and details like expiry of office and who appointed.
- name and address of chairman of governing body and clerk.
- arrangements for next parent governor election, where known.
- a financial statement based on that provided by the LEA and indicating how the governing body used their sum of money. (This will not be possible for the first annual report which must be submitted before the end of the 1987 academic year, which predates the implementation of the Finance Section 25).
- details of public examinations – if applicable – as required by the 1980 Education Act.
- details of how the governing body has sought to strengthen links with the community, including police.
- reference to other governors' information about the educational provision at the school, e.g. syllabuses.

Governors are to consider the desirability of issuing this report in a language other than English, and to do so if directed by the LEA; the report is to be free to all parents and employees of the school, available at least two weeks before the annual meeting, and copies, free of charge, should be available for inspection at the school.

ANNUAL PARENTS' MEETINGS (SECTION 31)

The governing body has a duty to hold an 'annual parents' meeting', open to all parents of registered pupils at the school and headteacher and other invitees, at which the annual governors' report is discussed, including the discharging of the functions of the LEA, governing body and headteacher. The governing body is to control proceedings, and if enough parents are present (a number equalling at least 20% of the number of registered pupils at the school), they can pass relevant resolutions which must be considered by the governors, head or LEA, whichever is most appropriate, and which must result in written comments for inclusion in the next annual report – only parents of registered pupils may vote on any issue put. (This section is not applicable to special schools in hospitals or schools where at least 50% are boarders or the governors deem it impracticable.) This came into force on 7 January 1987.

Consequently, by the end of the summer term of 1987 almost every governing body will have had to produce its annual report, and not less than two weeks later, have held its annual parents' meeting. The LEA is to bear the costs of this annual exercise as part of the running costs of the school. Governing bodies can, if they wish, produce additional reports and hold other parents' evenings, provided the costs for these can be met. Circular 8/86 suggest that:

'Governing bodies may subsequently find it convenient to issue their reports and convene the parents' meeting during the autumn term in each school year.'

It will be for governing bodies to decide the best pattern for their particular school. In some respects an autumn meeting is sensible if you wish to make a feature of the examination results, whereas a summer meeting affords opportunities for a review of that actual school year. In autumn meetings parents will be able to bring attention to issues which they hope will be looked into, and possibly improved, by the end of that school year, whereas summer meetings preclude such action.

Where there is a requirement to give addresses, this does not mean that home addresses are necessary: the school address in the case of the chairman, or the LEA address in the case of the clerk, are quite acceptable.

Since great importance is attached to the annual parents' meeting as a device by which parents are encouraged to become more closely involved with the school to everyone's mutual benefit, the governing body is to give its careful consideration to the conduct of the meeting. Establishing the correct atmosphere for a full and free discussion is essential. Circular 8/86 suggests that your clerk attends, and that a few non-governor members of the teaching and non-teaching staff are invited, as is a representative of the LEA, and, in secondary schools, possibly even representatives of the more senior pupils. It is not thought 'desirable' to invite the press or general public to such meetings.

Since parents can raise any matter concerning the governors' report on the running of the school, certain controversial issues could emerge which will require strong and firm chairmanship, especially in large meetings. If individuals are criticised, they should be given the right of reply, either at that meeting or at a subsequent governors' meeting or a meeting with the LEA or headteacher. The annual meeting must take place even if only a few parents attend. It is envisaged that some governing bodies will despair of ever recruiting sufficient interest from the parent body for such a meeting. This is why they need to pay particular attention to the wording of the annual report and to the arrangements for the annual meeting. Parents will attend if the governing body makes it an annual event not to be missed. It need hardly be said that the requirements of Sections 30 and 31 place enormous administrative burdens on LEAs, clerks and schools. Governing bodies need to give very careful thought to their role in what will become, eventually, a major feature of every school year.

REPORTS BY GOVERNING BODY AND HEADTEACHER (SECTION 32)

The LEA may ask the governing body and/or headteacher for reports at any time, and the head is also obliged to produce reports for the governing body if required.

This came into force on 1 September 1987.

ADMISSIONS (SECTION 33)

Where the governing body is responsible for determining admission arrangements, they are to consult the LEA at least once a year, especially before determining or varying such arrangements. In cases where the LEA is responsible for such arrangements it has to consult the governing body similarly.

This section came into force from 7 January 1987.

APPOINTMENT AND DISMISSAL OF STAFF (SECTIONS 34–41)**

(These sections apply to all schools other than aided or special agreement schools which will continue their existing practice, but may wish to take notice of these procedures.)

The LEA determines a school's complement of teaching and non-teaching staff, including part-time; staff employed solely in connection with provision of meals and/or midday supervision are not part of the school's complement, although the LEA, as employer, determines how many there should be. The appointment and dismissal of staff is under the control of the LEA. Where selection is concerned for headteacher appointments, at least three LEA representatives and at least three governors are to constitute the selection panel (articles of government may provide for the governing body to have a majority); an LEA cannot impose a headteacher, but can appoint, in consultation with the governing body, an acting headteacher. All headteacher vacancies are to be advertised nationally by the LEA. The selection panel is responsible for interviewing suitable applicants, but if the panel cannot agree a shortlist, the nominated governor interviewers have the right to nominate not more than two applicants for interview, the other panel members sharing a similar right. If the panel cannot recommend an appointment they either repeat the process, or readvertise. The LEA may decline to appoint the recommended applicant, in which case the panel may interview other candidates, or readvertise. At all stages of this process the chief education officer, or his nominee, has a right to attend and give advice.

A similar procedure is to apply to the appointment of other staff, although the size of interview panel is not specified. (Deputy head appointments may follow the procedures for headteacher if desired.) If a post is advertised, the governing body is responsible for selecting and interviewing candidates, although it can delegate its functions to the headteacher, to one or more governors, or to a combination of these. The LEA has a duty to decide whether or not the post should be retained, and can appoint an existing LEA employee by redeployment; in such circumstances the governing body, in consultation with the headteacher, can give the LEA a personnel specification and has a right to be consulted by the LEA. If the LEA subsequently makes an appointment with which the governing body disagrees, the LEA is to report this fact to the next appropriate education committee.

The LEA is to consult the head and governing body before dismissing, suspending or early retiring a teacher; (foundation governors are allowed to require the LEA to dismiss a reserved teacher). It also has to consult the governing body and headteacher before extending a teacher's probationary period or deciding whether it has been completed successfully. Both governors and the head have the power to suspend a member of staff, but they must inform the LEA, and each other, immediately, and reinstate if directed to do so by the LEA (consult Section 41 for precise details).

The clerk to the governing body of every county and maintained special school is to be appointed and/or dismissed by the LEA in consultation with the governing body. In the case of controlled or special agreement schools, this process will be determined by the school's articles of government. The LEA has a duty to consider any representations such governing bodies make concerning dismissal of their clerk.

SCHOOL PREMISES (SECTION 42)**

The governors of every county and maintained special school have control over the use of school premises outside school sessions subject to any LEA direction. In exercising this control they are to have regard to the desirability of the premises being made available for use by members of the community served by the school.

ABOLITION OF CORPORAL PUNISHMENT (SECTION 47)

This provides for the abolition of corporal punishment and applies to children in all schools (even those educated at home), except most independent schools, although children receiving financial assistance at such schools under the Assisted Places Scheme are also covered. Children in Scottish schools are also affected.

This came into force on 15 August 1987.

APPRAISAL OF PERFORMANCE OF TEACHERS (SECTION 49)

This enables the Secretary of State, after consulting local authority and teacher associations, to make regulations for the regular appraisal of teachers' performance. These regulations may make provision 'requiring the governing bodies of such categories of schools or other establishments as may be prescribed:

(i) to secure, so far as it is reasonably practicable for them to do so, that any arrangements made in accordance with the regulations are complied with in relation to their establishments; and

(ii) to provide such assistance to the local education authority as the authority may reasonably require in connection with their obligations under the regulations.'

(This controversial section, which applies from 7 January 1987, covers schools and colleges of further education. Since it is closely connected with the teachers' long-running pay negotiations, and since the consultative process has not, at the time of writing, been completed, governors will need to consult their clerk and/or chairman as to the up-to-date position.)

SCHOOL TRANSPORT (SECTION 53)

This amends the relevant section of the 1944 Education Act and seeks to clarify the grounds which have to be taken into account by an LEA in deciding whether free school transport is required (e.g. pupil's age, nature of route, alternative routes). It came into effect on 7 January 1987.

CHANGE OF STATUS OF CONTROLLED SCHOOL TO AIDED SCHOOL (SECTIONS 54 and 55)

The governing body of any controlled school can apply to the Secretary of State for Education for the school to change its status to an aided school. The governors will need to consult their LEA and publish their proposals. They must make a convincing case to satisfy the Secretary of State that they can meet both the financial costs by way of compensation to the LEA for its past capital expenditure on the school, and their share of the running costs (governing bodies who wish to take this step are advised to consult these sections in full and take the advice of their Diocesan Board of Education, if applicable). Governors of any voluntary school affected by any such proposals, any LEA, or ten or more local government electors in the area may, within two months of any such proposal, submit objections. This came into effect on 1 April 1987.

REPORTS TO SECRETARY OF STATE (SECTION 56)

Requires governing bodies of every school in the maintained sector (and certain other educational establishments) to submit reports and returns to the Secretary of State if he requests the information. This came into effect from 7 January 1987.

INFORMATION AND TRAINING FOR GOVERNORS (SECTION 57)

LEAs 'shall secure' for every governor in schools maintained by them free copies of their Instruments and Articles and any other relevant information connected with governors' duties, and (more importantly for our purposes) free training opportunities 'as the authority consider necessary for the effective discharge of those functions'. (See Chapter 11 for a full discussion of training.) This came into effect from 1 September 1987.

TRAVELLING AND SUBSISTENCE ALLOWANCES FOR GOVERNORS OF SCHOOLS AND FE ESTABLISHMENTS (SECTION 58)

An LEA *may* pay travelling and subsistence allowances for its governors. However desirable this may seem, it is unlikely that any LEA will, in the current financial climate, comply with this section. This came into effect from 1 September 1987.

ACCESS TO PAPERS ETC. OF GOVERNING BODIES (SECTION 62)

This enables the Secretary of State to make regulations requiring governing bodies to give public access to any relevant documents relating to the meetings and proceedings of the governing body, and came into effect on 1 September 1987.

(In some instances grouping of schools under one governing body is still permissible with the approval of the Secretary of State for Education, or at the discretion of the LEA in consultation with the governing bodies where two primary schools are concerned *if* they serve the same area (and provided neither is a special school, and both, if in Wales, share the same language policy). Grouped schools may choose to hold separate or joint annual parents' meetings: if they issue joint reports, provision must be made for the separation of items particular to one school. Governors of grouped boards should consult the relevant sections of the 1986 Education Act for precise details.)

Governors will find that they are given advice by their local education authority as to the implementation of these various sections, to which LEAs will add their own interpretations, e.g. what sum of money will the LEA give over to the governing body, and when? How will LEAs interpret the free governor training provision?

Full implementation of the following sections:

8 (governors' proceedings and tenure of office)
16 (general responsibility for conduct of certain schools)
20 (information about syllabuses for parents)

36 (the selection panel)

54 (change of status of controlled to aided status)

62 (access to governors' papers)

will depend on the making of appropriate regulations which were not issued at the time of writing. Consult your clerk about these, and any other aspect of the legislation.

As well as dealing with the above points of particular relevance to school governors, the 1986 Education Act contained other miscellaneous provisions, the most important of which related to freedom of speech in universities, polytechnics and colleges; recoupment of costs between LEAs; grants for teacher training; and the discontinuance of the Secretary of State's duty to make annual reports to Parliament, which had been an annual duty since 1944. (The final such report was given by Sir Keith Joseph in 1985. In view of the fact that the Secretary of State can call for such reports as he desires, and the obligation of LEAs, heads and governing teachers to furnish each other with reports, the discontinuance of this annual duty (see Section 60) may be seen by other partners in the education system as rather inequitable.)

When the Act received the Royal Assent, the Secretary of State for Education, Kenneth Baker, said:

> 'This Act provides new opportunities for parents, teachers, local education authorities and others to work more effectively together in providing the best education for our children.'

Governors, who it is assumed are alluded to in Mr Baker's 'others', may wonder how this legislation will help raise standards and whether their responsibilities have been clarified and strengthened. In places the legislation is indeed complicated, and many governing bodies will ponder long over the significance of the wording of those sections, among others, which outline the relative functions of the LEA, the headteacher, and the governors – especially in the light of the sections in this book which discuss the curriculum (Chapter 4), appointment of teachers (Appendix C) and the suspension of pupils (Chapter 9). As the 'Times Educational Supplement' (24.10.86) commented:

> 'The path is now littered with new pitfalls for the unwary. Litigious parents, governors who fancy themselves as barrack-room lawyers, heads who are jealous of their prerogatives (as they jolly well should be) – all will be tempted to rush to their solicitors every time one protagonist or another fails to observe the letter of this complicated (and, for much of its length) unnecessary law.'

It is hoped that such drastic measures are not resorted to, but governors will have noted from reading the above summary of the legislation the obscurity of some of the provisions. For example, who do governors see as members of their local business community? (And who represents the local community generally?) Why, for the first time ever in education legislation, do we see provisions made for the involvement in the curriculum of the chief officer of police? Indeed, who has control over the curriculum? The headteacher is placed in a very difficult position if the governing body decide to amend the LEA curriculum policy statement, since staffing will be in line with the LEA's policies, and the head may not be able to resource particular curriculum decisions made by the governing body. What do governors do if they do not judge that the expenditure of their school is economic, efficient and effective? And although the troubles at the Poundswick School (see Chapter 9) were much in the Government's mind when it drafted the clauses on discipline, the new Act will not be able to prevent a future Poundswick dispute if teachers refuse to teach reinstated pupils; however, the new procedures for suspensions, although complex, are an improvement, even though the scope for conflict remains – the National Association of Head Teachers, for example, feels that heads have too little power in this respect. (Incidentally, we have the Royal Wedding of Prince Andrew and Sarah Ferguson in July 1986 to thank for the fact that corporal punishment is now abolished in our schools. The relevant clause was debated in Parliament on the wedding day and the anti-caning lobby won by only one vote: two pro-caners, the Prime Minister and Peter Bruinvels, MP, were delayed by the wedding crowds and consequently could not register their votes.)

Additionally, whilst the teacher unions, in the main, have welcomed increased parental involvement on the governing body, they would have liked equal representation; and, needless to say, they were largely critical of the Act's provisions for enforced teacher appraisal. Moreover, is it really sensible in adjusting the size of governing bodies to establish a procedure in which the longest serving governor may have to leave the governing body? This person could be the most valuable and hardworking governor; many governing bodies may rue this procedure if they cannot persuade other governors to resign in their stead.

Many of the above questions will only be answered when, if at all, somebody takes legal proceedings against a governing body, LEA, or headteacher alleging a breach of a particular provision of this Act. It will take some time for the LEAs, headteachers and governing bodies to come to terms with the changes brought about by this legislation. However, imaginatively handled, the potential for change is exciting.

1944 AND ALL THAT

The 1986 Education Act can be seen as the final step on the long road travelled from the 1944 Education Act. Details of major milestones along this road – particularly the 1980 Education Act, the 1984 Green Paper and the 1985 White Paper – are given so that governors have an understanding of how they arrived at their present destination.

THE 1944 EDUCATION ACT

This Act is seen to be the cornerstone of our education system and the most important and substantial advance in public education this country has ever known; it attempted to spell out the elements of partnership in the education system more effectively. This Act created a Minister of Education (now known as the Secretary of State for Education) whose duty was 'to promote the education of the people of England and Wales and the progressive development of institutions devoted to that purpose and to secure the effective execution by local authorities, under his control and direction, of the national policy for providing a varied and comprehensive educational service in every area'. In other words, the Secretary of State has to initiate national policies, and to execute oversight and supervision of the local education authorities. All major educational policy is initiated by Parliament; various Acts provide the framework to our education system and impose certain duties on LEAs; for example, they have to organise their education system in three distinct stages – primary, secondary and further education; they have to arrange for 190 days schooling in every year; they have to conform to the relevant provisions of the Sex Discrimination Act and Race Discrimination Act; they have to alter the school leaving age when required; from 1985, they have to have (in most cases) individual governing bodies for each school composed of elected parents, teachers and other groups. The government does not own or run schools, nor does it employ teachers; it does, however, have the duty, via the Secretary of State, to *influence,* and this it does by issuing circulars (advisory documents), asking for reports (e.g. Taylor, Warnock, Swann, Bullock, Cockcroft – all mentioned in this book), calling for inspections, dispensing grants, controlling the building programme, regulating the training and supply of teachers, settling disputes, e.g. between a parent and an LEA, or between an LEA and a governing body, and carrying out national surveys (for example through the Assessment of Performance Unit (APU), established by the DES in 1975 to assess and monitor pupil achievement and to identify any incidence of under-achievement; this it does by mounting annual national surveys in the major curriculum areas and comparing them over time. Governors can obtain further information about the APU's valuable work by writing to the address on page 259).

The Secretary of State supervises the way in which the LEAs perform their very extensive duties and powers. The LEAs are required by the 1944 Education Act 'to contribute towards the spiritual, moral, mental and physical development of the community' by securing that sufficient schools are available and that these are run efficiently. Consequently, it is the LEAs who build and maintain most schools; appoint and pay teachers; allocate resources; control the secular curriculum in their area. Certain duties the LEAs cannot escape, e.g. to follow health and safety regulations in their schools; to ensure that school premises conform to national standards; to ascertain which children need special educational provision; to provide a careers service. However, they are allowed a significant number of discretionary powers, for example, in providing nursery education or school meals; in dispensing certain educational grants.

Where parents are concerned, they have a legal duty under the 1944 Education Act to cause any child of compulsory school age 'to receive efficient full-time education suitable to his age, ability and aptitude either by attendance at school or otherwise', and the LEA has a duty to ensure parents fulfil this legal requirement.

Because our national education system is locally administered, we find an enormous variation in practice throughout the country, different LEAs interpreting the legislation in their own way or ignoring parts of it where they choose to; this is why across county boundaries we find different systems of school organisation, or governing body practice or even vast descrepancies in LEA educational spending (see pages 68–69 for an illustration of this). Since there is no standard national practice, governors are advised to have regard to their local rules and regulations and practice; it may be, for good reasons, different from that which is stated in this book – each of the 104 LEAs in England and Wales jealously clings to its autonomy. An example of this is the way the LEAs interpreted the legislation contained in the 1944 Education Act. Among many other things, the 1944 Act required there to be managing or governing bodies in all primary and secondary schools. However, LEAs used their discretionary powers concerning the composition and procedures of such bodies, often grouping schools in large numbers under one body which was packed with political appointments. And, although the government issued Model Articles of Government in 1945, many LEAs chose to ignore them so that the governing bodies' functions were minimal. However, during the 1960s and 1970s, change was in the air, and some LEAs chose to alter their grouping practices, and to widen representation on the governing body to include parent and teacher representatives (and even non-teaching staff in some areas), even though there was no legal requirement for them to do so; (indeed, teachers in voluntary schools could not legally become governors, and parental involvement was strictly unofficial). Consequently, by the beginning of 1980, it was estimated that some nine out of ten LEAs had teacher or parent governors, and eight out of ten had both.

We have seen how the Taylor Report recommended a major review of the composition and powers of governing bodies. There is no doubt that the appearance of the Report stimulated changes of varying degrees throughout the country. The 1980 Education Act made significant changes to the composition of governing bodies, but failed to grasp the nettle concerning powers. This Act was the eighteenth occasion on which the 1944 Education Act had been amended, and it is important in that it made major changes to the framework of that Act.

THE 1980 EDUCATION ACT

Five clauses of this Act, which concerned England and Wales, specifically related to school government; the bulk of the Act dealt with parental choice, information for parents and the appeals procedure (as detailed in Chapter 8 of this book); school attendance orders; procedures for establishing a new school, school closures and changing the character of a school; awards and grants, including the Assisted Places Scheme; arrangements for school meals and milk; provisions for nursery education, and a number of miscellaneous matters.

Some of these amendments to previous legislation were welcome, for example those on the composition of school governing bodies – to be detailed below – and those concerning school closures – objectors to a closure submit their objections to the LEA rather than direct to the Secretary of State; where there are no objections, either to school closures or to proposed new schools, LEAs can proceed without the Secretary of State's approval, provided that they have given due notice. However, other clauses were the subject of some controversy; for example, the reduction of an LEA's statutory duties to provide school meals except for needy children; the funding of the Assisted Places Scheme to enable children from 'poorer' families to attend independent schools. (Interested readers should consult this Act, and others to be mentioned in this book, in full at their local library as all the detail cannot be given here.)

As far as the clauses relating directly to school governors are concerned, all the provisions were new, even though some LEAs had already used their discretionary powers and had pre-dated such provision.

As from 1 May 1980, the distinction between primary and secondary school lay involvement was to disappear with the word 'manager' being absorbed into the word 'governor'.

The representation on the school governing body was widened so that *all* schools had elected parent and teacher governors. Where parents were concerned, two had to be elected by secret ballot in county, voluntary controlled and special schools; one parent to be *elected* in voluntary aided and special agreement schools, and one *appointed* by the foundation. (There was no reason why an LEA should not exceed these minimum requirements.) Schools of under 300 pupils were to elect one teacher governor, with an additional elected teacher governor for larger schools; headteachers to be full voting members unless they chose otherwise. Additionally, it was left to the LEA to decide the number and representation from other groups for county schools, although LEA representatives there had to be, and, for primary schools, at least one representative of the minor authority (i.e., in England, the parish council, or parish meeting, if there is no council; in Wales, the community council; or, if these do not exist, a non-metropolitan district council). In voluntary schools there would have to be some changes in proportions to accommodate for elected parent and teacher governors, consequently foundation governors were to be in a majority of three in aided schools with a board exceeding 18, or a majority of 2 for smaller boards; or a proportion reduced from one-third to one-fifth for controlled schools.

These provisions were gradually introduced, applying to all new or newly-merged schools from July 1981; from September 1984 in the case of elected parents and teachers to special schools; and to all schools from September 1985. Of course, such provisions have been superseded by the 1986 Education Act, as outlined on pages 30–31.

To encourage all schools to have individual governing bodies grouping was no longer allowed after July 1981 (although there was evidence of it up to 1985), except where specific approval was given by the Secretary of State, or in the case of two closely linked primary schools.

As far as the proceedings of governing bodies apply, detailed regulations have been applicable to *all* schools since August 1981, the most important of which are:

- that governorships are not considered to be collectable items; no governor can hold more than five governorships (those with more were given until April 1983 to offload their surplus, or forfeit all such appointments)
- undischarged bankrupts cannot hold governorships, nor can those who have served more than three months' imprisonment, without the option of a fine, within five years of appointment (it is good to know that the governors sitting around the table with you are honest and upright citizens!)
- failure to attend three consecutive meetings disqualifies
- governors to elect their chairperson annually (employees of the school cannot stand as chair or vice-chair)
- any three governors may request a special meeting
- three, or one-third, whichever is greater, constitutes a quorum (subsequent Regulations issued later empowered the LEA to choose its own quorum rule)
- decisions to be made by majority vote, the chair having a casting vote
- governors with a pecuniary or personal interest concerning any governors' business to declare it, take no part nor vote, and to withdraw if requested; if the business concerns disciplining a teacher governor, or the pupil of a parent governor, then that governor *must* withdraw, although he/she must be allowed to put his/her case to the governors
- the agenda and minutes to be available at the school for

consultation by any person with a legitimate interest, with the exclusion of any item concerning a named person or deemed confidential

• parent governors whose children cease to attend the school, and teacher governors who cease employment at the school, to forfeit their office.

Although this Act did not give governors more *powers*, it did, by way of the 1981 regulations dealing with proceedings of the governing body, allow governors to exercise much more *influence*.

Of course, up until the relevant sections of the 1986 Education Act came into force, LEAs were empowered to decide for themselves the actual composition of the governing body, so that parent and teacher representation could be effectively swamped by a large contingent of LEA nominees; and LEAs could still impose restrictions on who could hold governorships, e.g. some LEAs debarred any LEA employee. The overall effect of the 1980 Act, then, was to leave a national mosaic of LEA practice concerning governing bodies as confusing as previously, even though at least the Taylor Report idea of 'partnership' was introduced.

Coincidentally with the initiation of increased influence and partnership, central government was busy stimulating action on curriculum reform, as Chapter 4 of this book outlines. A DES publication, 'The School Curriculum', was widely circulated, which made it clear that governors had a more positive role to play in curriculum development. This point was reinforced by Circular 6/81 (circulars are advisory papers sent by Government to LEAs) which, among other things, called for governors' advice and consultation over the curriculum. Hence, governors' duties in this important area were emphasised, and LEAs were asked to involve them in their consultative processes. A further development came with the arrival, in May 1984, of a Government Green Paper, 'Parental Influence at School: a new framework for School Government in England and Wales'; a Green Paper is issued as a discussion paper, and signals a government's intention to introduce legislation subsequently.

'PARENTAL INFLUENCE AT SCHOOL: A NEW FRAMEWORK FOR SCHOOL GOVERNMENT IN ENGLAND AND WALES'

This Green Paper started with the statement: 'Parents care about their children's progress – how they develop and what they learn', and made the point that insufficient scope had been given to parents to enable them to 'discharge their unique responsibilities'. Consequently, the government wanted each school to have a degree of independence from the LEA so that it could promote 'a life of its own'.

The state of governing bodies at that time was summarised thus:

'The Education Act 1944 provided for school governing bodies which were designed to play a substantial role in giving each school identity and purpose and in managing its affairs. The Education Act 1980 brings that objective nearer by ending the practice whereby the governing bodies of many schools were merely an offshoot of the LEA, and by giving parents and teachers a limited right to be represented on the governing bodies of their schools. But at present most governing bodies do not adequately serve the aim of promoting the school as a force for good in the life of the pupils, their families and the community which it serves.'

The Government therefore proposed to change the law in two fundamental respects:

1 by altering the composition of governing bodies to give elected parents the right to form a majority, as Table 2 shows:

Parents *or, for voluntary controlled schools:*		Local Education Authority *or, for primary schools in shire counties & inner London:*		Headteacher	Teachers	Total
Parents	Foundation	LEA	minor authority			
size of school:						
fewer than 100 pupils						
5		2		1	1	9
3	*2*	*1*	*1*			
100–299 pupils						
6		3		1	1	11
3	*3*	*2*	*1*			
300–599 pupils						
8		4		1	2	15
5	*3*	*3*	*1*			
600 pupils or more						
10		6		1	2	19
6	*4*	*5*	*1*			

Table 2: *The proposed composition of governing bodies*

2 by more clearly defining the functions of governing bodies, and
   strengthening their status in relation to the LEA and headteacher.
The main proposals of the Green Paper can be found in Appendix A,
pages 232–234.

'BETTER SCHOOLS'

The arrival in Spring 1985 of the Government's White Paper 'Better
Schools' was a gathering together of many of the Government's recent
thoughts on such issues as standards, the primary and secondary
curriculum, examinations and assessment, teaching quality, the
education of the under fives, discipline, the role of parents and pupils
from ethnic minorities. As far as proposed legislation was concerned,
the main interest was focused on Chapter Nine of the White Paper,
'The Legal Framework', which, in spite of its somewhat incongruous
title, dealt with school governing bodies, outlining proposals to
reform the composition, functions and powers of all governing bodies
of county, controlled and maintained special schools – only minor
changes being envisaged for aided and special agreement schools.

It was clear that the Green Paper had served its proper function of
stimulating discussion, and the Government acknowledged that it
took into account those views hostile to its Green Paper proposals;
consequently, there would be no parental majority. However, the
White Paper sought to remove those obstacles which stood in the way
of governing bodies realising their 'full potential … as a force for
good' in the life of a school. These obstacles were:

- insufficient account being taken 'of parents' natural and special
  interest in their child's education and progress'
- the piecemeal development of the governors' powers and duties,
  and the governing body's restricted role in relation to the LEA or
  the head
- the LEAs' common practice of appointing a dominating
  majority.

The main proposals of this White Paper are to be found in Appendix
B, pages 235–237. Having read a summary of the 1986 Education Act,
readers will decide for themselves whether the legislation has removed
more obstacles which have prevented governors playing their full part
in the life of their schools.

The various provisions of the above Papers and Acts have been
detailed at some length so that governors can trace for themselves the

basis of their present duties and powers. The modern school governor occupies a much more specifically legally defined position than ever before, but along with this comes a vastly increased burden of duties than has hitherto been recognised. However, it is one thing to have extra powers, but quite another to know how to use them effectively.

The following chapters aim to give governors some of the knowledge they need in order to become more effective in the varied and important tasks which confront them.

4 Governors and the curriculum – tread carefully in the secret garden

I have in front of me a very interesting 'Information Booklet for Parents' issued by a primary school in 1982/83, which, after listing all the governors, states:

'The Governors meet at least once a term. Their work is largely unseen by the public but it is of very great importance. They are part of the series of checks and balances on which the system of education by local authority is built up and are a safeguard against arbitrary decisions being taken by the Authority on the one hand or by the Head on the other. They have a general responsibility for the care of the fabric of the school building and for its letting to outside bodies, if this is requested. They should also call the attention of the Authority to such things as inadequate accommodation or below standard facilities in the school. They are responsible, in close consultation with the Headteacher, for the appointment of staff.'

All this sounds excellent as far as it goes, and I turn the page to read on, only to find a new section on the PTA. It appears then that this booklet is quite prepared to foster a view of its governors' role which is fundamentally inaccurate, and omits, presumably by design, the crucial area of governors' general direction of the conduct and curriculum of the school.

THE CURRICULUM AND THE LAW

Your exact legal duties with respect to the curriculum and the responsibilities you share with the LEA and headteacher have been discussed in the previous chapter. Pre-1987 your Instruments and Articles may have contained a passage similar to the following:

'The Governors are responsible in consultation with the Head for the general direction of the conduct and curriculum of the school. This does not mean that they have to consider all the necessary details from day to day but they have an overall authority and should make sure that they inform themselves with the Head, not only about the conduct and discipline within the school, but also the general principles on which the curriculum of the school is based.'

The vagueness of such wording reveals why the relevant curriculum sections of the 1986 Education Act have been written in an attempt to clarify the situation, and to specify the relationship between the LEA, headteacher and governors where the curriculum is concerned. And it is important to remember that there is now a legal obligation for the governors and LEA to produce and maintain up-to-date, written policy statements regarding the curriculum.

It is interesting to note that neither the word 'education', nor 'curriculum' is defined in any Education Act. We know that LEAs are charged with securing in their area sufficient primary and secondary schools which:

'shall not be deemed to be sufficient unless they are sufficient in number, character and equipment to afford for all the pupils opportunities for education offering such variety of instruction and training as may be desirable in view of their different ages, abilities and aptitudes, and of the different periods for which they may be expected to remain at school, including practical instruction and training appropriate to their respective needs'. (Section 8, 1944 Education Act)

and that:

'It shall be the duty of the local education authority for every area, so far as their powers extend, to contribute towards the spiritual, moral, mental and physical development of the community by securing that efficient education throughout those stages (i.e. primary, secondary and further) shall be available to meet the needs of the population of their area.' (Section 7, 1944 Education Act)

Moreover, since there exist regulations which prescribe standards for secondary school gyms and playing fields for primary and secondary schools, it is assumed that both P.E. and sports are a requirement of the curriculum. In other words, we are given clues that the curriculum should be appropriate to the age and need of the child, should provide a variety of instruction and training, some of it practical, and should comprise spiritual, moral and physical elements. Consequently, if a school were to offer an exclusive diet of sports-related subjects, it would be seen to be failing according to the law – just as it would if all its teaching dwelt on the spiritual. Indeed, recently some privately-run schools provided by a religious cult have been censured by HMIs for offering too narrow a curriculum diet which dealt almost exclusively with the spiritual. And, paradoxically, as everyone seems to know, the only subject legally required in the curriculum is Religious Instruction:

> 'religious instruction shall be given in every county school and in every voluntary school.' (Section 25(2), 1944 Education Act)

Nowadays it is more customary to talk about Religious Education (R.E.) rather than R.I., to signify the changing nature of the way the subject is taught; the following discussion reflects that change.

The above clause is a result of the settlement made between Church and State when we decided to restructure our education system during World War II. There is, of course, an exclusion clause, but this requirement was, and still is, subject to much controversy, especially in county schools. Evidently, governors of voluntary schools have an especial interest here, and extra responsibilities, particularly in aided schools where governors have the powers to dismiss an unsatisfactory R.E. teacher *without* the LEA's consent; governors of voluntary schools will do well to pay particular attention to this area of their duties, and to seek the advice of the appropriate authority, (e.g. the Diocesan Board of Education) where necessary. All LEAs have an agreed R.E. syllabus, and governors should consult this occasionally to see that it is being followed. Recent evidence suggests that many schools, and governors are in default over this curriculum area. One report which talked of a collapse of moral and religious education in schools found that 18% of schools provided no R.E. at all, while only 58% taught R.E. up to the 4th year in secondary schools. The relevant government minister stated:

> 'We look to LEAs, governing bodies and schools to live up to their statutory responsibilities.'

In an increasingly secular world, governors may find themselves in an invidious position with respect to the teaching of R.E., but you are reminded of the fact that a necessary element of your school's curriculum should be R.E., efficiently and suitably taught. This may prove difficult in view of a 1984 report which showed that schools had fewer than half the R.E. specialists required and not enough teachers were receiving the relevant training, with the consequent result that over half of all R.E. teachers were untrained. Additionally, Section 25 of the 1944 Education Act states that:

'the school day in every county school and in every voluntary school shall begin with collective worship on the part of all pupils in attendance at the school, and the arrangements made thereof shall provide for a single act of worship attended by all such pupils unless, in the opinion of the local education authority, or in the case

	Maintained schools		
	County	Voluntary	Total
Number of schools responding	253	43	296
Schools with convenient assembly area for whole school:	% 32.0*	% 60.5	% 36.2
Schools holding a full assembly:[1]	%	%	%
Daily	1.9	4.7	2.4
Three times per week	7.1	16.3	7.8
Weekly	21.7	39.5	24.3
At least once per term	37.2	58.1	40.2
At least annually	44.3	60.5	46.6
Schools regularly holding:	%	%	%
House assemblies	35.6	34.9	35.5
Upper and lower school assemblies	61.3	53.5	60.1
Year assemblies	73.1	76.7	73.7

*34.4% when regarding separate sites of split-site schools separately
[1]Figures are cumulative (e.g. 44.3% of county schools hold full assemblies at least once a year)

Table 3: *Schools holding assemblies*

Number of assemblies* per week per pupil:	Maintained schools	
	County	Voluntary
	%	%
0	0.7[1]	2.3[1]
1	17.8	9.3
2	34.4	25.6
3	13.8	20.9
4	18.6	25.6
5	12.3	11.5
More than 5	2.4	4.7
TOTAL	100.0	100.0

*excluding voluntary or classroom acts of worship
[1]Sixth form colleges

Table 4: *Frequency of assembly per pupil*

Number of schools responding	Maintained	
	County	Voluntary
	252	43
	%	%
Never	9.9	4.6
Sometimes	47.8	9.3
Usually	38.9	62.8
Always*	3.4	23.3
TOTAL	100.0	100.0

*respondents volunteered information, in addition to 'never', 'sometimes', 'usually'.

Table 5: *Frequency of assembly as an 'act of worship'*

(TES Survey © Times Newspapers Ltd 1985).

of a voluntary school, of the managers or governors thereof, the school premises are such as to make it impracticable to assemble them for that purpose.'

There is, of course, an exclusion clause which parents can take advantage of, as well as teachers.

Do you know whether this section of the Act is followed in your school? A survey of one in ten secondary schools in England and Wales in 1985 showed widespread non-compliance with this regulation, sometimes because of inadequate facilities (two thirds of county schools do not have a sufficiently large assembly area) but generally because in an increasingly secular and multi-faith society, the requirements of the Act are seen to be outdated. Tables 3, 4 and 5 show the extent to which this legal requirement is recognised in our secondary schools, only 6% of which actually follow section 25 to the letter.

As we have already seen, Section 18 of the 1986 Education Act placed a duty on governing bodies to decide whether or not to include sex education in the school curriculum. This controversial clause establishes the precedent that for the first time governors have exclusive control over a specific named component of the secular curriculum. If sex education is included in the curriculum, the LEA, the headteacher, and the governors are to 'take such steps as are reasonably practicable to secure that where sex education is given ... it is given in such a manner as to encourage those pupils to have due regard to moral considerations and the value of family life.' (Section 46, 1986 Education Act). A discussion about sex education in the curriculum is to be found later in this chapter, see pages 79–86.

Even though you have clearly defined legal duties to be involved in the curriculum, you may well find some opposition to this in your school. Indeed, if you look back through the minutes of your governing body, you may find that the curriculum issues are rarely dealt with, even in the head's report. Some heads are very protective about what they see as being their responsibility, since they are required to be in charge of the day-to-day management of the school – they are the captains of the ship.

This is quite understandable. From a head's point of view, she/he was appointed apparently because of appropriate professional expertise acquired after some years of specialist training and proved success in the classroom. From such a point of view, there is no sense in governors having a dog and barking themselves. Not only can many heads not understand why governors should have this legal duty of oversight of the curriculum, they also fail to appreciate why governors should want it. This is territory denied to governors for so long that heads possess squatters' rights, and a great deal of subtle diplomacy and negotiation is required by governors in asserting their claim. When I mounted my first series of training courses, the course leaflet stated that there would be discussions about the curriculum and governors' role. I received a most excited phone call from the chairman of one governing body who enquired whether the leaflet was accurate: could governors really discuss the curriculum? His head had told him quite firmly, 'I don't allow my governors to discuss the curriculum.' Needless to say, that phone call resulted in a course enrolment! Of course, there are many heads who are very open about the curriculum and welcome governors taking an active part in curriculum discussions. You will be able to judge your own head's position on this issue, and the stance you and your governing body should take in light of the curriculum sections of the 1986 Education Act as outlined on pages 33–36 of this book; what these sections aim to do is to ensure that the intentions of the 1944 Education Act are at long last realised for all schools, even though you may feel that the actual wording of the legislation leaves a lot to be desired.

THE CURRICULUM DEFINED AND REFINED

What is the curriculum? Have you ever tried to define it? If you have, no doubt some mention is made of subjects offered and teaching styles. This limited definition of the curriculum may account for teachers' sensitivity about your role. The curriculum, properly defined, is more than this. The Taylor Report called it:

'The sum of experience to which a child is exposed at school.'

What do you understand from this? Should teachers be worried about your curriculum role if such a definition is accepted? Does it cause you to tread willy-nilly on holy ground? My feeling is that we need a more precise definition before we can proceed, and the following seems to say it all:

'The curriculum in its full sense comprises all the opportunities for learning provided by a school. It includes the formal programme of lessons in the timetable: the so-called 'extra-curricular' and 'out-of-school' activities deliberately promoted or supported by the school, and the climate of relationships, attitudes, styles of

behaviour and the general quality of life established in the school
community as a whole.'
('A View of the Curriculum' DES 1980 p. 1)

If governors argue their case from this total perspective of the
curriculum, then they will be on much firmer ground.

How can this be done? You will need to be able to discuss the
curriculum from a position of some knowledge, so it is important that
you do your homework well. The recent background to the increased
public debate about the curriculum can be traced back to James
Callaghan's 'Great Debate' speech at Ruskin College, Oxford, when
he was Labour Prime Minister in 1976. Since we do not have a
centralised education system in this country as they do in some others
(e.g. in France where centralised control means that the curriculum (in
its limited sense), decided in Paris, is the same in every French school),
and since successive governments have been content to maintain their
non-interventionist position, especially about the curriculum,
Callaghan's speech can be seen as a milestone. It kicked off a wealth of
initiatives right up to the time of writing this account, so that the issue
of the curriculum was brought centre stage. No longer could schools
and teachers treat this as their secret garden, not to be entered by
anyone outside the 'profession', nor could the role of central
government be ignored.

In 1977 the then Labour Government issued Circular 14/77
requiring LEAs to report on their curriculum policies and practices.
Although the government changed in 1979, the new Conservative
administration became most active in calling for curriculum change
and reform. Having looked at the submissions to the 14/77 Circular,
the government called for a consensus for a national curriculum
framework. HMIs were active in the field, too. Her Majesty's
Inspectorate have been around since 1839, having an independent role
to inspect educational provision and to assess the work of our schools.
Their reports on individual schools are now published for all to see
(since 1983), and they also publish national reports on a variety of
educational issues. In some respects they are the eyes and ears of the
Department of Education and Science (the DES), the ultimate
controller, via the Secretary of State for Education, of the education
system in this country. In 1977, an HMI survey on school provision
for 11–16 year olds outlined eight broad areas of experience which
were considered to be important for all pupils:

- aesthetic/creative
- ethical
- linguistic
- mathematical
- physical
- social/political
- scientific
- spiritual

(Since the curriculum is constantly evolving, a ninth area of experience, namely technology, is now considered to be an essential addition to this list.)

Looking at the secondary school curriculum in this light takes you away from considering it as merely a list of subjects. Does your school – assuming it to be in the 11–16 age range – contain a reasonable balance of the above categories? Balance in the secondary school curriculum is most difficult to achieve considering the demands made upon it. The DES has made firm proposals that the following subjects should be a feature of such a curriculum diet:

English, Maths, Science, Religious Education, Physical Education, Modern Languages, Arts and Crafts, Careers Education, History, Geography and Economics.

You as governors may equally as firmly recommend that such subjects as:

Civics, Law, Politics, Peace Education, Computer Studies, Rural Science, Domestic Science, Technology, Sex Education, Multicultural Education, Parent Education, Social Studies, Health Education, Media Studies and others

should feature on the curriculum of your school.

The problem is one of squeezing a quart into a pint pot. Remember that your school meets for less than 1000 hours per year; legally the school day for pupils of eight years of age and above is fixed at a minimum of at least four hours daily of secular instruction, divided into morning and afternoon sessions (for under eights the figure is three hours minimum daily) for 190 days per year. You will find a remarkable degree of local divergence in hours worked by various schools, but the daily average is around five hours of instruction. How is all this subject knowledge going to be catered for? Thinking of the curriculum in terms of areas of experience will help your governing body in analysing the curriculum of your school. One suggested curriculum model is as follows:

%

12.5	LINGUISTIC	
12.5	MATHEMATICAL	
10.0	PHYSICAL	
10.0	MODERN LANGUAGE	
15.0	SOCIAL/POLITICAL	Second Modern Language
5.0	ETHICAL	
20.0	CREATIVE/AESTHETIC	
15.0	SCIENTIFIC	Technology

Table 6: *Example of curriculum model for 10/11–14 high school based on 8 areas of experience*

You will find it illuminating to subject the timetable of your own school to such a percentage analysis.

Where primary schools are concerned, a 1978 HMI Primary School survey listed a similar list of ideal components in the primary curriculum:

Language and Literacy, Mathematics, Science, Aesthetics (including P.E.), and Social Abilities (including R.E.).

Again, applying the above analysis to your primary school would be a useful exercise.

Generally, HMI reports favour a wide curriculum in primary schools, since such a curriculum provides many opportunities for the practice and application of the 3 Rs. Where primary schools are concerned, there is evidence of a high priority being given to the 3 Rs, with gradually improving standards. Teachers are found to be hard-working and caring, and pupils polite and friendly. The only reservations expressed concern about the occasional failure to meet the needs of the least able and the most able, generally inadequate craft and science provision, and scarcely any evidence of work which takes into account the nature of our multi-ethnic society. Additionally, one report stated:

> 'The majority of schools do not have any spare resources; as a result desirable and important extensions of the present curriculum may be prevented or stultified ..., almost all schools are short of books, especially ones of good quality. Overall the condition of books in schools seems to be deteriorating and there are insufficient funds available to replace them or to extend the range available.' (Education Observed, 1984, p. 3/4)

Indeed, it is important that you realise the resource implications of the curriculum and calls for curriculum change. What goes on in the classroom costs money: change costs even more. It is ironic that the many DES curriculum reports, which usually call for some change or another, have printed in small, sometimes minute, lettering inside the front cover:

> 'Nothing said in this report is to be construed as implying government commitment to the provision of additional resources'!

You are probably aware that between LEAs there is an enormous discrepancy in the amounts found per pupil in the education budget, as Table 7 comparing four LEAs shows.

You would find it illuminating to compare these statistics, which are published annually, with those of your own LEA. One interesting comparison is with the Inner London Education Authority which in the same year incurred unit costs per pupil of £1170 per primary child and £1778 per secondary (figures which are almost double that of

PUPIL TEACHER RATIOS – 1984-5

	Nursery	Primary	Secondary
Hereford & Worcs.	———	23.8	17.2
Kent	22.0	23.6	16.8
Lancs.	22.4	22.7	16.7
Notts.	18.4	20.8	15.3
Worst			
(English counties)	50.0	25.0	18.1
	(Suffolk)	(Oxon.)	(IoW)
Best			
(English counties)	15.0	20.2	15.3
	(Surrey)	(Humber)	(Notts.)

(Source: CIPFA)

UNIT COSTS PER PUPIL – 1984-5

	Primary Schools	Secondary Schools
Hereford & Worcs.	659	936
Kent	637	965
Lancs.	645	997
Notts.	775	1061
Highest	785	1069
(English counties)	(Humberside)	(Avon)
Lowest	637	936
(English counties)	(Kent)	(Heref'd & Worcs.)

(Source: CIPFA)

CAPITATION AND BOOK SPENDING (PRIMARY SCHOOLS) 1983-4

	Total Capitation	Books Only
Hereford & Worcs.	22.11	9.6
Kent	20.52	4.95
Lancs.	20.48	7.53
Notts.	36.37	10.48
English counties: Lowest :	16.27 (Surrey)	4.52 (Surrey)
English counties: Highest:	36.37 (Notts).	12.48 (Bucks.)
English counties: Average	24.06	7.49

CAPITATION AND BOOK SPENDING (SECONDARY SCHOOLS)

	Total Capitation	Books Only
Hereford & Worcs.	40.07	11.44
Kent	39.73	8.95
Lancs.	36.68	8.10
Notts.	53.28	13.42
English counties: Lowest:	18.29 (Derby)	5.89 (Cheshire)
English counties: Highest:	55.64 (Beds.)	18.22 (Beds.)
English counties: Average	40.26	10.15

(Source: DoE and Ed. Publishers' Council)

Table 7: *Education budget per pupil*

Hereford and Worcestershire LEA). ILEA's pupil/teacher ratio was also very favourable, being 17.2 for primary schools and 12.8 for secondary. (However, pupil/teacher ratios, although interesting, do not tell us much about the *actual* number of children in a class; in reality, as you will know from your own experience, the ratios are much higher.) Such discrepancies are the result of the local political character of your authority and the ability, or willingness, to raise the necessary cash through the rates. In reality, you will find that because of a lack of resources, your school may not have much leeway for undergoing any curriculum change which necessitates the spending of scarce financial resources.

Now that LEAs have a duty under Section 29 of the 1986 Education Act to supply governors with an itemised financial statement concerning their school, and to make available 'a sum of money which the governing body are to be entitled to spend at their discretion ... on books, equipment, stationery and such other heads of expenditure (if any) as may be specified by the authority or prescribed by the Secretary of State', governors will have to take more notice of educational spending. Whether this legal provision means that all the capitation allowance is to be given over to the governors, or just part of it, is unclear. This is something for the governor to check locally. It is considered that most governing bodies are likely to delegate their sum to the headteacher.

If you do not already know it, you will find it interesting to find out from your head what the capitation allowance per pupil is in your schools. In Leicestershire in 1986/7 the following amounts applied:

    5–11 year olds – £19.41
    11–15 year olds – £30.87
    16+   – £45.85

Remember that this sum has to stretch over 190 days, and may well include paying for the school's phone bills, travel and other items. When you understand that less than the equivalent of a packet of crisps can be spent per pupil per day in the average primary school on books and materials, then you begin to realise how resourceful teachers need to be, why they clamour for more resources, and why PTA funds – supposedly for 'non-essential items'(!) – are so valued.

So inadequate are such capitation allowances considered by teachers, that heads in Gloucestershire took the unprecedented step in 1985 of disclosing their predicament in the face of the many Government reports which asked them to revamp the curriculum. They issued figures which showed that whereas £69 per pupil per year was allowed for pupils involved in government funded TVEI projects, they had just £24 per year per pupil below sixth form level after overheads for such things as cleaning and administration were allowed for. That amounted to 1.58p per lesson, or £3.00 annually for such subjects as Maths, Science, English and French and between 60p and £1.80 for 'minority' subjects like R.E., craft, drama, art, geography and history. When you realise that such triflings have to cover text books, art, craft and science materials, sports equipment, computers and associated software, other expensive audio visual aids, *and* furniture repairs, you can appreciate the Gloucestershire heads' concern.

(To show how typical Gloucestershire's problem was, compare its figures for educational spending with those in the tables on pages 68–69. In 1984/5 Gloucesteshire's total unit costs per primary pupil were £658, for secondary pupils, £998; the capitation allowances per primary pupil were £23, for secondary £34 (these figures do not tally with their pie chart – presumably some averaging out had been applied) and their pupil/teacher ratios were 22.7 and 17.2 for primary and secondary schools respectively.)

A similar problem of under-resourcing is found in secondary schools generally and has been noted by HMI reports. Whereas a wide curriculum is favoured in the primary school and is generally considered to be successful, in secondary education the very broadness

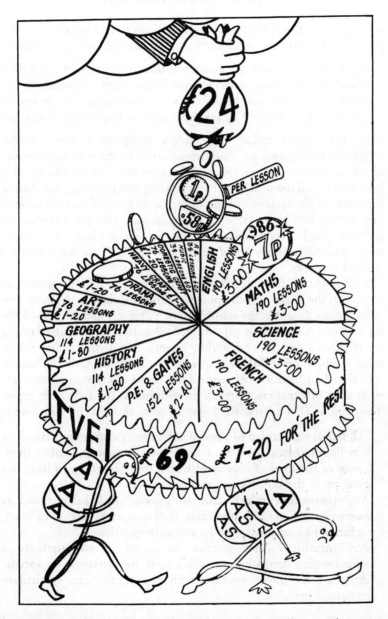

Fig 2: *Pie chart compiled by Gloucestershire heads to illustrate their acute problems*

needed can be a problem: it is indeed difficult to fit a quart into a pint pot. As the HMI Report 'A View of the Curriculum' (1980) stated:

> 'There is apparently no guarantee that five years of secondary education will have provided the pupil with opportunities to acquire, at whatever level, skills or knowledge or forms of understanding universally acknowledged as important'. (page 14)

This HMI report called for a larger compulsory core element supplemented by options. And this seems to be the pattern emerging in our secondary schools today. Where weaknesses are found, they have to do with too much teacher direction; dull teaching; unbalanced curricula for the extremes of the ability range particularly; not enough oral work; low expectations of pupils; not enough attention to political and economic literacy, technological awareness, environmental education and teaching which reflects this country's cultural diversity.

Whilst schools have developed an impressive range of options to cope with the quart-into-the-pint-pot problem, there is evidence that many pupils do not make sensible option choices, and are allowed to leave school with serious gaps in their education; particularly lacking are children's exposure to health, careers, social, moral and multi-cultural education. HMIs recommend that secondary school children are offered an 'entitlement curriculum' which takes into account the eight areas of experience already mentioned. As the 1983 DES report 'Curriculum 11–16: Towards a statement of entitlement' concluded:

> 'All pupils are entitled to a broad compulsory common curriculum which introduces them to a range of experiences, makes them aware of the kind of society in which they are going to live, and gives them the skills necessary to live in it.
> Any curriculum which fails to provide this balance and is overweighted in any particular direction, whether vocational, technical or academic, is to be seriously questioned.
> Any measures which restrict the access of all pupils to a wide-ranging curriculum or which focus too narrowly on specific skills are in direct conflict with the entitlement curriculum envisaged here.'

Admittedly, such discussions about the curriculum are complicated and technical. Your school will have been exhorted via the various reports listed above to subject its curriculum to a detailed analysis, and to have undertaken the vast project of putting in writing its curriculum aims and objectives for each subject. You should ask to see these written statements of intent. How far does the curriculum in your school measure up to the school's aims in general, and the individual subject's aims in particular? Is it suited to the individual needs of pupils? Are you involved as a governing body in a regular review of the school's curriculum policy? It is unlikely that many governing bodies up to 1986 would have been involved in such a formal way in curriculum reviews or in writing curriculum policy statements in the way proposed by the 1986 Education Act. They might not even have been aware that their active involvement as governors was being canvassed by the DES, and that schools had been asked to include their governors in detailed discussions about this secret curriculum garden. But, as one report stated:

> 'What schools teach and achieve is largely a measure of the dedication and competence of the headteacher and the whole staff and of the interest and support of the governing body.' ('The School Curriculum', HMSO 1981, page 3)

Moreover, the pressure from the DES for curriculum change continues apace with the issue since 1984 of HMI discussion papers on 'The Organisation and Content of the 5–16 curriculum', papers on the primary curriculum, 11–16 curriculum, objectives in English, policy statements on science, foreign languages (generally considered to be the disaster area of the curriculum), a statement of objectives for maths based on the Cockcroft report (1982) on the teaching of maths, discussion papers on art and music, and a government paper reviewing all the LEA submissions made to the DES following the issue of Circular 8/83 which asked LEAs for a progress report on their review of school curriculum policy. With all this activity going on, you will understand why the wise school consults its governors. In fact, an enormous amount of debate, much of it hostile, has been engendered by this wealth of discussion papers and it is likely that whilst most of the submissions to the DES have been from professional groups, some governing bodies will have made their views known.

After almost a decade of discussion and curriculum reform, most schools are now getting their curriculum act together. Whilst recognising the constraints of time available for schooling, and lack of resources, a coherent progressive curriculum is emerging. Sir Keith

Joseph said in a speech in 1984:

'The curriculum should be relevant to the real world and to the pupils' experience of it. Judged by that test, HMI reports show that much of what pupils are now asked to learn is clutter.'

You may find it instructive to list any unwanted 'clutter' you may have seen in your school to which you think Sir Keith referred. According to Sir Keith Joseph, the four principles of curriculum reform should be:

- BREADTH
- BALANCE
- DIFFERENTATION (i.e. taking into account the different capacity children have for learning a subject)
- RESPECT FOR CAPABILITY (i.e. acknowledging in particular the special needs of all pupils, from the least to the most able)

The 1985 'ideal' curriculum menu is outlined below:

For the primary phrase:

- a substantial emphasis on achieving competence in the use of language (which, in Wales, may be Welsh as well as English) and in mathematics;
- science;
- worthwhile offerings which develop understanding in the area of history, geography and R.E.;
- a range of aesthetic activities;
- opportunities throughout the curriculum for craft and practical work leading up to some experience of design and technology and of solving problems;
- physical and health education;
- computers;
- insights into the adult world, including how people earn their living.

You will find no place for foreign languages – something enthusiastically encouraged for primary schools in the mid-1960s. Such a curriculum, it is suggested, offers breadth, coherence and progression. In what ways does such a 'curriculum menu' differ from that of the 1978 Primary Survey outlined on page 67?

For the secondary (11–16) phase, it is government policy to include:

- R.E.
- English and English Literature

- Mathematics
- Science – physics, chemistry, biology
- a worthwhile offering of the humanities
- aesthetic subjects (Art, Music, Drama)
- practical subjects (craft, design, technology, domestic science)
- physical education
- a foreign language (for most able pupils)
  (For both the primary and secondary phases, Welsh has a place in the curriculum.)

This is a large compulsory core, and it is recognised that the secondary phase needs to be split into two stages: years 1–3 and 4–5. After years 1–3, it is assumed some subjects may be dropped. For example, many pupils may wish to drop a foreign language, while a few will wish to take on a second; humanities is given a low priority, and it is suggested that history or geography is dropped after three years; a similar case is made for domestic science and P.E. Dropping subjects after year 3 makes way in years 4–5 for an optional element in the curriculum. The concern is what proportion of the total time at school should be allocated to optional classes – the suggestion is 15% – and should options be free or constrained? It is accepted that room needs to be found for pre-vocational studies (assisting young people to prepare for the world of work), possibly following the model of the Technical and Vocational Education Initiative (TVEI); social education (including health education, careers, social studies); or environmental education; or short courses for these subjects, including also computer studies.

Contrary to the 1977 HMI Survey 11–16 mentioned on page 65, these government proposals view the curriculum in terms of subjects rather than areas of experience. However, for both the primary and secondary phase it is recognised that schools have a socialising function and that schools provide opportunities for pupils to develop personal qualities and 'desirable modes of behaviour' as well as to become 'familiar with the broadly shared values of our society'. Consequently, even though it is thought desirable that pupils, especially 11–16, need to understand the principles underlying a free society and have some basic economic awareness, the thorny subject of 'Peace Studies' is not considered worthy of an independent place in the curriculum, but should be allowed to 'arise naturally in various parts of the curriculum'. Such proposals have come under considerable attack, especially from the supporters of the humanities, history and geography; it is also questionable whether the whole range of additional extras can be squeezed into the suggested 15% optional category.

How does your curriculum measure up to these new proposals? Remember that these are discussion documents, and that LEAs and individual schools have much freedom in interpreting the proposals. For example, in some LEAs, Peace Studies constitutes a compulsory element in the secondary curriculum. The problems are greater for the governor of a secondary school. What is your school's compulsory core?

For example, an ILEA document, 'Improving Secondary Schools' (1984), argues for a compulsory core to include:

English Language and Literature	– 5 periods – 12½%
Mathematics	– 5 periods – 12½%
Science	– 4 periods – 10%
Personal and Social Education +	
Religious Education*	– 3 periods – 7½%
At least one Aesthetic subject	– 4 periods – 10%
At least one Technical subject	– 4 periods – 10%

(*to include careers education; citizenship; community studies; comparative R.E.; consumer education; education for parenthood and family life; health education; industrial education and work experience; mass media and leisure; moral education; political education; social impact of science and technology; economic education; social and life skills; information technology; and study skills. These to be studied over the five years of schooling in units of six to eight weeks – as is advocated for other areas of curriculum.)

This core would leave 37½% of the school week or 15 out of 40 periods for either additional periods in compulsory subjects or a free range of option choice from:

Classical and modern languages
History
Geography
Economics
Commercial and business studies
P.E.
Additional 'aesthetic' subjects
Additional technical subjects
Additional English and Mathematics

This influential report, produced under the Chairmanship of Dr

Hargreaves, ILEA's Chief Inspector and hailed by some as the new guru of curriculum innovators, has been widely publicised and its effect may well be to encourage other local authorities to offer a similarly flexible curriculum design. (Incidentally, this report recognised the valuable role governors had to play in the life of the school, especially parent governors. Since only one seventh of ILEA secondary school governors were shown to be representatives of parents, it recommended that governing bodies should be increased from 20 to 23, and that parents should constitute one quarter of the governing body – 4 to be elected by the parents and a fifth parent to be co-opted to ensure that minority groups are represented.)

Compare this curriculum scheme to one from a large Leicestershire Comprehensive which split its week into 25 periods, 40% of which were compulsory, (in Humanities, English, Maths, Sound and Movement), 24% of which offered constrained options (in Design and Science) and 36% of which allowed for free options from the following list:

Children and Parents
Computer Studies
Dance
Drama
English Literature
Fitness for Life
French
Film and Television
Geography
German
History (Modern World)
History (Schools' Council Course)
Journalism
Music
Physical Education
Spanish
Community Service
Typing

Now that all schools are required to publish information booklets, governors can compare their own school's curriculum with others, to see how schools, especially secondary schools, cope with the enormous logistical problem of supplying a well-balanced, progressive, coherent, individualised curriculum taking into account

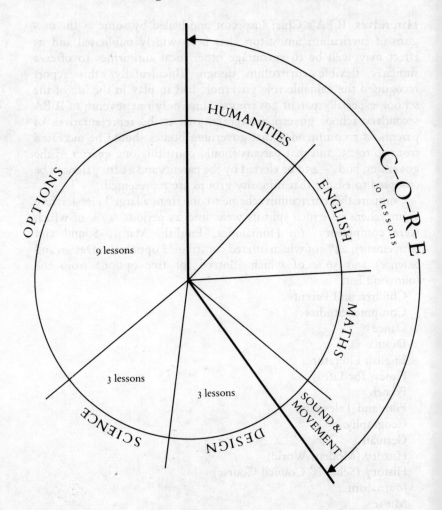

Fig. 3: *Curriculum scheme from a large comprehensive*

not only resources but also staffing availability, not to mention keeping abreast of the latest government advice in this area. Indeed, this modular approach to curriculum design is one which is gaining increasing support nationally.

Governors have a duty to monitor and understand this host of curriculum initiatives and innovations in their schools. Not only does the governing body have to write a curriculum policy statement, but it also has to account for itself annually by way of the annual report and the annual parents' meeting, both of which are likely to be heavily curriculum-oriented, and by making syllabuses available for inspection.

A potentially highly controversial feature of the curriculum is the governing body's policy regarding sex education. Those governors whose boards decide to include sex education in the curriculum may find the following section of interest.

SEX EDUCATION

A clause inserted into the 1986 Education Bill by the House of Lords brought the highly charged subject of sex education centre stage in mid-1986. It is important to point out that there has been no reliable evidence that sex education is badly taught in our schools; rather there is evidence that schools, especially primary schools, do not teach much sex education, and that health education in general is approached in a piecemeal fashion. Indeed, education for parenthood seems to have a low profile in our schools. An international study of children's sexual knowledge, 'Children's Sexual Thinking', which included research in England, revealed a frightening measure of ignorance about sex which supports the observation that sex education is not only absent from schools, but, more importantly, from the home, too; one of the conclusions of this research was that *parents* needed sex education.

Sex education has featured in the school curriculum for many years: you may remember your own school's treatment of the subject. Remember that, under the 1944 Education Act, LEAs have a duty to contribute to the moral, spiritual, mental and physical development of the community. Taking account of the 1980 Education Act which requested schools to include a statement about 'the manner and context in which education as respects sexual matters is given', your school prospectus has, since May 1981 when this particular regulation came into effect, had to go public in this area. Consequently, many schools have simply stated that they offer no sex education, and parents have had the choice of sending their children to such schools if they preferred to deal with this sensitive subject themselves. Schools which have chosen to provide sex education will have sought the advice of various professionals, will have studied any guidelines issued by their LEA, and will have paid heed to documents like the 1981 DES publication, 'The School Curriculum', which stated that 'sex education in one of the most sensitive parts of broad programmes of health education and the fullest consultation and co-operation with parents are necessary before it is embarked upon'. Such schools will also have had regard to statements like that made in the 1985 'Better Schools' White Paper that sex education, 'taught within a moral framework', is a central task for schools in preparing children for responsible adulthood. Such a view is expanded in the 1986 HMI discussion document, 'Health Education from 5–16', to be discussed below.

With this background, we may ask why the House of Lords saw fit to include the following clause into the 1986 Education Bill:

> 'The local authority by whom any county, voluntary or special school is maintained, and the governing body and headteacher of the school, shall take such steps as are reasonably practicable to secure that where sex education is given to any registered pupils at the school it is given in such a manner as to encourage those pupils to have due regard to moral considerations and the value of family life.'

This exact clause became Section 46 of the 1986 Education Act.

An anti-sex education movement – or at least the most recent one – can be traced back to the Gillick campaign of 1984/85 which made it illegal for contraceptive advice without parental consent to be given to under-16 year olds. This ruling caused problems for teachers and for organisations like the Family Planning Association which had been active for over a decade in supplying sex education tutors to schools; this ruling was subsequently overturned by the Law Lords in 1985. However, as a DES briefing paper on sex education sent to the LEAs in 1986 stated:

> 'The circumstances in which the Law Lords considered it might be justifiable for a doctor to offer contraceptive advice to a girl under 16 without the knowledge and consent of her parents do not have a parallel in school education.'

(This is, in my view, a debatable point. Since the Government's AIDS campaign, which has gained momentum rapidly since the Spring of 1987, much explicit advice, especially concerning condoms, has been directed at schoolchildren of every age – indeed the word 'condom' and its various derivatives is now a common feature of playground and classroom conversation. Additionally, all teachers have been sent a DES booklet 'AIDS: Some Questions and Answers' (available free charge from the DES Publications Despatch Centre – address on page 259), which presumably is an encouragement to them to answer frankly any questions children may have; some LEAs have, in fact, instituted AIDS in-service training for their teachers. This causes a dilemma for those governing bodies which do not wish to promote sex education in school, and to Roman Catholic Schools which want to deal with sex education, yet disapprove of contraception. However, there are estimated to be some 200 schoolchildren carrying the AIDS virus (Spring 1987 estimate), and AIDS is clearly an issue which schools, and governing bodies, cannot duck. As a way out of this dilemma, schools may decide that AIDS education comes under the umbrella of health education, rather than sex education).

The sensitivity which surrounds sex education is perhaps best highlighted by Brent and Haringey Education Authorities who hit the headlines in 1986 for pursuing sex education policies which included dealing with homosexuality in ways which offended some who heard about them; the mass media seized upon their use of a textbook, since withdrawn, called 'Jenny lives with Eric and Martin'. How many people, or children, ever read the offending literature is not known. Apparently the book, which could only be used with parental consent, was a Danish book, written by a female writer, which the publisher's blurb described thus:

'When you are grown up, you can live together in different ways. Some women fall in love with a man and live with him. And some men fall in love with a woman and live with her. But women do also fall in love with other women, and men do fall in love with other men. In this book you will read about Jenny and Eric. Jenny is a little girl. Martin is Jenny's dad, and Eric is Martin's lover. They all live happily together, and this is the story of how they spend their weekend.'

The ensuing furore was heightened by the fact that this was a picture book, which included a photograph of five-year-old Jenny in bed with her father and his lover, and could be read by very young pupils. Without knowing the full facts, or reading the offending literature, it is difficult to pass judgement, but this illustrates the need for governors and teachers to ensure that they treat this important subject with due regard being made to parental and public sensibilities.

Schools, then, found themselves in a difficult position: on the one hand there seemed to be a revolt against the provision of sex education, yet on the other hand they were being exhorted, particularly by the DES, to include moral education, health education (including sex education) and preparation for family life and adulthood as essential elements of the school curriculum. Most schools which include sex education on the curriculum are careful to solicit the co-operation of the parents, usually inviting them to a parents' evening at which teaching materials are reviewed. As the 1986 DES document, 'Health Education 5–16', states:

> 'Schools should be ready to discuss fully and sensitively with parents any of their particular concerns, emphasising the complementary nature of the roles of parents and schools and stressing the importance of balance and objectivity in teaching children about sex and personal relations in a world where much in everyday conversation and the media trivialises and sensationalises these areas of life.'

It should be noted that international research shows that countries which encourage sex education have lower teenage pregnancy rates and lower abortion rates than countries which shun sex education; there is even the suggestion that the spread of AIDS is also slower in countries which accept sex education. For example, a NAGM conference on Health Education in the autumn of 1986 heard of research which showed that in Holland some 18 girls out of 1000 in the 15–19 age range became pregnant in 1980–81, compared to 43 out of 1000 girls in England and Wales and 96 out of 1000 girls in America. The significance of these statistics is that sex education is encouraged in Holland and Scandinavian countries (it is compulsory in Sweden), treated in a piecemeal fashion in England and Wales and largely discouraged in the United States where deep religious feelings surround the issue. However, it is interesting to note that in those American States which encourage sex education, rates of teenage pregnancy are significantly lower than in those states which do not.

Furthermore, a number of British surveys in 1986 reached the overwhelming conclusion that both pupils and parents want schools to include sex education in the curriculum: many parents are uneasy about having sole responsibility in this area. However, governors with schools which contain Muslim girls will understand that while subjects like childcare and human biology are acceptable, Islam prohibits the teaching of sex education, seeing this as a matter for parents.

It was to be expected that when sex education was debated in Parliament, feelings would run as high as they do outside. (Interested governors can read the complete three-hour debate in Hansard (Volume 102, No. 160, pages 1056–1096) – details from your local library.)

As we have already seen, the effect of the legislation is to remove sex education from the control of the teachers, and from the LEA, to the governing body. The legal position now is as follows:

'The articles of government for every school shall provide for it to be the duty of the governing body –
(a) to consider separately ... the question whether sex education should form part of the secular curriculum for the school; and
(b) to make, and keep up to date, a separate written statement –
  (i) of their policy with regard to the content and organisation of the relevant part of the curriculum; or
  (ii) where they conclude that sex education should not form part of the secular curriculum, of that conclusion.' (Section 18 (2), 1986 Education Act)

Consequently, governing bodies can choose not to offer sex education, due regard having been given to their LEA's curriculum policy statement. If the governing body chooses to offer sex education, then it must provide a written statement about the content and organisation of sex education and ensure along with the LEA and headteacher that 'reasonably practicable' steps are taken to ensure that any sex education has 'due regard to moral considerations and the value of family life.'

The governing body will have a right, and a duty, to examine the school's sex education provision, to monitor materials and teaching styles, and to reject any aspects they dislike; teachers and heads will be obliged to comply with the governors' decisions. It is assumed that this is an area in which governors may choose to spend some of the finance allocated to them for books and equipment. It seems likely, then, that discussions about sex education will constitute a significant proportion of governors' meetings. Moreover, this issue is also likely to feature in the annual governors' report and annual parents' meeting. Governors will also have to give careful consideration to parental requests to withdraw their children from lessons where sex education is offered, and also to consider what alternative arrangements will be made for such children.

With the above discussion in mind, governors may care to consider the following:

- If sex education is taught in your school, does it have 'due regard to moral considerations and the value of family life'?
- Do you favour sex education being taken out of the control of teachers and of the LEA and being given over to the governing body – the only curriculum area with this special status?
- As a governing body, will you be able to discharge your responsibilities for sex education effectively, or will you opt out and decide that sex education will not be taught in the school?
- If you opt out, are you content to leave such an important subject to playground tittle tattle and the sensationalism and trivialising of the popular press?
- If the governing body opts out, what do you expect your teachers to do when pupils ask questions relevant to sex education as they do spasmodically in all areas of the curriculum? Is the teacher to give no reply? What will the governing body's response be if a teacher gives an incidental sex education 'lesson' in response to a pupil's legitimate concern, especially if the child says that her/his parents will not or are unable to, give the necessary information?
- If the governing body decides to teach sex education, how will it recommend tackling the thorny issues of AIDS, sexually transmitted diseases, abortion, homosexuality?

Further advice in the form of a Government Circular is to be issued, but at the time of writing this was not available; ask your clerk for details. Meanwhile, to help you answer such questions, it is worth quoting at length from the 'Health Education 5–16' booklet which was widely circulated in 1986:

'*The scope of sex education*
The importance of sexual relationships in all our lives is such that sex education is a crucial part of preparing children for their lives now and in the future as adults and parents. In sex education factual information about the physical aspects of sex, though important, is not more important than a consideration of the qualities of relationships in family life and of values, standards and the exercise of personal responsibility as they affect individuals and the

community at large. It is therefore quite common to find sex education taught as part of a programme of personal and social education, sometimes in conjunction with religious education, as well as of a health education programme.'

... 'In aided and special agreement schools, although the topics within a sex education programme might cover a range similar to that in other schools, the teaching will rest on the principles upon which the school is founded.'

... 'Pupils of secondary school age will inevitably become more directly aware of their own physical development and feelings of attraction towards another person, as well as of adult attitudes, sometimes conflicting, towards sexual behaviour. For this reason alone, schools need to deal sensitively and appropriately with such issues as contraception, sexually transmitted diseases, homosexuality and abortion. But such treatment is essential for other reasons also. All these issues involve not only knowledge, but moral and legal questions, are of concern to parents, and may prompt pupils to seek advice from the teacher, either in the classroom or more informally. How the school approaches these issues may also be affected by its legal status and the principles on which it was founded. Nevertheless it remains necessary to include all these issues as part of the secondary school's programme of sex education since they are brought to pupils' attention in a variety of contexts both inside and outside school. The discussion of these issues should be objective and attempt to explore all sides of the argument honestly. Some account of the law applying to sexual relationships involving children under 16, to homosexuality and to abortion should be given.'

... 'Given the openness with which homosexuality is treated in society now it is almost bound to arise as an issue in one area or another of a school's curriculum. Information about and discussion of homosexuality, whether it involves a whole class or an individual, needs to acknowledge that experiencing strong feelings of attraction to members of the same sex is a phase passed through by many young people, but that for a significant number of people these feelings persist into adult life. Therefore it needs to be dealt with objectively and seriously, bearing in mind that, while there has been a marked shift away from the general condemnation of homosexuality, many individuals and groups within society hold sincerely to the view that it is morally objectionable. This is difficult territory for teachers to traverse and for some schools to accept that homosexuality may be a normal feature of relationships would be a breach of the religious faith upon which they are founded. Consequently, LEAs, voluntary bodies, governors, heads and senior staff in schools have important responsibilities in devising guidance and supporting teachers dealing with this sensitive issue.'

Sex education is an emotive, controversial subject, and reaching a collective decision about its exclusion or inclusion in the curriculum is likely to strain relations in some governing bodies. However, it is useful to ground your discussions in the fact that we are preparing today's children for the twenty-first century and that, consequently, governing bodies, now that they have control of this important curriculum area, are being less than helpful to their schools if they adopt the ostrich position.

FURTHER READING

DES	'Health Education from 5–16', *HMSO* 1986
Goldman R & J	'Children's Sexual Thinking', *Routledge and Kegan Paul* 1982
Lee C.	'The Ostrich Position: Sex, Schooling and Mystification', *Unwin Paperbacks* 1986.

THE HIDDEN CURRICULUM

Alert readers will have spotted that the discussion so far has tended to deal with only the formal part of our curriculum definition given on pages 63–64. This is because of the need to have informed you about the recent curriculum debate, which has centered on the formal aspects. But you will remember that our definition of the curriculum included:
  'the climate of relationships, attitudes, styles of behaviour and the general quality of life established in the school community as a whole.'
Not much of the above discussion touches on this equally vital part of the curriculum over which you have oversight. Whilst it is appreciated that you may feel – unwarrantedly – that you can have little influence in the formal, technical, professional side of the curriculum, you must not shirk your responsibilities here. But what of the second part of the definition? What does it mean and how can you exert any influence?
  We might say that the formal part of the curriculum is what the headteacher will write about in your governors' report; it describes

timetable, the special ways in which the various subjects are being taught and matters to do with staffing the curriculum. It is the kind of detail to which you are directed on your school visit, and which is also described in the school prospectus. It is what the school likes to pat itself on the back about. But there is more to a school than this – hence the second part of the definition. This is something which is rarely described in reports, but pervades everything that the school does. It is the undocumented aspects of school life – the reading between the lines, the climate, the ethos – it is the *hidden curriculum,* which is, arguably, even more important and influential than the formal curriculum.

We know that in many situations in life we receive and/or interpret messages from the various settings and cues which confront us. To put it in the vernacular, we get vibes; the setting tells us something. Moreover, different people receive different vibes from the same setting, and at different times. And this is no less true of the school. The very way the school organises itself, its rules and regulations, its methodologies, transmit messages. Unfortunately, messages are not always received and understood as the sender intended. For example, what messages do you receive from the following:

A The wearing of school uniform is compulsory in this school.
B It is the policy of this school to stream children according to their ability.
C If you want to go to the toilet, you must first put up your hand.
D Parents are not allowed beyond this point.

If you discuss these statements with fellow governors, you may elicit a range of responses concerning these messages like:

A 'We feel that a school uniform shows the outside world that this is a disciplined, caring school' *or*
'Schools only recommend the wearing of school uniform to impose a set of standards, to squeeze out individuality, to reward mindless conformity.'
B 'It is the school's duty to recognise individual excellence and to make special provision so that each child receives an education which suits her capabilities' *or*
'This school still thinks it's a grammar school. Streaming children serves to sponsor a few at the expense of the many, because it shows that only certain kinds of learning and certain kinds of pupil are really valued.'

C 'We can't run our lessons unless children are properly trained.
We can't cope with interruptions, and, anyway, we have break
times of this kind of thing' *or*
'It's embarrassing enough having to answer a call of nature when
you're involved in a group task in a busy building without
having to draw attention to yourself as well. It's humiliating.'
D 'The teachers can't have the responsibility for looking after
children and be bothered by mums and dads at the same time.
They're busy people, and we shouldn't interfere with the
professionals' *or*
'What have teachers got to be scared of? They're our children.
It's our school. Without us and all the hard work we put into our
children, their job either wouldn't exist or would be even more
difficult. Don't they know that the latest trends are to involve
parents more closely, since by so doing they improve the quality
of schooling?'

In other words, the hidden curriculum does not only just concern
what teachers teach, but also what children and their parents learn,
which may well be the *unintentional* consequences of the teaching
and/or organisation. This will clearly be different from school to
school, from class to class, from teacher to teacher, from time to time.

Teachers are often not in the best position to assess the hidden
curriculum, which is where you as governors come in. You bring a
different pair of eyes and ears to the school. Since you are not
immersed in it daily, you are able to look at it more objectively. For
instance, it is likely that you will be able to spot examples of sexism
and racism in the curriculum which teachers are not conscious of (see
Chapters 5 and 6 for more detailed discussion of these concepts).
Moreover, children are very adept at picking up the cues which are
sent to them intentionally or unintentionally. For example, in large
comprehensive schools it is not unknown for non-examination groups
to be given inferior classrooms (perhaps in mobiles located in odd
corners throughout the campus) and inferior teachers. The message is
quickly understood: 'little is expected of us, little is given to us;
they've lost all hope in us.' No wonder such children often rebel; just
as nothing succeeds like success, nothing fails like failure. Indeed, the
fear and boredom which result from much school organisation and
teaching are themselves unintended products of the hidden curriculum:
school intends to turn children on to learning, yet, paradoxically, it
progressively turns many of them off.

Schools must be very careful about such unintended consequences. Two more examples should give you other insights into the hidden curriculum.

A parent was collecting his 4¾ year old daughter from her reception infants class during the early part of her first term at school. While he was waiting for his daughter to tie her shoelaces, he asked the teacher how his daughter was doing at school. The teacher looked down at the child saying, 'Shall I tell Daddy the truth?' to which she received a sheepish nod. The father braced himself for the worst. 'Well, she's been a bit naughty. You see, David and Ian came up to my desk and said, 'We like Alice, she does our work for us.' Well, I had to tell Alice that she mustn't do that kind of thing in my class, must you, Alice?' At which father and daughter took leave of the teacher. What does the little girl learn from this? Probably that school is a competitive place where individuality is promoted, where initiative is penalised, and where helping your friends, even though they may be floundering, is a punishable offence. Admittedly, this may not have been the message intended, but can there be a guarantee it was not the one received?

Finally, read this little dialogue taken from a different infants class during a cookery lesson. Having read it, you should jot down some of the things the children have learnt other than cookery.

COOKERY LESSON – INFANTS

Teacher	What must you do before starting?
Children	Wash hands, put on an apron.
Teacher	Well remembered – girls go first and girls put on blue aprons and boys red so I know the difference.
	Boys go and get out the big heavy bowls.
	Now go and wash your hands – hurry back.
John	Can I weigh the margarine?
Teacher	Yes – you can go first, then Marjorie, Sundip, Tim, and Ruth. Next time Ruth will be first in the queue.
Ruth	Is this butter, Miss?
Teacher	No, it's margarine – just as good as butter but cheaper.
Sundip	My mum uses oil in the chapattis. She says it's like melted margarine.

Teacher	We must ask your mum to show us sometime.
Ruth	My mum uses margarine in scones. Can she show us too?
Teacher	We can't have everyone's mum here.
John	Can I go to the toilet?
Teacher	No, you should have gone at playtime before we started work. Now, who will mix the cake? Someone who doesn't shout out.

Well, what aspects of the hidden curriculum did you discern? Will the children have received similar messages? Was the teacher aware of these messages? Would it help her if she were?

GETTING INVOLVED

It is only by frequent, well-planned and purposeful visits to your school that you will be able to understand the curriculum in all its diversity. As a member of a governing body, you have much to offer and to contribute. No school is an island. All schools can profit from the carefully considered views of others. All teachers benefit from discussing their work with another adult – too much of what they do is with young people. If you see something you do not understand, feel free to ask the expert:

Why is this done?

Do children benefit from this?

Can they learn adequately this way?

How do you keep tabs on them?

What reading scheme do you use?

What's all this modern maths about?

How do you use computers in the classroom?

What problems do you have as a result of lack of resources?

What's the school going to do when it loses its drama specialist?

All these questions, and many others, are curriculum-related. They are not busy-body questions. You are not poking your nose in. They are legitimate questions of committed, concerned supporters. Without answers to these kinds of questions, you will not be able to do your job properly. You will not know if the school is doing the job it purports to be doing. And you need to seek out the answers if you are to be informed. Since it is unlikely that answers to these kinds of questions will be in print, you have to get used to talking to teachers, and they have to get used to talking to you. If teachers feel that you come to the school in a caring, supporting, befriending way, they will be pleased to be your guide through this secret curriculum garden. If your questions seem unreasonably aggressive, and if you adopt an inspectoral role, then you will appreciate that your motives will be questioned and the ensuing dialogue will not be to your advantage.

Tread carefully in this secret garden: its secrets are important, and you have a duty to find them out. Whatever type of school you are a governor of, it is important that you maintain an interest in all new educational developments; after all, the primary school governor may become a secondary school governor and vice versa. We are in a period of rapid curriculum change, especially at the secondary level, and governors will find that discussions about the curriculum will occupy a greater proportion of their time than hitherto, not least because of the provisions of the 1986 Education Act. That this is the case is to be applauded since schooling has more to do with the curriculum than with smelly toilets and peeling paintwork.

The following three chapters concentrate on certain aspects of the curriculum which need particular attention from governors: sexism, racism and special needs.

FURTHER READING

Cockcroft W.	'Mathematics Counts' (known as the *Cockcroft Report*), HMSO 1982
DES	'Curriculum 11–16', HMSO 1977
"	'Ten Good Schools', HMSO 1977
"	'Primary Education in England', HMSO 1978
"	'Aspects of Secondary Education in England', HMSO 1979
"	A View of the Curriculum', HMSO 1980
"	'A Framework for the School Curriculum', HMSO 1980
"	'The School Curriculum', HMSO 1981
"	'Curriculum 11–16: Towards a Statement of Entitlement', HMSO 1983

DES	'English 5–16', *HMSO* 1984
"	'Mathematics 5–16', *HMSO* 1985
"	'The Curriculum from 5–16', *HMSO* 1985
Fletcher T.	'Microcomputers and Mathematics in Schools', *DES* 1983
Galton M. *et al.*	'Inside the Primary Classroom', *Routledge and Kegan Paul* 1980
Inner London Education Authority	'Improving Secondary Schools' (known as the *Hargreaves Report*), *ILEA Learning Resources* 1984

NB: Your school may have copies of many of the above.
It is worth writing to:

The Publications Despatch Centre,
DES,
Honeypot Lane,
Stanmore,
Middlesex

which issues summary versions of some of the above free, e.g. a four-page leaflet, 'Cockcroft: An introduction for primary schools' is a useful guide. When writing, ask for a list of the DES free publications, which cover every curriculum area.

5 Sexism in the curriculum – sorting out the girls from the boys

Many governors are unsure about how to go about eliminating sexism, or are yet to be convinced of the need to concern themselves with the issue. This chapter presents them with evidence that, it is hoped, will begin to shed light on this most important aspect of schooling and the governors' monitoring role.

A booklet published by the Equal Opportunities Commission in 1985, 'Equal Opportunities and the School Governor', advised governors to undertake a three-stage plan of action:

- Get the issue raised
- Take positive action
- Keep up the momentum

This chapter aims to equip you with the necessary information, and inspiration, to effect this three-stage plan of action.

GIRLS AND UNDER-ACHIEVEMENT IN EDUCATION: SOME FACTS

'Giving them a boy's education will damage their reproductive organs.' (The Lancet 1863)

'A girl is not necessarily a better woman because she knows the height of all the mountains in Europe and can work a fraction in her head; but she is decidedly better fitted for the duties she will be called upon to perform in life if she knows how to wash and tend a child, cook simple food well, and thoroughly clean a house.' (Board School Report 1874)

What have the above to do with a discussion of today's schools? Surely such attitudes do not still hold? Well, compare them with two quotes, each a century later:

> '... the incentive for girls to equip themselves for marriage and home-making is genetic.' (Newsom Report 1963)
>
> 'Our girls need to be able to read and write well, to add up and to have the right manner. 'A' levels would simply give them ideas and make them restless.' (Departmental Store Training Officer 1977)

Girls have been gradually catching up boys, and in some cases overtaking them in certain aspects of their schooling, since the mid-60s particularly. For example, more girls than boys used to leave school as soon as it was legally possible, but since 1967 there has been a gradual increase in the number of pupils, particularly girls, who stay on at school; in England and Wales in 1983, 30% of boys and 33% of girls stayed on an extra year, compared to 1967 figures of 23% and 21% respectively. Although girls' success in 'O' and 'A' level has been superior to boys' – in 1985 11% of girls left school with five or more 'O' levels, compared to just over 9% of boys; fewer girls than boys left school without any exam results; and, for the first time, more girls than boys passed at least one 'A' level, 18.5% compared to just under 18% for boys – there is no room for complacency. We shall examine the sex differences in relation to subjects later in the chapter, but the crucial point is that fewer girls than boys enter full-time higher education – 199,000 girls and women under 24, compared to 246,000 boys and men in 1983/4, and of the 75,000 university first degrees awarded in 1983, only 40% went to women. And, although fewer girls than boys were unemployed in 1983/4 – 11% compared to 14% of 16-year-olds - fewer girl school leavers take on any form of job training and those that do gravitate towards sex-stereotypical training. For example, in 1983/4 on Youth Training Schemes there were 22% of girls compared to 28% of boys, with girls almost overwhelmingly in placements related to Community and Health Services, Food Preparation, Clerical and office services, and only one in five took places in Information Technology Centres. Only 20% of employed women have positions in the manufacturing, technical and scientific sectors of industry. Indeed, fewer girls than boys have employment which includes part-time study – 4% compared to 8% of boys.

Moreover, not only do girl pupils under-achieve once they have left school, but evidence suggests that their female teachers do also. Although women primary school teachers outnumber men by three to one, only four in ten primary school headteachers are women. In secondary education, where 45% of teachers are women, only one headship in six is held by a woman. Furthermore, in higher education, only 2% of professors are women; there is only one female chief education officer in our 104 LEAs; the first female polytechnic director was not in post until 1987; and there is no female university vice chancellor. In other words, there seems to be sex discrimination in our education system, and there is clearly a need for governors, with their exercise of control over the curriculum, to examine their school very carefully to see whether, for example, school admission procedures, curriculum, subject choices, the appointment and promotion of teachers, are perpetuating such inequalities.

This is no easy task, and many governors will need to be convinced of the above figures and some of the arguments which follow. Indeed, the sensitive nature about any discussion in this area is well highlighted in the case of a 1978 Working Party on sex equality in Devon's schools, which was headed by that county's chief education officer. The report simply asked teachers to examine more closely their attitudes and expectations about girls and to provide compensatory experience and equal opportunities for boys and girls to follow the same curriculum. This report, which clearly recognised that discrimination was occurring in Devon schools and that girls were under-achieving, caused an uproar locally, the ripples of which were felt nationally. The chairman of the education committee is quoted as saying:

> 'If boys are to be turned into fairies, and girls into butch young maids, it should be for parents to decide, and not for the education authority or schools. If parents wish to bring up boys as boys and girls as girls, this would seem to be highly desirable and fundamental to family life.'

Such a view seemed to be supported by some parents, especially those who objected to boys doing cookery and needlework. It is safe to assume that some governors, and even teachers, would also think similarly.

WHAT CAN GOVERNORS DO ABOUT THIS UNDERACHIEVEMENT? THE SEX DISCRIMINATION ACT 1975

Whatever you feel about the arguments and findings, it is as well to remind you that British law requires that all boys and girls enjoy equal educational opportunity. The Sex Discrimination Act (1975) which applies to the whole of Great Britain – but not to Northern Ireland – makes sex discrimination unlawful, not only in employment, training and the provision of goods, services and facilities, but also in education. It applies to discrimination against both women and men – and girls and boys. Two kinds of discrimination are outlined:

Direct discrimination, in which a person treats a woman or girl less favourably, on the grounds of her sex, than he or she would treat a man in similar circumstances; and *indirect discrimination,* in which a condition or requirement may be described as being equal as between the sexes, but discriminatory in its effect on one sex, because, for instance, a considerably smaller proportion of girls can comply with it.

Consequently, it is unlawful for a school to discriminate against a girl (or boy) on grounds of sex

(i) in the terms on which it offers to admit her to the establishment as a pupil, or

(ii) by refusing or deliberately omitting to accept an application for her admission to the establishment as a pupil, or

(iii) where she is a pupil of the establishment –

(a) in the way it affords her access to any benefits, facilities, or services, or by refusing or deliberately omitting to afford her access to them, or

(b) by excluding her from the establishment or subjecting her to any other detriment (Section 22).

Single sexed schools are still allowed under the Act.

How can you, as a governor, check whether any of your pupils (or staff for that matter) are subjected to detriment, directly or indirectly, as a result of their sex? The following case is a good example of unlawful discriminatory practice:

This case, known as the case of 'Debell, Sevket and Teh versus the London Borough of Bromley', concerns three 10-year-old primary school girls of the above surnames. After their 1982 summer break, they returned to school expecting to be members of the fourth year class 10. However, at assembly on the first morning they learnt that they were to be placed in a third year class – class 9 – along with five other girls: all the boys from their previous class being placed in class 10. Their parents were naturally concerned to know the reasons for this arrangement, arguing later that their daughters felt they were being kept down, with the result that both their self-esteem and confidence were affected, since others would perceive this new class organisation to be based on ability. They also argued that work in class 9 was of a lower level than that of class 10, and that this would cause their daughters to do less well in the examinations taken before transfer to secondary school. They were, furthermore, unhappy that their daughters would be deprived of association with their former classmates and friends.

On complaining, the parents learnt that there were 39 children in the fourth year: 17 boys and 22 girls, which was too many for a primary class. Consequently, there would be 31 pupils in class 10 – 17 boys and 14 girls. This meant that the eight youngest girls were to be accommodated in class 9 with other third year pupils. It transpired that there were four boys younger than Debell, Sevket and Teh, but they were being placed in class 10, ostensibly to balance the numbers of boys and girls in that class. (Mathematicians will want to know why the 'balance' could not have been achieved by a formula of 16 girls to 15 boys, or by a proportional split of 17 girls to 14 boys.) Since quite clearly the pupils had not been separated according to age, but according to sex, the parents made repeated requests to their LEA, the London Borough of Bromley, for the re-allocation of their girls to class 10. The requests being refused, the parents took the LEA to court under sections 1(1) (a) and 22(c) of the Sex Discrimination Act: their daughters as fourth year pupils were being treated less favourably than boy fourth year pupils. Their case was that this discrimination subjected their daughters to a detriment in that they would not be able to compete on an equal footing in the allocative tests at transfer to secondary school, the results of which would be used in streaming pupils. Moreover, these tests were also used as a measure of ability for entrance to the two local selective schools.

The LEA case was that in this particular school there had to be mixed-age classes; that teachers were used to teaching such groups; that children in classes 9 and 10 did mix socially and share some lessons; and that the curriculum was not based on teaching whole age groups on a progressive yearly basis, but on the progressive needs of each individual pupil as she moved through the school. Where these three girls were concerned, the head was of the opinion that they would do better educationally in class 9 which had a female teacher; she also admitted she had to endeavour to achieve an even mix of the sexes for the benefits this afforded to the curriculum and to the pupils' socialisation.

As it happened, the three girls did not do as well as their parents expected in the fourth-year examinations; one girl was sent to an independent school at her parents' expense; another was given private tuition at her parents' expense. Meanwhile, on advice from the Equal Opportunities Commission (EOC) classes 9 and 10 were rearranged in the summer term on the basis of age alone. Since this did not satisfy the parents (the rearrangement was made *after* the crucial tests in which their daughters were alleged to have under-achieved), and since both the school and the LEA were not inclined to admit that their conduct had been unlawful, proceedings were instituted at the County Court in the summer of 1983.

In the 1984 court case that followed, both the school and the LEA admitted that they had inadvertently contravened the 1975 Sex Discrimination Act, their class organisation in this instance being made on the grounds of sex. The girls were awarded £351 each, an additional sum of £278 being paid to cover the costs of private tuition incurred by one girl.

The implication of this case for governors and schools is clear: pupils should be treated on their individual merits, regardless of their sex.

The following practices have been deemed by the EOC to contravene the 1975 Act:

- The use of separate tests for boys and girls.
- The use of different norms in the calculation of test scores.
- The preparation of separate lists of scores for boys and girls.
- The operation of a quota system based on pupils' sex.
- The exclusion of pupils from courses of study solely on the ground of sex.
- The exclusion of pupils from visits, community/social service projects and out-of-school activities solely on the ground of sex.
- The exclusion of pupils from other benefits, facilities or services provided by a school solely on the ground of sex.
- Sex discrimination in careers guidance.
- Sex discrimination in the appointment and promotion of staff.

Before we go on to look at some common school practices which seem clearly unlawful, it would be appropriate for you to study carefully the following definitions:

Sexism = prejudicial discrimination based on gender, usually having the effect of relegating women to secondary and inferior roles.

Sex stereotype = a fixed and over-simplified idea of the usual behaviour, the abilities or the aspirations of persons of one sex.

With these in your mind, think about the following four themes – classroom behaviour, teaching materials, role models, option choice – which research demonstrates adversely affect girl pupils (especially in secondary schools).

CLASSROOM BEHAVIOUR

Have you ever stopped to look carefully at the children's behaviour as you make your school visit? You probably have the impression that, just as in your own family and circle of friends, it is the boys who are more mischievous and unruly, and the girls who are quieter and more keen to co-operate with the smooth running of the life of the home or school. You may be aware of research which shows that girls are better than boys both at reading and writing at the age of 11, and obtain better examination results than boys. How then do we explain the paradoxical view that girls are disadvantaged in the school where classroom behaviour is concerned?

The view is that girls, especially in primary schools, find themselves in a homely enclosed world in which they are not stretched and face few challenges. It suits teachers, most of whom in the primary classroom are women, to foster quietness, politeness and conformity; with over 25 pupils facing them every moment of the day, these are the conditions of least tension. However, such classrooms can become stultifying, especially for girls whose very quietness and conformity ill-equips them for the increasing competitiveness of the secondary school; in other words, such a system is teaching girls how to lose, since they fail to speak up and make a case for themselves. Consider the various mixed groups in which you meet and work. Do you find, in general, that women defer to men; that men, contrary to common belief, talk more than women and make more interruptions? Is your governing body like this? Such research is easy to undertake: simply place a tape-recorder in a mixed gathering and note and time the various contributions.

This is what seems to happen in the typical classroom: boys hog the limelight; they dominate classroom discussion; they demand more individual attention from teachers, knowing how to subvert classroom activity, and to incite their male peers to join in. The amazing upshot of all this is that both male and female teachers like boys best, take more interest in them, ask them more questions in class, and give them more help. And boys are very adept at feeding on this attention. Not only are boys more likely to be the teachers' favourites, but teachers, both male and female, are more likely to know their boy pupils' names, be more concerned about their academic progress and to have higher expectations of them. No wonder girls react to such discriminatory treatment. When the pupils themselves are asked who in the class they would rather be, girls choose boys; boys do not choose girls. When asked to rank their own ability, boys tend to exaggerate their own performance, whereas girls play down their own. Indeed, it is quite common for girls to under-achieve, not wishing to be seen as 'boffs'; they seem to realise that unpopularity is the price of competing with boys in class. As one study concludes:

> 'Girls may follow the same curriculum as boys – may sit side by side with boys in classes taught by the same teachers – and yet emerge from school with the implicit understanding that the world is a man's world, in which women can and should take second place.'

Many of these classroom practices you may consider trivial, and not intentionally discriminatory in any way. But here it would be well to remind you of the discussion on the hidden curriculum in the last chapter. As you go on your school visits, ask yourself these questions:

- Are boys and girls listed separately on the register?
- Do they line up according to their gender?
- Are the girls allowed to leave the classroom first?
- Do boys do the heavy lifting jobs?
- Do girls do all of the cleaning jobs?
- Are the boys and girls punished differently? Why?
- Are boys 'punished' by being made to sit next to girls, and vice versa?
- Do the teachers give equal attention to the demands of the boys and girls?
- Are girls allowed to wear trousers to school?
- Are girls allowed to wear earrings (or earstuds) whilst a similar concession is denied to boys?
- Are boys called 'cissies' if they cry?

Add your own questions to this list, or encourage your fellow governors to discuss their observations following their school visits.

TEACHING MATERIALS

There is no doubt that one of the ways in which attitudes may be influenced is through reading. Equally important is the influence which books can have on influencing boys' and girls' views of themselves as male of female. Have you ever really tried to read the books available in your school through the eyes of a child? This is admittedly a difficult task, but one of the more fruitful outcomes of the women's movement from the 1960s onwards has been to attract our attention to the overt sexism in most children's literature, from pre-reading books upwards. Again, such research is comparatively easy to do and a group of governors could quite quickly subject a range of the books used in their school to a content analysis and elicit quite disturbing results. The chances are that in story books the central character will be a boy (or male animal or male object) who will be active and adventurous, whilst girls will be passive and unadventurous. Indeed, one study found that even though 80% of writers for children's books are women, less than 1% of their books depicted girls as heroines or leaders. Moreover, the likelihood is that the amount of illustration concerning girls or female-related items will be significantly less than that depicting boys. This is compounded by the stereotypical representation of girls in books; they are likely to be involved in tasks related to housework, or to be playing at, or asking for, a narrow range of occupations such as secretary, nurse, teacher. It is for this reason that the immensely popular Janet and John series of reading books, in use for some 30 years, was phased out by Dudley LEA in 1985, having lost favour in that authority – as well as in schools up and down the country.

But it is not only children's fiction which is the culprit. Even in subject text books over the whole range of age ability, girls and women are relegated or lost. The Maths case study which follows gives some examples. You may also like to consider why very few women seem to appear in school anthologies concerning famous explorers, scientists, writers, historical figures? Indeed, one secondary school pupil who had been studying 'early Man' in a humanities class asked her teacher quite innocently whether women were not in existence in that period; a content analysis of the text book used showed no pictures of women or girls, and the text had to be read very carefully to glean only a passing reference to them.

Most teachers, and nowadays most publishers, are well aware of the amount of sexism in books, and non-sexist books are a feature of many publishers' catalogues; Penguin even published a lengthy catalogue in 1984 entitled 'A Penguin Non-Sexist Booklist: Ms Muffet Fights Back'. However, many of the 'offending' sexist books are likely to be on the school shelves for many years to come; governors and teachers can alleviate the damage done by campaigning for the removal of the more overtly sexist.

The struggle is likely to be a long one. Even the examination boards have yet to learn, as the following questions taken from a selection of recent papers show:

- By selling a refrigerator for £63 a shopkeeper makes a profit of $12\frac{1}{2}\%$ of the price to him. How much does he pay for the refrigerator?
- Two towns A and B are 26 km apart. A cyclist leaves A at 13.00 ... He then rests ...
- A salesman was paid his annual salary in 12 monthly instalments. In addition ... he was paid a bonus.
- A farmer who intended to keep sheep and cows in his farm asked each of his four sons how many sheep and/or cows he should keep ...
- A man pushed a packing case at mass 8 kg ...
- The average weekly expenditure on food is a major item in the family budget. How can the mother ensure that in time of inflation she can provide nutritious and interesting meals for her family of husband and two teenage children?
- An applicant for a job in which a high level of colour sense was required was given ten colour cards each of a slightly different shade of green. He was told ...

(All these are taken from 'O' level papers from 1981, 1982 and 1985.)

ROLE MODELS

Children are quickly and subtly socialised into their sex roles from the moment of their birth; by the clothes we make them wear, the toys we give them, the stories we tell, the role models we surround them with. Schools are a vital part of this socialisation process, and they make a substantial contribution to providing pupils with a view of the world which legitimises such differentiation: boys will be boys, and girls will be girls; women teachers teach girls' subjects; women fill the caring and welfare positions (school nurse, cleaning staff, catering staff, secretary, school counsellor); men fill the leadership roles, having the major share of senior posts in the school (they are even in charge of the cleaning ladies!). All of the above are bound to make their impact on the future aspirations of girls and boys in the school, and to be reinforced by other discriminatory practices in the wider society.

It is likely that the younger teachers, especially the female ones, in your school are fully aware of all the above points and are doing their best to eradicate the discrimination, and to increase their own and their pupils' chances of equal opportunities. Training courses for teachers are oversubscribed, more female teachers are being encouraged to apply for positions of authority, and many projects up and down the country, e.g. the Girls into Science and Technology (GIST) project, Women into Science and Technology (WIST), Girls and Mathematics (GAMMA), are reporting encouraging signs. However, there is still a long way to go before significant changes will occur; just as there were only 25 women MPs before the 1987 election (fewer than at any time since World War II. Indeed the maximum had been 28 until the 1987 election which increased the number of women MPs to 41), so too the number of women in senior teaching posts is woefully small as Tables 8 and 9 illustrate:

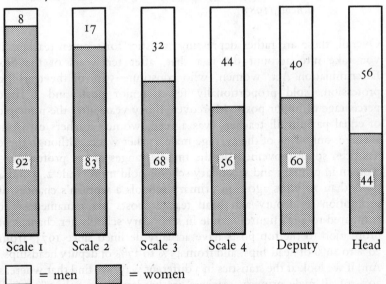

Table 8: *Women as percentage of teachers on each scale in primary schools,* *1983*

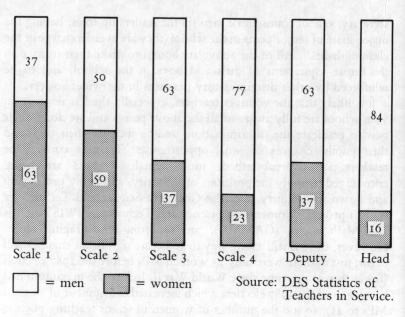

Table 9: *Women as percentage of teachers on each scale in secondary schools, 1983*

Overall, these are rather depressing statistics for women teachers if you take into account the fact that, after ten years of the Sex Discrimination Act, women, who constitute 59% of the teaching profession, hold proportionally fewer senior posts and a large percentage of junior posts. Moreover, thirty years after the principle of equal pay for all teachers was agreed, women teachers earn, on average, only 87% of the average male teacher wage. Although there has been some movement in the middle ranges of the profession – women in primary and secondary schools hold more Scale 2, 3 and 4 posts than 10 years ago – in primary schools a woman's chances of promotion to deputy and head teacher posts has remained static compared to 1973 figures, while in secondary schools her chances of promotion to the top posts have actually declined since 1973, from 20% to 16% of headships, and from 45% to 37% of deputy headships. And if we look at the statistics in a different way, we find that whereas 30% of all male primary teachers are headteachers, only 7% of all female primary teachers are heads; similarly, over 3% of all male secondary teachers are heads, whereas less than 1% (0.7%) of secondary school headships are filled by women. In other words, male teachers in primary and secondary schools are between four and five times more likely to become headteachers than women.

How can you best protect the interests of the staff of your school where equal opportunities are concerned? You have already been referred to the important role you play in interviewing new members of staff, and it is perhaps as well to outline for you Section 6 of the Sex Discrimination Act which refers to sex discrimination against employees and applicants:

'(1) It is unlawful for a person, in relation to employment by him at an establishment in Great Britain, to discriminate against a woman –

    (a) in the arrangements he makes for the purpose of determining who should be offered that employment, or

    (b) in the terms on which he offers her that employment, or

    (c) by refusing or deliberately omitting to offer her that employment.

(2) It is unlawful for a person, in the case of a woman employed by him at an establishment in Great Britain, to discriminate against her –

    (a) in the way he affords her access to opportunities for promotion, transfer or training or to any other benefits, facilities or services, or by refusing or deliberately omitting to afford her acess to them, or

    (b) by dismissing her, or subjecting her to any other detriment.'

It was only in 1944 that the practice of dismissing women teachers on their marriage was stopped by Parliament, but there is still a strong suspicion that discrimination against women occurs, notwithstanding the Sex Discrimination Act. How else would you explain the above tables?

In 1983, the EOC undertook an investigation into the appointment and promotion of staff in a well-known Midlands' school which reached some disturbing conclusions as far as governors are concerned. It found that the governing body had failed to play its correct role in relation to staff selection as outlined in the Articles of Government, which had led to dissatisfaction within the staff, particularly among female members. The governing body were quite firmly reminded of their duties in this respect. As the EOC stated, although the employer of teachers is seen to be the LEA, the governors, too, have an important part to play; they may be used to relinquishing any responsibility and deferring to the LEA in this respect, but their attention is drawn to section 42(1) of the 1975 Act:

> 'A person who knowingly aids another person to do an act made unlawful by this Act shall be treated for the purposes of this Act as himself doing an unlawful act of the like description.'

So, beware! As a governing body you must be particularly careful if you are involved in interviewing new staff members. The EOC has dealt with a growing number of complaints, from those, especially female, who feel they have suffered unlawful sex discrimination, and many of these complainants have been found to be justified at industrial tribunals. For example, in the summer of 1985 a female Lancashire deputy headteacher of 19 years' experience as deputy was awarded £600 compensation when it was found that her repeated attempts to become a headteacher in that county had failed. Since Lancashire had only two women heads out of 104 mixed secondary school headships (1.9% of female headships compared to the national average of 16%), it was admitted that sex discrimination was probably one cause of this low proportion of women headteachers. It is likely that your LEA has an Equal Opportunities Policy which must be rigorously observed in all selection procedures. However, as governors you need to be especially vigilant in this area, as the abstract from the following letter to a Midlands newspaper in 1985 showed:

> 'I applied for a teaching post with very good experience and qualifications, and good references, and I was asked several questions about my husband at the interview. On finding out that he did not work in Leicester I was asked why I was applying for a job here. To this I simply said that we were separated. I felt the questions quite irrelevant but answered politely and briefly. I was then asked to withdraw from the interview 'until my personal life was sorted out'. Obviously I felt insulted but what is especially ironic is that this happened in a community college where the Principal is a woman.'

It is important, then, in your role as governors to consider these and other questions, where the staffing of your school is concerned:

- Who holds the posts of responsibility in your school?
- How are the scale points distributed? Do female teachers receive their fair share of the total points allowance? For example, it is

not unknown for female teachers to receive only 20% of the points allocation, even though they constitute over 50% of the school's staff. If this is so, investigate the cause(s). Is it due to previous discriminatory practices? If so, what are you as a governing body proposing to do about it? Can you do anything about it? (If you are not sure how your school's scale points arise, consult the Appendix at the back of this book.)

- Are female teachers encouraged to attend in-service training courses?
- As far as non-teaching members of staff are concerned, have you ever considered appointing a female caretaker? A male cook/ supervisor? A male ancillary? A male secretary? Male cleaners?
- If you discern evidence of past discrimination, what can you do to remedy it?

OPTION CHOICE

The DES Education Survey 21, (1975) wrote:

'Some of the patterns of curriculum developed in the first three years of secondary schooling produce, either purposely or by accident, restrictions on what appears to be a free choice of options for the fourth year stage. One example of this is a school which separates home economics and needlework (girls) from woodwork and metalwork (boys) in years 1 to 3. In the fourth form, technical drawing is introduced as a supposedly free choice for boys and girls. The craft department, in line with contemporary thinking, is unwilling to teach technical drawing in isolation and insists that it must be linked with metalwork. Only those pupils who have previously taken metalwork are allowed to study technical drawing.'

Do all boys and girls receive the same curriculum diet, or are some subjects still seen to be girls' or boys' subjects?

Does the timetabling allow for boys and girls to make sensible options, or does it exclude them by offering no choice? Are boys and girls given equal facilities, encouragement, and coaching for the wide variety of sports and extra-curricular activities in your school?

The following case study of maths and computer science subjects shows you what you need to pay attention to, how complex the issue is, the need for research, the need to make your case; it could be applied equally well to other areas of the curriculum. Maths is chosen because it is widely recognised to be one of the curriculum areas which is least well covered by schools. It also incorporates elements of the preceding arguments concerning classroom behaviour, teaching materials and role models.

DO GIRLS COUNT? – A CASE STUDY

(Interested readers should consult the Cockcroft Report from which some of the facts from this section have been taken.)

> 'The first thing of importance is to be content to be inferior to men – inferior in mental power in the same proportion as you are inferior in bodily strength.'

So wrote an early nineteenth century popular writer of books for women, one Mrs Ellis. And there is much evidence that the prevailing attitude was that the curriculum for girls should be inferior to that of boys, with the emphasis on domestic subjects. It was generally considered unimportant for girls to take arithmetic. Indeed, even when some resourceful women, like the notable Mrs Somerville (born 1780), did begin to acquire a degree of scholarship, this was frequently scorned; for instance, Mrs Somerville's father is said to have been very concerned about her speedy acquisition of mathematics, uttering:

> 'we must put a stop to this, or we shall have Mary in a straitjacket one of these days.'

Such attitudes were common throughout the nineteenth century, and well into this century, and there can be no doubt that this historical legacy is one of the reasons for girls' relative lack of performance and success where mathematics is concerned; the lessons of history are forgotten very slowly. Little opportunity for a mathematics education for girls meant that there were few women mathematics teachers to spread the message of the importance of a mathematical education to girls.

How significant is this historical legacy today? Of the 7748 mathematics graduates in our schools in 1979, only 2484 (less than one third) were women; of the B.Ed. student teachers in 1980, 17.4% men chose mathematics as a specialist teaching subject, compared to only 8% women. So even today, men maths teachers are the predominant role model for pupils. This is compounded by parental attitudes. Current research suggests that parents have lower educational expectations for their daughters than for their sons; and that they are prepared to accept lower levels of achievement in maths for their daughters. As Germaine Greer wrote in 'The Female Eunuch', 'a girl faces one relentless enemy – her family'. If children seek homework advice on a maths problem, it is likely to be father who is consulted. Not surprisingly, maths is not seen as a career option, even for gifted daughters. (How far have we progressed since Mrs Somerville's day?)

There have been many studies which have tried to point to innate biological differences to explain the differential mathematical abilities of boys and girls. Tests do seem to show that up to the age of 13, girls have consistently higher scores than boys on tests of verbal ability, reading and general intelligence, whereas boys do slightly better on non-verbal tasks and tests of spacial ability. This is one reason why 11+ test scores were 'skewed' in boys' favour, otherwise there would have been many more girls in grammar schools than boys. Whether these results are the product of biology or child-rearing practices is debatable. Witness the ways parents, and teachers, reinforce sex-stereotypical behaviour in their choice of toys for children. Boys are more likely to be given constructional toys, craft toys (woodwork sets, chemistry equipment), and to play with sand and water and so on. No wonder their spatial ability is more keenly advanced than girls'! And consider the opportunities given to girls to help with measuring and DIY tasks around the house, and classroom, and compare such experiences to those of boys; the results are almost certain to be sex-stereotypical – boys helping dad, girls mum. It is even argued that the consequence of encouraging boys to be more independent and assertive than girls, is to give boys an advantage over girls in the problem-solving aspects of mathematics, added to which the very obedience which schools and society inculcate into girls causes them to be more anxious and wary of authority, whereas a successful mathematician needs to be enquiring and challenging – characteristics which we encourage in boys almost exclusively. Of course, there are many exceptions to prove the rule: it seems, for example, that in the primary school, girls perform better at mathematics than do boys. This may be explained by the type of non-competitive classroom characteristic in such schools; by positive role models; by non-sexist materials in such schools; by the very fact that, in the initial stages of learning the subject, the ability to follow and apply the rules without challenging them is crucial; by the proved intellectual supremacy of girls over boys at this stage; by the relative absence of perceived sex role differences amongst the pupils themselves. However, girls' relative superiority in the subject progressively deteriorates, so that they gain fewer 'O' levels (44% compared to 56%) and 'A' levels (28% compared to 72%) (1982 figures) than boys, consequently failing to pursue a career in mathematics, and subsequently perpetuating the very cycle of discrimination outlined above.

You have only to examine the maths text books your school uses to see how interesting many of them are for girls.

- John's first jump measured 83 cm. His second jump measured 79 cm. Altogether John jumped 162 cm.
- A man expects to walk at 5 km p.h. for 6 hours a day. How far will he walk in: (a) 1 day? (b) 1 week? (c) 10 days?
- A hiker is walking at 5 km p.h. This means that in 1 hour he walks 5 km. How long will it take him to walk:
  (a) 10 km? (b) 25 km? (c) 5000 km? (d) 2½ km? (e) 1 km?
- A man walks 18 km in 3 hours. How far will he walk in 1 hour? Hence, what is his speed?
- A man starts out on a 65 mile cycling journey at 10.45 am and arrives at 3.45 pm. What was his average speed?
- Fred walks at 5 km p.h. for 2 hours, then at 3 km p.h. for 2 hours, then stops. How far has he walked?

Only occasionally will girls see the relevance of maths to their lives. But only slight changes in the wording of such questions could have significant effects. For example:

- A woman training for the marathon runs for 2 hours at 11 km p.h. and then for 1 hour at 9 km p.h. and then for 1 hour at 8 km p.h.
  (a) How far has she run?
  (b) Draw a graph to show her speeds during the training session.
- Of 25 girls, 18 like pop music, 13 like classical music and 10 like both.
  (a) Show this information on a Venn diagram.
  (b) How many girls like neither pop nor classical music?

Or is this question sexist in its presumptions? Quite clearly, merely substituting girls/women for boys/men in questions will not be sufficient, if it is the girls who are seen to be doing the shopping and house-related tasks, and the boys sports and adventurous activities. Nor should we forget that both classroom and teacher behaviour play their part in this story. Studies do show that, at the secondary stage especially, boys, who are beginning to creep ahead of girls in performance, receive correspondingly more teacher attention and praise, and that even high achieving girls receive less attention than high achieving boys. Just as nothing succeeds like success, nothing fails quite like failure. The lesson is quickly learnt.

Fortunately, teachers have begun to realise the damage that such discriminatory practices cause. Special conferences, courses and projects have drawn attention to the issue, so that, for example, there are moves afoot to change sexist materials in schools; to alert teachers to the unintended consequences of their classroom performance; to give girls more encouragement to take maths-related subjects at school – computer studies, physics, technical drawing, craft, design and technology; to offer more relevant careers advice, especially outlining the importance of a maths qualification for various occupations. The 1982 Cockcroft Report, 'Mathematics Counts', which enquired into the teaching of maths in our schools, even recommended:

> 'that active steps to encourage more girls to take mathematics at 'A' level and then proceed to study at degree level could lead to an increase in the supply of well-qualified teachers of mathematics.' (p.197)

Indeed, some schools have decided on a policy of positive discrimination for girls by establishing single sex groups in maths. Because such projects have been small scale, results are inconclusive, although it appears that separation of the sexes in class, even for short periods, can be useful. Some girls positively enjoy the break from boys and the comradeship of an all-girl group where they are not made to feel inferior to boys and they do not suffer from the many distractions caused by boys; against this it must be said that some girls are offended by the assumption that their performance will be increased by single-sex setting, and prefer the competition of mixed-sex groups! One Midlands school did find that girls in single-sex classes achieved slightly better examination results, finding the subject so much more rewarding that twice as many girls as usual opted for 'A' level maths. Unfortunately for them, timetabling difficulties meant that eventually the 'A' level groups became mixed, and teachers noticed that the girls' performance subsequently deteriorated.

Giving girls a fair deal in maths as well as the range of maths-related subjects on the school curriculum is necessary if we accept that in this major curriculum area, girls are receiving unequal treatment and opportunities. You only need to remind yourselves of the relative performance of the sexes in such subjects as physics, chemistry, technical drawing, computer studies (see pages 114–115), to show that governors need to be constantly vigilant in this area.

It is interesting to see the manner in which male teachers and boys seem to have colonised the latest, and maybe most important, maths-related curriculum area, computer studies. In a period of job stagnation and fewer career opportunities for teachers, the emergence of computers on the school scene was a boon, particularly to maths staff in schools. They transferred to become better paid computer studies specialists; male teachers predominate in this field, and not surprisingly, we find that a similar position is occurring in this area as in maths teaching: boys are benefiting at the expense of girls. As a recent report, 'Computers in the Primary Curriculum', stated:

> 'There are increasing signs that computers are being used more by boys and male teachers than by girls and female teachers. Primary schools may need to take positive steps to ensure that both sexes have equal opportunities.'

Also, one survey of third year primary pupils found that whereas 29% of girls owned their own calculator, 56% owned their own digital watch and 36% had access to the family computer, the corresponding figures for boys were 58%, 80%, and 59%; no wonder boys are more confident in this area. Indeed, national figures do suggest that boys use computers more than girls; one 1983 survey found that at home boys were thirteen times more likely to use a computer than girls, only one in twenty-five of whom used them. In schools, similar trends are reported: boys are much more keen on computer-based work and predominate in computer clubs. It seems that the software available appeals more to boys (much of it is based on war games and space-related topics) and that boys enjoy data processing more. Not surprisingly, this results in more boys gaining 'O' and 'A' levels in computer studies – 1982 figures show that of those taking the subject, 69% of 'O' level and 77% of 'A' level entrants were boys. Since future career opportunities can be very much influenced by such results, it is important for schools to see that such a curriculum topic becomes more 'girl-friendly', perhaps by timetabling girls-only computer lessons and arranging girls-only computer clubs. As the director of the national Microelectronics Education Programme is reported to have said:

> 'We are very worried about girls losing out, but it is hard to combat. Society says gadgets are for boys, yet some of our best

computer people are women. I wish these girls would ignore what the boys say and get interested. Give up the dolls, for God's sake.'

It is hoped that this case study, involving as it does the themes of option choice, classroom behaviour, teaching materials and role models, will have alerted governors to subject other areas of the curriculum to a similar analysis. In this way, you will come to know your school in a way which will reinforce your important duties concerning oversight of the curriculum and the need for a sensitive awareness of staffing requirements and strengths throughout your school.

If these arguments don't convince you, look at your school's exam results – if this is pertinent. This will clearly show you the degree to which sex-stereotyping occurs in your school. Compare your own school's results with others in the locality. Remember, schools have to publish their results by law, although many are less than honest about the way they present their statistics. As you read any such data, keep an enquiring mind.

You may find Table 10 overleaf illuminating. It seems to exhibit quite firmly by its results the existence of sex-stereotyping in our schools.

If what you have read so far inspires you to action, refresh your mind about the EOC's three-stage plan of action as outlined at the start of this chapter: get the issue raised, take positive action, keep up the momentum. 'Getting the issue raised' should prove to be no problem if you take notice of the many points highlighted in this chapter; however, finding time on a busy agenda may well be a problem! Governors are encouraged to take positive action by establishing a working party; drawing up an equal opportunities policy statement for the school; having one governor with a watching brief for equal opportunities; involving LEA advisers where they exist (e.g. the London Borough of Newham has an advisory teacher to combat sexist influences in primary schools). Your own school may have a member of staff with special responsibility for equal opportunities – one school which prided itself as being one of the first to fight such discrimination created a special post of responsibility for promoting equal opportunities in the school, and appointed a man to the post!

If you constantly remind yourself of your legal duties where the curriculum and staffing are concerned, keeping up the momentum should be relatively straightforward, since you will appreciate this is an important and considerable aspect of your work as a governor.

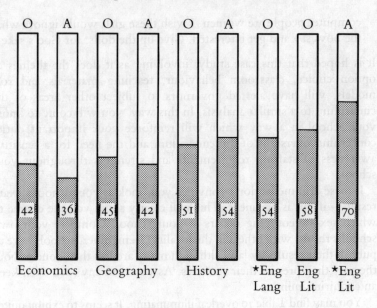

*Eng Lang includes CSE English and English Literature includes 'A' Level English

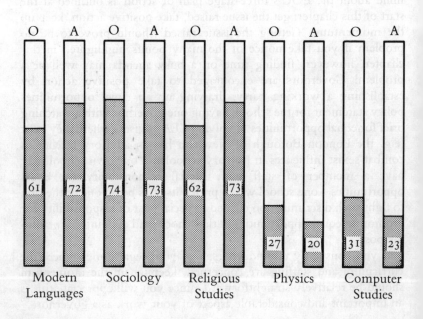

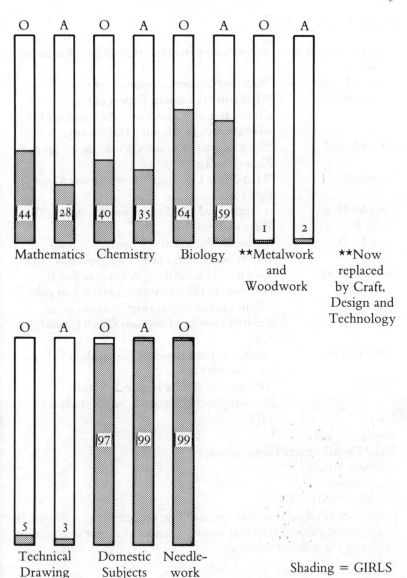

Source: DES, Statistics of Education, 1982

Table 10: *Percentage of girl entrants for selected subjects in 'O' and 'A' level examinations, England 1982*

FURTHER READING

There is now an enormous variety of texts on this subject. Particularly useful are:

Arnot M. (ed)	'Race and Gender', *Pergamon* 1985
Cockcroft W.	'Mathematics Counts: Report of the Committee of Enquiry into the Teaching of Mathematics in Schools', *HMSO* 1982
Deem R. (ed)	'Schooling for Women's Work', *Routledge and Kegan Paul* 1980
Spender D.	'Man-Made Language', *Routledge and Kegan Paul* 1980
Spender D. & Sarah E.	'Learning to Lose: Sexism in Education', *The Women's Press* 1980
Spender D.	'Invisible Women: the Schooling Scandal', *Writers and Readers Publishing Cooperative* 1982
Stanworth M.	'Gender and Schooling. A Study of Sexual Divisions in the Classroom', *Hutchinson* 1983
Stones R.	'"Pour out the cocoa, Janet": sexism in children's books', *Longman/Schools Council* 1983
Whyld J. (ed)	'Sexism in the Secondary Curriculum', *Harper and Row* 1983
Whyte J.	'Beyond the Wendy House: Sex Role Stereotyping in Primary Schools', *Longman* 1983

Some useful addresses

Equal Opportunities Commission,
Overseas House,
Quay Street,
Manchester M3 3HN

Offers free advice and a wide range of free publications on all aspects of sex discrimination; state that you are a school governor to be sure of obtaining the relevant material.

The Letterbox Library,
1st Floor,
5 Bradbury Street,
London N16 8JN

A women's group which supplies non-sexist children's books and a regular newsletter.

6 Schools since Swann: towards a multicultural education for all

'... all areas of the country should work through a curriculum that has a multi-cultural approach – and not just ... areas of high ethnic population.'

Such was the important central message of a 1985 report, the Swann Report, whose main arguments are summarised later in this chapter. If this message is accepted, then all governors, even those with few or no pupils from ethnic minorities in their schools, should find this chapter pertinent, especially when read in conjunction with Chapters 4, 5 and 10. Indeed, the 1985 White Paper 'Better Schools' stated unequivocally that the government accepted and was concerned at the Swann Committee's findings, especially regarding under-achievement. This White Paper made a commitment to reduce such under-achievement, to remove educational obstacles holding back particular groups of children and

'to support the work of the education service in preparing pupils for an ethnically mixed society which is working towards racial harmony'.

When you have read this chapter, it is hoped that you will appreciate why the Swann Report stated that:

'School Governors... can ... play a leading role in formulating policies for the curriculum which reflect cultural diversity and which accord true equality of opportunity to all pupils.'

THE FOURTH R

'... people are really rather afraid that this country might be swamped by people with a different culture. And, you know, the

British character has done so much for democracy, for law, and done so much throughout the world, that if there is a fear that it might be swamped, people are going to react and be rather hostile to those coming in.' (Mrs Thatcher, quoted in the 'Daily Mail', 31 January 1978)

We live in a multicultural society, but public statements like the above show that we have failed, by and large, to accommodate ourselves to the fact that hundreds of languages and dialects, scores of different religions and ethnic groups now constitute the fabric of our society, and that the threads of this fabric can be traced back to Celtic and Nordic invaders to our shores.

The central theme of this chapter, the fourth R, racism, is a response to the increasing importance in recent years of the role of a multicultural and anti-racist philosophy in our schools. It will be argued that governors have important duties in respect of this issue. Indeed, in many ways the structure and arguments presented here follow very much those relating to sexism: both deal with ways in which anti-discrimination policies can help to eradicate significant inequalities in the education system; both outline the main features of recent legislation aimed at combatting such inequalities (the 1976 Race Relations Act was, in fact, very closely modelled on the 1975 Sex Discrimination Act); both have been influenced by powerful arguments from their respective movements – the feminist movement and the 'black' movement; and both have drawn on evidence from government-sponsored agencies established to ensure that the relevant legislation was followed: the Equal Opportunities Commission and the Commission for Racial Equality (CRE).

Why should governors be concerned with racism? We live in a multi-racial and multicultural society which presents our educational system with many opportunities, challenges and problems. It is estimated that ethnic minority pupils constitute some 750,000, or 8% of the school population, (in this area statistics are very much guesstimates, because for various reasons we do not as yet have such accurate and comprehensive records as we do regarding sex differences and education). However, we do know that the non-white population, chiefly composed of Afro-Caribbean (or West Indian), Indian, Pakistani, African and Asian immigrants with significant proportions of groups such as Greek Cypriots and Chinese, are concentrated in only a few local authority areas, such as the Industrial Midlands and the London Metropolitan area; consequently, whereas some local education authorities are virtually all white, others have non-white proportions of up to 25%. However, no LEA, school or governing body can escape its obligations in respect of multicultural and anti-racist education.

Great Britain has a long and not very honourable tradition of encouraging, and discouraging, immigration to this country. In 1983, about 96% of the population in Great Britain was white, including significant proportions (some 3%) coming from such countries as Ireland, Italy and Poland. Only 4% of the population was black, principally of Indian, Afro-Caribbean or Asian origin, over half of whom were born in this country. Consequently, and contrary to many people's belief, we have a relatively small black population, just over 2 million, which is of British citizenship and therefore entitled to receive the same benefits and opportunities as the majority white community.

However, there is a substantial body of evidence which shows that our non-white, 'black', or 'ethnic minority' citizens do not share equal opportunities with their white neighbours, experiencing more un-employment, worse housing, lower wages, inferior access to the available range of social services, and an inferior education; added to this there are many horrific instances of such citizens being the victims of racial hatred and attacks. Until 1987, there were no black MPs. In other words, there is evidence of much racial discrimination in this country. This chapter focuses on such discrimination in the education system and offers governors guidance on how it can be eradicated from schools. During the discussion, the term 'black' will refer to those of Afro-Caribbean, Asian or other New Commonwealth origin or descent; the more acceptable term, Afro-Caribbean, will be used instead of West Indian, unless otherwise quoted in the source material referred to.

UNDER-ACHIEVEMENT OF BLACK CHILDREN IN OUR SCHOOLS

The tendency for black children to percolate downwards in our schools' streaming systems has long been well known, and has been graphically illustrated in 1985 research from Warwick University's Multicultural Studies Unit. This research showed that while Afro-

Caribbean children entered secondary school with reading scores at least as good as, if not better than, their white or Asian colleagues, they tended to be allocated to the lower streams, were denied opportunities to take 'O' levels, and subsequently left school with inferior results. In fact, the ability of Afro-Caribbean children placed in the lowest ability groups in one sample was found to be, on average, higher than that of similar groups not so placed. This government-sponsored research revealed that it was both racist attitudes and practices which were restricting the educational achievement of black pupils; indeed, cases of racist remarks by teachers were mentioned. The very fact that young black students tend to do well in FE colleges is shown to be evidence that schools and teachers fail to capitalise on their ability. Black pupils are, understandably, hostile to and resentful of any racist treatment by their teachers and show this hostility and resentment by living up to (or down to) their teachers' low expectations, and by anti-social behaviour. Moreover, another 1986 survey of Afro-Caribbean pupils found that their poor school performance was caused by language difficulties: some four out of five interviewed found difficulty in understanding what their teachers were saying, failed to ask teachers to repeat instructions lest they were accused of inattentiveness, and subsequently got themselves into trouble by asking their classmates for clarification. Again, this research mentioned the mutual mistrust and dislike between teachers and pupils. Such findings were echoed in the 1985 Swann Report (of which more below) which found that in a 1981/2 DES survey of five multicultural LEAs, only 6% of 'West Indians', compared to 17% of Asians, left school with five or more higher grades at CSE or 'O' level – the national average for England as a whole being 23%. Where 'A' levels were concerned, only 5% of 'West Indians' gained one or more passes compared with 13% of Asians (the national average being 14%).

Such poor relative results by the 'West Indian' sample lead to the following post-school experiences:

- only 1% of West Indian children attend university, compared to 4% of Asians and white children.
- On YTS schemes there is some concern that, in certain cases, black school leavers are directed towards courses which are less likely to lead to employment; even more serious are allegations that some employers have refused to accept black YTS trainees on work placements. Indeed, the Commission for Racial

Equality has investigated claims of racial discrimination in the way trainees were recruited on to Youth Training Schemes in one LEA, particularly the case of one college of further education which it was claimed operated an unofficial quota scheme which ensure that half its YTS trainees were white, even though it was in an area with a large ethnic community.

- While the 1985 national figures show that 11.5% of all men and 10.5% of all women were jobless, the figures for non-white were 21.3% and 19.1% respectively. However, such figures looked at on a regional basis are much more extreme; for example, in Leicester, a fairly typical case, the 1985 figures for unemployment in the 16–19 age-group show that whilst 24% of white youths were unemployed, 38% of Asians and 45% of Afro-Caribbeans were jobless (in certain local authority housing estates in Leicester, and elsewhere, the figures were even higher).

Add to these points the fact that Afro-Caribbean children are far more likely to find themselves allocated to special needs provision, or to be placed in 'disruptive units', then the message seems to be that such children are the victims of discriminatory practice. It must be said that the available statistical evidence has, for good reason, been queried (e.g. samples are small, and local – we need national samples), and that much of the debate concerning under-achievement is controversial and ideological. However, all the modern evidence rejects any accounts for such discrepancies being based on alleged IQ differences between the races, so we are left with incontrovertible evidence of a degree of racism in our education system which needs to be tackled. The relatively favourable standing of Asian children in such surveys disguises the fact that Bangladeshi children under-achieve to a similar degree to Afro-Caribbean, and there is also evidence to suggest that Asian children in general have to struggle much harder than white children, for example by repeating years and taking resits, to achieve similar results to white children, so there is no room for complacency about this group.

It must be remembered that such figures represent the situation some ten years after the passing of the 1976 Race Relations Act (which came into effect in 1977), which outlawed discrimination on the grounds of colour, race, nationality or ethnic or national origin, and which covered discrimination in housing, employment, the provision of goods, facilities and services, and education. Governors need to be aware of their responsibilities under this Act.

THE 1976 RACE RELATIONS ACT

Section 1 of the Act identifies two types of discrimination, direct and indirect:

Direct discrimination – treating somebody less favourably than another on racial grounds – would refer, for example, to a school's refusal to allow entry to a black student; to allocation of black children to streams or to exam entry purely on the basis of their colour, or on the teachers' stereotypical assumptions concerning such children; it would also refer to the alleged taunting by a Bristol teacher of a black colleague:

'Here comes the foreigner. Wogs, Pakis, Coons, they're all the same to me. All Wogs should go back to Wogland. I'm a racist you know.'[1]

(¹ quoted in A Dorn, 'Education and the Race Relations Act',
p 12 – in 'Race and Gender', Arnot M (ed).)

Indirect discrimination – applying, irrespective of motive or intention, a condition or requirement such that a considerably smaller proportion of a particular racial or ethnic group can comply with it – is a more tantalising, but probably more common, phenomenon; it must be shown that failure to comply with the condition or requirement is not justifiable on non-racial grounds and that its effects are detrimental. For example, rules and regulations concerning school uniform, school meals, access to certain courses (say because of English language qualifications) or to certain schools (because of admission criteria based on religion) could be covered by this section, *even though* discrimination was not intended, but whose consequences, nevertheless, discriminate against a racial group. A racial group is defined by the Act with reference to colour, race, nationality or ethnic or national origins. Since it failed to mention religion there were doubts as to whether Sikhs, Jews or Travellers (Gypsies) were racial groups. (A 1978 case determined that Sikhs were not a racial group, but a 1983 Lords ruling reversed this ruling.)

Sections 17, 18 and 19 of the Act make it unlawful for LEAs, proprietors and governors of educational establishments to discriminate on racial grounds with respect to:

- admissions policy (e.g. refusing to admit, or having differential admission criteria)
- access to any benefits, facilities or services provided by the school or college

- exclusion, or subjecting a student to any other detriment.

Governors would need to ask themselves whether their school's streaming policy, admissions criteria, exam policy, option choice, meal arrangements, careers advice, disciplinary policy (for example with respect to suspensions) subject any of their black children to any detriment in relation to these sections. Moreover, LEAs under Sections 18 and 19 would have to ensure that their educational facilities, ancillary benefits and services (e.g. grant awards) are provided without discrimination.

Compensatory provision in the form of special arrangements for teaching English as a second language to particular racial groups is allowable under Section 35 of the Act, as is the provision of special access courses in further or higher education.

Section 70 of the Act, which deals with incitement to racial hatred, can be used by LEAs, schools, teachers, parents and governors in coping with the increasingly common practice of racist organisations using schools as recruiting grounds and handing out racist literature; consequently, it would be in order for a governing body to disallow the use of their school premises to an extreme political group under this section, except in the case of general election campaigns when, under the Representation of the Peoples Act 1983, there is a duty to allow candidates representing such groups a public platform.

LEAs, schools and governing bodies are not only in the business of supplying services, they must also remind themselves of their obligations as employers. Section 4 of the Act covers discrimination in recruitment, promotion, dismissal, conditions, training, or any other benefits, facilities or services. Although evidence is scanty, due to lack of research, there is a general feeling that black teachers have suffered discrimination in their employment conditions as witnessed by their lack of access to promotion, and secondment, and by treatment they receive from their colleagues. That this was the case was supported by the Swann Report, quoting evidence from the CRE which estimated that there were only some 800 teachers of 'West Indian' origin, and 'a rather larger number' of Asian origin in our schools; there was, additionally, evidence that black teachers found difficulty in obtaining permanent posts, many being on supply contracts. The fact that few held promoted posts led to what the CRE called 'a widespread sense of frustration and bitterness among ethnic minority teachers about what they see as their subordinate and disadvantaged position in the teaching profession'. A 1986 CRE survey of 20,000 teachers in eight urban areas with high ethnic populations found that only 1 in 50 were black, and that 80% of them were on the lowest salary scales 1 and 2 compared to 57% of white teachers. There is some evidence that black teachers are now forming into associations in order to counter such discrimination, and at least one LEA is now offering special in-service training courses for black teachers concerning promotion and preparation for headship and is ensuring that those responsible for appointing teachers, including school governors, are given race awareness training. Ethnic monitoring is a feature of many LEAs now, and governors would do well to monitor their own school's performance regarding equal opportunities for all staff.

Section 71 of the Act makes it the duty of every local authority to make appropriate arrangements to ensure that their functions are carried out with due regard to the need both to eliminate racial discrimination and to promote equality of opportunity and good relations between persons of different racial groups. Many LEAs have, in consequence, produced policy statements in multicultural education and have started a number of initiatives to put such policies into effect. It is likely that governing bodies will have been consulted and some governing bodies have, at the school level, been responsible for issuing their own policy statement. If you have not seen your LEA's multicultural policy, if one exists, you should ask to receive a copy with a view to discussing it at an appropriate governors' meeting. There is a line of argument that some LEA multicultural policy statements are not worth the paper they are written on, since Section 71 of the Race Relations Act does not contain any enforcement provisions; this view is quite erroneous since the local education authority has a responsibility for ensuring that its practices are non-discriminatory in effect, a responsibility which applies to making, and enforcing, 'appropriate arrangements'. However, recent research suggests that such LEA policy statements may only have a limited and partial impact on schools. Nevertheless, the very production of such policy statements indicates that the LEA has at least recognised its duty under the 1976 Race Relations Act. Although enforcement of this Act has proved to be less than satisfactory, due to individuals' reluctance to make use of it, and due to ignorance of its provisions, it does offer scope for the imaginative governing body to subject its school's policies to review, to ensure that the Act's provisions are adhered to.

A first step towards this, if it has not already been taken, would be to place discussions of racism, like sexism, on the agenda of governors' meetings. It must be admitted that some governors, especially of all-white schools, may fail to see the relevance of multicultural and anti-racist policies to their situation. Such doubting governors would find it instructive to refer to the Swann Report.

THE SWANN REPORT

This report was referred to at the outset of this chapter. It had its origins in 1979 when a Committee of Inquiry, initially under the chairmanship of Anthony Rampton until his resignation in 1981, was established to review the educational needs and attainments of children from ethnic minority groups. The report, known as the Swann Report after its eventual chairman, was published in March 1985. In fact during the Committee's deliberations there were a number of resignations due to differences of opinion, which highlights the controversial nature of the subject matter at hand. Unfortunately the Report is extremely long and costly, so you may prefer instead to read one of the available summaries (details at the end of this chapter). The following brief account will alert governors to the nature of the issues which schools need to address, and gives a flavour of the Report.

The Swann Report argues that a democratic pluralist society like Great Britain has to acknowledge that historically it is an amalgam of a variety of groups and traditions, that society is constantly changing and that we need to escape the tendency to expect recently arrived ethnic minority groups to assimilate into 'our' way of life; rather, we should encourage diversity within unity – a multicultural society.

It is acknowledged that prejudice – a preconceived opinion or bias for or against someone or something – is a feature of society, and that there is now a heightened level of awareness that it is the role of education to equip children with the knowledge and understanding to counteract such prejudice which, in its most insidious and negative form, amounts to racism. Lack of knowledge and understanding leads to stereotypical views of other racial groups, usually regarded in some way or another as inferior to the indigenous 'white' population. It is clear that some teachers (and governors) hold stereotypical views of certain ethnic groups; for example, that Afro-Caribbeans are good at sports, that Asians are hard-working and industrious. Such racist views, whilst not as overt and intentional as many in society at large, may still be, by the very nature of their covertness and unintentionality, more damaging in their *effect,* since they influence the teachers' actions and expectations and lead to self-fulfilling prophecies. Moreover, 'colour blindness' – the failure to recognise distinctions between white and black children – widespread amongst teachers (as amongst other groups, including governors?) can be just as harmful as intentional racism, since it rejects the validity of important aspects of a person's identity.

Institutional racism – a set of long established taken-for-granted practices and procedures which have the effect of depriving particular racial groups of equality of opportunity in comparison with indigenous white groups – is perhaps the most important concept which governors need to grasp. For our purposes it concerns the organisational dynamics of the school which probably pre-date the influx of ethnic groups and into which they are expected to fit (practices like streaming, setting, subject choice, discipline policy), but which, by not making any allowances, deprive ethnic minorities equality of access to the full range of educational goods on offer. Such institutional racism is, by its very nature, endemic, and because it is unintentional, most harmful. We may compare this concept with that of the 'hidden curriculum' mentioned in the curriculum chapter.

Schools, if they are to win the trust of all their pupils, need to be aware of the influence both of intentional and unintentional racism by checking all instances of racist attitudes and behaviour; to fail to do so is a dereliction of their duty and can be seen by ethnic minority groups as complicitous. It is for this reason that the Swann Report is entitled 'Education for All' because it seeks simultaneously to change attitudes amongst the white majority and to develop an education system which gives all children, regardless of colour, equal opportunities to give of their best.

As schools have slowly awakened to the needs of ethnic minority children, they have adopted a number of approaches, which range from assimilation, integration, multicultural education and anti-racist education. Assimilationists believe that we should disrupt the education of white children as little as possible, instead directing our attention to the deficiencies in the ethnic minority culture (for example, lack of English) so that they can fit into 'our' way of life. Integrationists have a slightly more positive view of ethnic minority pupils, recognising their different culture and seeking to find out more about it, whilst at the same time encouraging integration into the host community. The Swann Report rejects both these positions since they are discriminatory, treat ethnic minority pupils as 'problems', do nothing about under-achievement, and lead to negative stereotypes. Rather, Swann preferred a multicultural approach which met the educational needs of all ethnic minority children whilst at the same time preparing all children for life in a multicultural society. The problem about multicultural education – and one which the Swann Report fails to emphasise sufficiently – is that is it an ill-defined concept and tends to indicate policies which merely provide information about the various ethnic communities so that we can better understand them (an approach becoming known as the 3 S's – Saris, Samosas and Steel Bands), but which generally fails to take the next important step, that of confronting the racism which exists in society and in schools. A truly multicultural education policy would incorporate anti-racist strategies. Governors may like to consider where their LEA, school or governing body lies in the assimilationist – to – anti-racist spectrum outlined above.

The Swann Report recognises that there is a wealth of languages spoken in British homes and that the linguistic needs of ethnic minority children need to be catered for. However, it does not support any other medium for teaching in our classroom than English, whatever the ethnic mix of the classroom. The practice of removing 'black' children to special classes or units for English as a Second Language (generally known as E2L or ESL) is seen as a form of institutional racism, since it deprives such children of all the benefits offered in the normal classroom and also treats them as if their lack of English implied a lack of ability. Consequently, such language needs should be met within the normal classroom and E2L provision given appropriate support through training of teachers.

Mother tongue provision, either as a means of instruction in bilingual education or as a means of developing fluency, is rejected by the Report which sees a good command of English as the basis for equality of opportunity; mother tongue teaching is best done after school by appropriately qualified tutors. There is, however, a place for such teaching in the modern language curriculum as an option for *all* children, provided suitable teachers, teaching materials and exam syllabi can be provided. By treating E2L provision, and the bilingualism and even multilingualism of many of our pupils as inferior to English, the Report is guilty of the racism it seeks to eradicate. Although it quotes the 1975 Bullock Report, 'A Language for Life', about the benefits of language across the curriculum, it fails to acknowledge that Bullock was also an *advocate* of bilingualism as is evidenced by its view that:

> 'the school should adopt a positive attitude to its pupils' bilingualism and wherever possible should help maintain and deepen their knowledge of their mother tongues'

– a point of view since buttressed by a Directive of the European Economic Community.

The problem of language is indeed a thorny one – the Swann Committee received more evidence over this issue than any other – but it will not disappear by pursuing an almost 'colour blind' attitude to its existence and by maintaining a view that actively encouraging the mother tongue will in some way impoverish the education of ethnic minority pupils. To perpetuate such a line of argument shows us how difficult it is to escape the euro-centric white view of the world, and how racism can be quite unintentional. Great Britain is a multilingual society, indeed much of the world's population is bilingual, even multilingual. In some LEAs there are dozens of languages spoken: for example, in Haringey there are 87 spoken languages, in Waltham Forest 65, in Bradford 64, Leicester 50 and Peterborough 42. A 1985 research project, the Linguistic Minorities Project, spotlighted the multilingual nature of Great Britain. It specifically concentrated on five local authorities, showing that the percentage of bilingual pupils ranged from 7.4% in Peterborough to 30.7% in Haringey. Moreover, such pupils often had, and used, a third language, making them truly multilingual. There was also a level of demand from parents that schools should offer support to mother tongue teaching.

The Swann Report's failure to incorporate the significance of multilingual education into its multicultural strategy is a clear indication of its failure to recognise that the school curriculum not only has to reflect a multilingual world, but also to prepare for it. It can be argued that we have failed to live up to our obligations if our response to multilingualism is to subsume the languages spoken by significant proportions of our pupils into the modern languages department (usually French and German). And by failing to exploit the considerable linguistic skills of such bilingual children because we find it difficult to escape our euro-centric view of language, which is that English (and French and German) are superior to any other languages, we deny the reality of the league table of the most widely spoken languages in the world, which is as follows:

1	Chinese	700	million
2	English	395	"
3	Russian	250	"
4	Spanish	230	"
5	Hindustani (a combination of Hindi and Urdu)	220	"
6	Bengali	135	"
7	Arabic	135	"
8	Portuguese	135	"
9	German	120	"
10	Japanese	110	"
11	Malay-Indonesian	100	"
12	French	95	"

The Swann Report at least grasped the religious education nettle, proposing a review of the provisions of the 1944 Education Act which were, 40 years later, out of synchronisation with the fact that Britain was now a multifaith society. However, although it was recognised that the 1944 Act allowed the existence of voluntary-aided schools for Roman Catholic, Jewish or Church of England pupils, Swann did not feel it appropriate to recommend the creation of separate Muslim schools – or for any other religious group – for which there were strong claims being made. It was argued that such schools could more easily cater for the special cultural and educational needs of their own community, whilst escaping the racist impediments of much of the anglo-centric education system. However, such schools were rejected by the Swann Report, although some black members of the Committee were in favour of experimenting with some separate schools. Nevertheless, the Report did recommend that LEAs should consider their policy regarding single sex schools which were declining in number, but for which there were definite benefits for Muslim girls especially. Overall, Swann advocated that the emphasis should be for *all pupils* to share a common educational experience which would prepare them for life in a pluralist society. The Swann Report made scant reference to the role of the governing body in its pages, but it did call for an increased representation of governors from ethnic minority groups who could help to exercise some influence.

Clearly, none of the policies advocated by Swann would have any effect if the initial and in-service training of teachers was not considered. Since many of our teachers received their training before we came to realise the need for multicultural and anti-racist education, there is a need for in-service courses and teacher exchanges, suitably funded and staffed; since much in-service training is school-based, Swann recognised that for such activities to be effective 'they must have the whole-hearted support of heads and senior staff, Governors and the LEA'. Where initial teacher-training courses are concerned they should give students a thorough multicultural education. If teachers and student teachers showed themselves to be temperamentally unsuited to such approaches they would not be able to promote the 'Education for All' philosophy of the Report and their suitability as teachers, current and potential, would be assessed accordingly. The under-representation of black teachers in our education system was a matter of concern to the Swann Committee which noted that:

> 'on many of our visits we were struck by the inherent incongruity of 'all-white' teaching staffs, often living well away from the catchment areas of their schools, seeking to meet the needs and respond to the concerns of a multiracial pupil population.'

Lest we forget the significance of the term 'ethnic minority' pupils, the Report concluded with an informative section on the particular educational needs of children of Chinese, Cypriot, Italian, Ukrainian, Vietnamese, Liverpool 'Black' and Traveller origin, all of whom have tended to receive much less attention than children of Afro-Caribbean or Asian origins. Indeed, a much more concerted and adequately funded approach was called for by the Swann Committee if the principles of an 'Education for All' were to be realised. This has implications not only for LEAs and teachers, but also for HMIs, Examination Boards, and, although they were not subject to any particular scrutiny in the Report, governors themselves. Evidently, multicultural and anti-racist education will not just happen; neither the passing of the Race Relations Act, nor the production and dissemination of a report can, by themselves, do much to change behaviour and attitudes.

WHAT CAN GOVERNORS DO?

As governors you can do much to help your school combat racism, attack inherited myths and stereotypes, and draw attention to the unintentional consequences of institutional racism, especially if you follow the strategies with respect to sexism as detailed on page 113 of this book, namely:

- Get the issue raised
- Take positive action
- Keep up the momentum

There is evidence from HMI Reports on schools throughout the country that they are failing in their obligations to provide a multicultural education. For example, the general conclusion from a review of HMI reports in 1984 was that, in primary schools:

'There is hardly any evidence of work that takes full account of our multi-ethnic society'

and, in secondary schools:

'The curriculum as a whole ... needs to reflect the cultural diversity of present-day society'.

Although the Swann Report examined the evidence for under-achievement, particularly of Afro-Caribbean pupils, noted the under-representation of black teachers in our schools, and mentioned the concept of institutional racism, it has been criticised for not giving enough prominence to the *school* as being one of the prime agents of such racism.

We have already noted the important role of teachers as role models; not only is there a dearth of black teachers as positive models, but there is, unfortunately, evidence that in some schools racist teachers act as negative models, and in other schools teachers who fail to appreciate the significance and importance of multicultural policies provide no model at all.

Where pupils are concerned, there is much evidence of racist views and behaviour by both white and black pupils. Extreme political groups like the National Front actively recruit amongst inner city pupils and many of the disciplinary problems in such schools are due to racist graffiti, insignia, abuse and attack. It seems that much of this racial prejudice is to be found amongst underachieving pupils who feel themselves to be vulnerable. Not that all this racism is white against black: one well-publicised case in 1985 concerned a young Conservative activist suspended from school for alleged racist remarks towards French pupils on an exchange visit. Such an instance reminds us that not all racism exhibits white/black characteristics, but can also be of a white/white and black/black nature.

Many schools are now monitoring the incidence of such racism. Is yours? There is a well-documented tendency to treat children of Afro-Caribbean origin as trouble-makers, as evidenced by the high proportion of them in special disruptive units, or on suspension from school. The Commission for Racial Equality took notice of the national concern for this tendency and undertook a lengthy investigation into suspension arrangments, choosing Birmingham as typical of a major urban, multiracial education authority. The CRE reviewed Birmingham's suspension procedures over a six-year period, finding that during 1974–1980 black pupils were almost four times as likely to be suspended from secondary school as white children, and that institutional, rather than direct or intentional, discrimination was the main reason for this differential treatment. Since this investigation, Birmingham LEA has reviewed its suspension procedures, and the CRE welcomed the fact that since 1979 the proportion of black pupils suspended has fallen, so that the rate of suspension of black children is close to the proportion of black pupils in Birmingham's schools. The two important points which emerge from this investigation, supposing Birmingham to be a typical authority, are that the evidence suggests that black pupils were too readily suspended, and that unless careful monitoring is undertaken and records taken and analysed, it is easy for discriminatory patterns to develop. The happy conclusion of this investigation is that Birmingham LEA took positive measures which included the production of a multicultural education policy statement, the appointment of multicultural inspectors and the establishment of a Multicultural Resources Unit and Multicultural Development (Teaching) Unit, and that these measures were capable of reversing a discriminatory trend.

Governors are reminded of the provisions of the Race Relations Act, especially sections 1, 17 and 18 which outline discriminatory practices which are probably illegal.

Thus, what goes on in the classroom in terms of relationships between teacher and taught is crucial, as is what children are actually taught or not taught. Consequently, we turn our attention here to the curriculum and the teaching materials used in the classroom. In any discussion of multicultural education, the curriculum must be a central focus, and again governors are reminded of their responsibilities for the general direction of the curriculum as detailed in Chapter 4.

There is incontrovertible evidence, built up over many years, that the curriculum as a whole, and individual subjects to varying degrees, exhibit a euro-centric bias, much of it dismissive of other societies, cultures and religions. Such subjects as history, geography, R.E., literature, domestic science frequently present a white, Christian, colonial view of the world, failing consequently to acknowledge, and to adapt to, an increasingly pluralist society. Governors could examine their school's curriculum content using similar guidelines to those described in the previous chapter, scrutinising not just what is included, but what is *ex*cluded, asking such questions as:

- Does the history syllabus pay attention to non-European aspects of history, or emphasise the achievements of non-European civilisations?
- Does the domestic science syllabus acknowledge the dietary delights of ethnic minority communities?
- Do the arts subjects recognise different cultural styles and techniques, for example, in music, drama, dance and art? Do pupils have opportunities to experiment with these styles and techniques?
- Is the literature of ethnic minority groups used in the classroom? Are folktales, short stories, plays, poems, novels, written by their authors, available and acknowledged?
- Does the teaching of mathematics and science acknowledge the influence and contribution of non-European societies to our knowledge of these subjects?
- Does 'Modern Languages' really mean what it says, or should it be known as 'European Languages'? Are any attempts made to offer a variety of world languages?

Geography syllabi in particular have been the focus of much criticism. One recent study of 20 geography examination syllabi found that 14 presented the developing world almost exclusively in terms of problems. Negative terms like 'backward', 'primitive agriculture', 'under-developed regions', 'the problem of the population explosion', feature as if the 'problems' of 'Third World' countries (notice the racist terminology traditionally used) were internal and not connected with global economic and political systems; the treatment of topics like plantation agriculture still follow a colonial perspective, without hinting that colonial exploitation brought with it many negative features. Typically, the non-European peoples described are seen to be dependent on the skills and expertise of European settlers. No wonder, then, that white Europeans see themselves as superior and more intelligent than 'black immigrants'.

Consider, too, your school's language policy, which will have an effect throughout the curriculum. Of course, in any school with significant proportions of non-English speaking pupils, English as a Second Language will be a high priority. But are suitable arrangements made? Are children excluded and segregated, or is provision made to teach E2L throughout the curriculum? Are such speakers seen as inferior and intellectually less able, or does the school acknowledge the positive benefits of these pupils' bilingualism? Most schools seek to foster special talents in the sporting, musical, academic and artistic spheres. Any school with sufficient numbers of expert chess players, swimmers, cricketers, model makers or whatever would make use of and extend such talents to the benefit of the school and pupils, especially where the kudos of success in competitions is the result of such talents. Why then do many schools fail to capitalise on the cleverness of the bilingual speaker? It was recognised by the Bullock Report that·

> 'no child should be expected to cast off the language and culture of the home as he crosses the school threshold, to live and act as though school and home represent two totally separate and different cultures which have to be kept apart.'

If schools want to gain the respect of the parents of such pupils, and of ethnic communities generally, then they would do well to recognise the varied talents in such communities, not least their multilingual abilities. A healthy respect for such skills would improve home-school links. Although the Swann Report is dismissive of bilingual teaching, evidence in this country, and others, does not bear out the conclusion that children's English suffers as a result; rather, the contrary is the result, since children are surrounded by this language, not their own. Nevertheless, mother tongue teaching remains controversial. Are you satisfied that your school makes appropriate arrangements for both E2L and mother tongue teaching?

The following brief summary of an investigation by the CRE between 1984–6 of the arrangements made by Calderdale LEA for teaching ESL should prove salutary. Some 6,500 (or 3.4%) of Calderdale's population is of Asian origin, and although Calderdale had adopted an equal opportunities policy in 1985, it seemed clear to the CRE that the LEA's practices for dealing with Asian children were discriminatory and contrary to the Race Relations Act of 1976. Since the mid-1960s it had been Calderdale's policy to separate ESL teaching from mainstream schooling. The procedures adopted by Calderdale for assessing the level of English and subsequently the segregation of such children for special language tuition were seen by the CRE to subject such children to a number of detriments, including:

- lack of access to a normal school environment
- having to travel outside their home area, either losing part of the school day, or spending more time in travel
- provision of a more restricted curriculum
- hindrance of their language development and learning process since they were deprived of an environment in which they could work alongside native English speakers with a full curriculum

Moreover, their parents were shown to be deprived of the expression of parental choice of schools, and consequent rights of appeal; additionally, the two special language schools did not issue prospectuses, contrary to the 1980 Education Act. The children's detriment was further compounded by the fact that their parents did not have the opportunity to elect or be elected as parent governors. The CRE concluded that Calderdale LEA's arrangements for ESL teaching amounted to indirect discriminatory practices according to Sections 28, 17b (and/or (a) and/or (c) taken together), 1(1) (b) and 32. Fuller details are available in the CRE's free report about the case – details at the end of this chapter. For the purposes of our discussion, the important point is that it could be argued that school governors, by default, had failed to monitor the LEA policy, which is now in the process of change as a result of the CRE investigation.

We have already noted the influence of books, TV and other teaching materials where sexism is concerned, and the situation is no less critical in connection with racism. Comics, for example, much in evidence in schools, particularly during 'wet' playtimes, are full of stereotypical, negative images of black people, Red Indians and Chinese, still treating them as savages in mud huts, cannibals, primitives or in some way servile and inferior. Such racism may be unintentional, but its very presence is indicative of a racist society. Every so often, controversy surrounds a particular book or series; for example, 'Little Black Sambo', withdrawn in certain areas, still raises hackles after ninety years in circulation, and Noddy books still abound, containing characters such as the offensive golliwogs.

Not all examples of racist material are so obvious and consequently appropriate guidance is available for teachers to enable them to subject their teaching materials to an anti-racist analysis. Governors, too, have a role to play here, at least as far as understanding goes, but great sensitivity is required, as the leaflet on the next page illustrates. Can you spot anything racist in this leaflet? It was withdrawn because of an alleged racial stereotype; the reason for its withdrawal is to be found at

EDUCATION FOR A MULTICULTURAL SOCIETY

Respect for self: Respect for others.

Fig. 4: *'Anti-racist' education leaflet*

the end of this chapter.

Just as we have noted the relative invisibility and subordination of girls and women in reading schemes, so too do we find even greater degrees of invisibility and subordination of black children and adults in school books. One recent survey of a popular new primary school reading scheme found no examples of a two-parent black family; only one black female child spoke; the very few black men illustrated far outnumbered black women; the only black occupation featured Indians working with elephants.

There is now a growing market of multicultural books and teaching materials of all kinds, but it is likely that in many schools this exists alongside material which was in use long before the Race Relations Act and the Swann Report, and with which teachers have become familiar: encyclopaedias and world atlases are a good example of the kinds of material which are rarely, if ever, replaced – mainly because of the cost.

What schools look for now are books which:

- offer a balanced view of the world, seen from different perspectives
- represent ethnic minority groups positively and non-stereotypically in both illustration and story line, (hence negative words like 'backward', 'primitive', 'mud huts', 'savages' are taboo)

- reflect Britain's multicultural society accurately, showing black people in a variety of occupations, (not only as bus conductors and hospital domestics), and in a variety of inner-city, rather than peasant, environments
- contain stories, poems, folktales from a variety of cultures: Chinese, Vietnamese, Bengali, Bangladeshi and so on
- acknowledge, and capitalise on, the culture, history and achievements of other societies, not just English
- tackle issues like racism, the problems of 'the Third World', and so on.

You may find it interesting to consult with the staff in your school to see how they have subjected their curriculum to such an analysis. Whilst it may be relatively straightforward for subjects such as English, Domestic Science, Arts, Music, R.E., to reflect our multicultural society, what is the situation regarding Mathematics, Science, Craft, Design and Technology? What is your school doing about multicultural education throughout the curriculum?

Don't forget the influence of school assemblies. Do these celebrate merely the traditional Christian festivals such as Christmas, Easter, Harvest Festival, Ascension Day, or do they also take in Diwali, Eidul Fidre, Ramadan, and other significant sacred days? It must also be remembered that the occurrence of such festivals has especial significance for some pupils, and could affect their response to the school curriculum. For example, the first time a London-based CSE examination board offered a Bengali examination it scheduled the aural examination on the day of Eidul Fidre, a sacred day with the significance of Christmas; this meant that some 20% of the candidates were not able to sit this component of the exam.

Additionally, does your school's general environment reflect a multicultural society through its displays and notices? Are signs written in other languages, where applicable? Do letters home and the school prospectus take notice of the linguistic traditions of the parents? Are visitors from the various ethnic minority groups invited to speak to pupils? Does your school ever exchange visits with schools of different types? Do your school meals acknowledge the dietary habits of your pupils? For example, what is your attitude to the provision of halal meat, kosher food, vegetarian dishes? What is the school's attitude to the dress of some of its pupils? Do any ethnic minority groups offend school rules regarding uniform because of their particular style of dress?

The above are aspects of the school's ethos, its hidden curriculum. As frequent visitors to the school you are therefore in a good position to assess the school's attempts to reflect multiculturalism and to challenge racism. Although teaching materials and displays are important components in attacking racism, they are redundant if the school pays scant regard to the less informal though no less important features of school, like life in the school playground, with evidence of racist behaviour and attitudes being allowed to go unchallenged by the pupils. As the Swann Report explained:

> 'it is difficult for ethnic minority communities to have full confidence and trust in an institution which they see as simply ignoring or dismissing what is in fact an ever-present and all-pervasive shadow over their everyday lives.'

Nor, too, should the influential role of teachers be overlooked. The issue of under-representation has already been dealt with, but are your teachers wholly in acceptance of the school's multicultural policy? Have they been keen to attend in-service training courses? Do your teachers know all the names of their pupils, and can they pronounce them correctly, or do they give them 'white' names? Do they know the names of the languages spoken by their pupils? (Do the governors?) Do they show a positive interest in the child's cultural heritage? Have the teachers attempted to learn an ethnic minority language? Is any of your teachers racist? If your school has ethnic minority teachers, is there evidence of indirect or direct discrimination against them where promotion prospects are concerned? It is a sad fact that there are regular complaints that they are passed over in the field of promotions. Although the difficulty of proof has meant that few cases have been successful, the very accusation of bias against ethnic minority teachers can do lasting local damage to a school; governors have an important role in ensuring that staff relationships are smooth and that potential conflict is snuffed out as soon as possible.

What of the governing body itself? How committed to mulitculturalism and anti-racism are you individually and collectively? Do you ever debate the issue? Are you assimilationists – 'When in Rome do as the Romans do' – or anti-racist? Does the governing body keep the school on its toes concerning multiculturalism? Do you consider this issue only appropriate to areas with a significant proportion of ethnic minority inhabitants, or should *all* schools pay attention to the issues? Do you encourage parental involvement, not only in the day-to-day life of the school, but also by means of community self-help with special Saturday Schools for supplementary or mother tongue classes? Have you ever been invited to see what happens in such schools? Is any of your governing body a representative of the ethnic community? If so, is this only token representation, or have attempts been made to establish proportional representation of such governors to the governing body? Not surprisingly, evidence shows a large disproportion of black governors in comparison with white. For example, the ILEA found that in 1985 fewer than 5% of its governors were black, even though it had over 22% of pupils of Asian or Afro-Caribbean background. What is the proportion in your area? Have any attempts been made to recruit more ethnic minority governors? Do you support such attempts?

It is hoped that this chapter, especially when read in conjunction with Chapter 10, will alert governors to the need for imagination, tolerance and tact in what must be one of the most sensitive and important aspects of their role – ensuring that their school makes every effort to deliver all-round, equitable education which reflects the diversity, not only of British society, but also of the world at large.

(The leaflet on page 136 was withdrawn because of its portrayal of the 'black' boy(!) dressed casually while his white friend wore school uniform – a situation which could be taken as projecting a racial stereotype.)

FURTHER READING

Arnot M. (ed)	'Race and Gender: Equal Opportunities Policies in Education', *Pergamon* 1985
Bullock Report	'A Language for Life', *HMSO* 1975
Klein G.	'Resources for Multicultural Education', *Longman* 1984
Klein G.	'Reading into Racism', *Routledge and Kegan Paul* 1985
Runnymede Trust	'Different Worlds', 1983
Swann Report	'Education for All', *HMSO* 1985

Summaries of this Report are available from the Runnymede Trust, and Lord Swann made his own summary, the appearance of which was widely criticised, partly because it failed to mention racism.

Some useful addresses
Centre for Research in Ethnic Relations,
Arts Building,
University of Warwick,
Coventry CV4 7AL.
(0203 24011)
– publishes a number of research and policy papers.

Commission for Racial Equality,
Elliott House,
10/12 Allington Street,
London SW1E 5EH
(01 828 7022)
– publishes a wide range of publications, many of them free, including
an Educational Journal.

The report mentioned on pages 134–135 is titled: 'Teaching English as
a Second Language: Report of a Formal Investigation in Calderdale
Local Education Authority', CRE 1986

National Anti-Racist Movement in Education
(formerly known as National Association for Multicultural Education),
P.O. Box 9,
Walsall,
W. Midlands WS1 35F

Runnymede Trust,
37A Grays Inn Road,
London WC1 8PP
(01 404 5266)
– an educational charity established in 1968 – provides information on
immigration and race in Britain – publishes monthly bulletin.

7 Special educational needs – Are you using 'your best endeavours' to ensure integration?

'Special needs' has featured highly on the educational agenda for many years now, and all governors, not just those governors of 'special schools', will need to have some knowledge and understanding of children with special educational needs according to their obligations under the 1981 Education Act, which is featured in this chapter. Local education authorities have been obliged by law since 1944 to make provision for children who were intellectually, physically or emotionally handicapped 'in special schools or otherwise'. Under 1945 regulations, eleven categories of handicapped pupils were recognised:

blind, partially sighted, deaf, partially deaf, delicate, diabetic, educationally subnormal, epileptic, maladjusted, physically handicapped, those with special defects. (Diabetics were absorbed into the 'delicate' category in 1953.)

Although those deemed seriously disabled – the blind, deaf, physically disabled and epileptic – had to be educated in special schools, children with other disabilities could attend ordinary schools if adequate provision were available. Indeed, it was the intention of the 1944 Act that the less severely handicapped – the greater majority – would be educated in ordinary schools. In effect, this did not happen, and there was a steady growth of special school provision so that by the early 1980s, getting on for 177,000 children (about 1.8% of the total school population) were receiving full-time education in 'special schools'. However, the percentage of children in an LEA deemed as needing 'special schooling' varied from between 0.5% and 3.00% – figures which represented that area's provision or interpretation of the categories, rather than differing need. Consequently, few school governors needed to concern themselves with such children. Moreover, these governors were not catered for by the provisions of the Taylor Report, so in many ways governors of special schools, of which there were 1650 in 1977 in England and Wales, found themselves very much in the wilderness, as did their pupils, being cut off from mainstream provision.

This sense of isolation is gradually decreasing as a result of a major report into the education of handicapped children – known as the Warnock Report – and resulting legislation, the 1981 Education Act, both of which, taken together, have brought special education out of its wilderness, and have placed specific duties on all school governors where children of special educational needs are concerned. The rest of this chapter outlines the major features of the Warnock Report and the 1981 Act, and deals with their implications for school governors.

THE WARNOCK REPORT

In late 1973 the Secretary of State for Education announced the establishment of a Committee of Enquiry into the educational needs of handicapped children. This was the first such committee specifically charged by any UK government to review educational provision for all handicapped children, whatever their handicap. The Committee, chaired by Mary Warnock, began its work in 1974 and published its Report in 1978: 'Special Educational Needs: Report of the Committee of Enquiry into the Education of Handicapped Children and Young People'. The Report is a comprehensive review of the educational provision in England, Scotland and Wales for such children. Northern Ireland is subject to different provision.

The major focus of the report was to turn our attention away from a consideration of children's handicaps towards decisions about their special educational needs. It took a broader notion of special education than the traditional one of education by special methods appropriate for particular categories of children in special classes, units or schools, embracing instead the notion of any form of additional help, wherever and whenever provided, to overcome educational difficulty. The Report made the important point that the goals of education were the same for *all* children, 'although the difficulties which some children encounter may dictate WHAT they have to be taught and the disabilities of some HOW they have to be taught'. The Warnock Report condemned the divisive statutory categorisation of certain pupils as handicapped, recommending that such a negative label should be abolished. In its place, Warnock introduced the concept of special educational need. It made the point that not only is 'handicap' difficult to define, but that also the old labels resulted in rigid dichotomies:

> 'To describe someone as handicapped conveys nothing of the type of educational help, and hence of provision, that is required. We wish to see a more positive approach and we have adopted the concept of SPECIAL EDUCATIONAL NEED, seen not in terms of a particular disability which a child may be judged to have, but in relation to everything about him, his abilities as well as his disabilities – indeed all the factors which have a bearing on his educational progress.'

Although almost 2% of the school population were receiving a special education, segregated from their peers, it was estimated that 1 pupil in 6 was likely to require some form of special educational provision at any one time, either permanently or for only short periods (e.g. while a particular problem, such as partial deafness, was treated); furthermore, up to 1 child in 5 was likely to require special educational provision at *some* time during their school career. In other words, in a primary school of 300 children, as many as 60 could require some form of special education provision at any given time.

Labels such as 'educationally subnormal' (who would want to be stigmatised thus?) were to go, to be replaced instead by the term 'children with learning difficulties'; in other words, a description, rather than a categorisation, would be used, in the hope that a special educational programme would follow. Such a learning difficulty could be mild, moderate, or severe; this wording would also apply to children with emotional or behavioural problems.

Children who came under this broad category of special educational need would require one or more of the following;

> '(i) the provision of special means of access to the curriculum through special equipment, facilities or resources, modification of the physical environment or specialist teaching techniques;
> (ii) the provision of a special or modified curriculum;
> (iii) particular attention to the social structure and emotional climate in which education takes place.'

Some children may have a combination of these forms of special educational need. In other words, since special education should be special, pupils so identified should have access to specially-trained teachers on a full or part-time basis, to special resources, and to a special curriculum.

The second most important theme of the Warnock Report was the central role of parents in the education of their 'handicapped' children. According to Warnock, 'Parents as much as teachers must see themselves as active educators.'

It was acknowledged that the successful education of children with special educational needs depends upon the full involvement of their parents; they should be equal partners, but since they have special burdens they need advice, encouragement and support. This not only includes access to professional workers of various kinds who deal with their child, but also refers to the special help parents need during the school holidays. As Warnock recommended:

> 'ways of enabling the premises of some special schools to remain open during the school holidays should be ... considered by the local authorities and teachers' associations and, where appropriate, school governors.'

Much of the report is given over to the discovery, assessment and recording of children with special educational needs. Although multi-professional teams would have an important function in this regard (the Report outlines the role(s) of the various professional agencies), parents too must be closely involved in the assessment procedures and in subsequent educational programmes. Parents would need access to information – a point taken up by the 1980 Education Act and discussed in Chapter 8 – and support. Not only would parents be able to request an assessment of their child, but they would also have the right of access to *all* records about their children; an LEA would need parents' co-operation if it were to initiate the request for an assessment. Such assessment procedures should be applicable to any child from birth, and important weight would be attached to any information supplied by the parents. Once assessed, children should receive an annual review of their progress, although parents should be able to initiate a review at any time. Particular sensitivity should be paid to the assessment of children whose first language is not English, because of the growing concern that a disproportionate number of children from West Indian families had found themselves in special schools or classes described as Educationally Subnormal (Moderate), ESN (M). As the Report stated:

'Any tendency for educational difficulties to be assessed without proper reference to a child's cultural and ethnic background and its effect on his education can result in a category of handicap becoming correlated with a particular group in society.'

If a parent were unhappy about an LEA's decision to record, or not to record, their child as in need of special educational provision, they should have the right to appeal to the Secretary of State.

The active involvement of the governing body was emphasised if the third major theme of the Report, integration, was to be a reality. If the old distinctions between handicapped and non-handicapped were to be removed, and all children where possible were to be educated in ordinary schools, then the principle of integration – the education of all children in a common setting – was to be given effect to. Although the 1944 Education Act allowed for integration and the 1976 Education Act had specifically called for integration, the Warnock Report, which had widened the scope of special education so that it was not just concerned with the 2% in special schools, but also the additional 18% who had never been segregated, but whose special needs may not have been met, sought a more positive response to integration.

The point was strongly made that 'if integration is to bring all the desired benefits there must be a sufficient proportion of the activities of a school, physical, social and educational, in which a child with a disability or significant difficulty can participate on equal terms with other children, and by which he can come to enjoy the realisation of personal achievement and gain acceptance as a full member of the school community by pupils and staff.'

Consequently, the governors should satisfy themselves that teachers have a whole-hearted commitment to accepting children with various categories of special educational need, that they are suitably trained, and that there are suitable resources. It goes without saying that governors should be consulted *before* arrangements are made to establish a special unit or class in a school. Additionally, if such a class or unit were established in a school, then it was recommended that a member of the governing body should be specifically concerned with that class or unit. If this person had previous experience of special needs, then so much the better, if not, he/she 'should be especially charged with informing himself of this aspect of school activities and with generally equipping himself to promote discussions of matters relating to special education'. Such a governor would also liaise with the headteacher and LEA advisory and support staff for additional information or about matters which caused concern. The important point here is that all governors would need to keep a watchful eye; successful integration needs nurturing, it will not just happen. It must also be remembered that the aim of integration is to enrich the education of both handicapped and non-handicapped children.

Clearly, there would still be an important place for special schools since they had the resources and expertise not available in ordinary schools. Such schools would continue to cater for the more severe cases of special need currently constituting part of the identified 2%. Integration for such children would not be in their best interests, because they would be deprived access to scarce specialist resources; such schools could include some of those residential boarding schools already available; they should have their own governing body and encourage more links, for example more weekend visiting, with the parents. Where special schools existed, they should encourage links with their local ordinary schools; such links should be educational and/or social, for each school has something to offer the other.

The Report recommended that although special schools were excluded from the Taylor Report's terms of reference, they should each have their own governing body on the same lines as those recommended by Taylor so that their separateness was minimised; they should not be grouped; their membership should be broadened to reflect Taylor's recommendations, and to be more representative of the parents and the community. Warnock also made the important recommendation that, wherever appropriate, the governing body of a special school should include a handicapped person, who should, preferably, be knowledgeable about the needs of the children for whom the school catered.

The Report concluded that:

'Special education must be seen as a form of educational activity no less important, no less demanding and no less rewarding than any other, and teachers, administrators, and other professionals engaged in it must have the same commitment to children with special needs as they have to other children.'

You will appreciate why we can add the word 'governors' to the above list.

Such were the major features of the Warnock Report. Much of the thinking expressed in the Report was used as the basis of the 1981 Education Act which amended the law on special education and came into effect on 1 April, 1983.

THE 1981 EDUCATION ACT

After an extensive period of consultation, the Government accepted that many of Warnock's recommendations should be enacted in law. The notion of various categories of handicap was abolished, to be replaced by the much wider concept of special educational needs: a child has special educational needs if she/he has a learning difficulty which requires special educational provision to be made. The Act states that a child has a 'learning difficulty' if she/he has:

'significantly greater difficulty in learning than the majority of children of his age', or
'has a disability which either prevents or hinders him from making use of educational facilities of a kind generally provided in schools, within the area of the local authority concerned, for children of his age', or
'is aged under five and falls into one of these categories or is likely to later if special educational provision is not made'.

Taking account of the evidence that a disproportionate number of children from ethnic minority groups found themselves allocated to special schools, especially in the old category ESN(M), Section 1 (4) of the Act stated:

'A child is not to be taken as having a learning difficulty solely because the language (or form of language) in which he is, or will be, taught is different from a language (or form of language) which has at any time been spoken in his home.'

'Special educational provision' is to be regarded as any educational provision for children under two (this would normally apply to those children who from birth, or shortly afterwards, were recognised as being in need of special provision); for children over two such provision is regarded as 'educational provision which is additional to or otherwise different from the educational provision made generally for children of his age in schools maintained by the local education authority concerned'. Notice the LEA's responsibilities at this young age; indeed the responsibility extends until the child is 19. In fact, the

1944 Education Act states quite clearly that *all* young people have the right to full-time education up to their nineteenth birthday, if they so request. This provision has generally been ignored, although it still applies irrespective of special needs. What the 1981 Education Act provides for is that the LEA's duty to identify, assess and provide for special educational needs continues for all those receiving a full-time education up to the age of 19; such special educational provision may take a variety of forms such as in special schools, special units attached to primary or secondary schools, in special classes, in day or boarding schools, in hospitals, or in a child's own home: the situation is slightly different where Further Education is concerned.

In other words, and for the first time ever, the law recognises the special educational needs of up to 20% of the school population who may at some time in their educational career require some form of special provision.

General duties are laid upon LEAs to provide sufficient suitable schools for such child, and upon parents to cause their child to receive 'efficient full-time education suitable to his age, ability and aptitude and to any special educational needs he may have, either by regular attendance at school or otherwise' (an amendment to the 1944 Education Act).

Most importantly, as far as we are concerned, a legal duty was placed on governors of *all* schools to '*use their best endeavours*' to ensure that:

- the special educational needs of pupils in the school are being met
- these special needs are known to their teachers
- the teachers are aware of the importance of identifying children with special needs so that appropriate provision is made
- as far as possible, any child with special needs engages in the activities of the school together with non-special-needs pupils.

Thus, governors are to play a significant role in what many see as the Act's most vital feature, the duty to integrate into the life of the school all children of whatever degree of special need, due regard having been taken of the views of the parents and, interestingly, the child. Such integration must be compatible with:

- the child receiving the special educational provision required
- the provision of 'efficient education' for other children in the class
- the efficient use of resources.

Much of the Act is given over to providing parents with new rights in making their views known, and in having these views taken into account, in being involved in assessments, in being given access to records about their children, and access to help and information.

If parents request or give their consent, LEAs have a duty to identify and provide for the special educational needs of children under two. For children aged 2–19, LEAs are responsible for identifying and assessing, with parental involvement, their special needs. The Act lays down very detailed procedures for such an assessment and the consequent Statement of Special Educational Needs. The important point is that once all the procedures have been followed, the LEA is legally bound to make the special provision called for by the Statement; the Statement is regarded as a form of protection for the child, and has to be reviewed annually. This complex procedure applies mainly to the 2% of children with severe disabilities. For the other 18% who do not require such detailed assessments, but who clearly have a special educational need, governors are reminded of their duty to 'use their best endeavours' to see that suitable provision is made. Additionally, there is an LEA appeals procedure (although the appeal committee's decisions are not binding on the LEA), and a further right of appeal to the Secretary of State.

KEEP A WATCHING EYE

The 1981 Act was called by some 'the parents' charter' because it gave them increased rights and access to professional workers, and by others 'the professionals' charter' because it created the need for more workers in the special educational needs field, and more work, especially of a bureaucratic kind, for them to do.

As in all things educational, different LEAs have responded differently to the challenges and opportunities afforded by the 1981 Act. In some areas, special educational needs teams of workers were created county-wide, and integrated education was fully encouraged. In others, the LEA took full advantage of the three opt-out clauses in the Act (see page 148), especially that integration should be compatible with 'the efficient use of resources'; since no additional government funding accompanied the Act, LEAs could agree with the spirit of the legislation, but fail to put it into practice.

Since this legislation is still comparatively recent, governors will wish to monitor their own authority's special educational needs policy carefully over the next few years because the system is an evolving one; it has been acknowledged that full implementation is unlikely before the end of the century. There is much evidence that parents do not know how they can contribute to the assessment procedure, have had their hopes raised unduly, have not been treated as partners by the professionals in the assessment procedures; that LEAs have ignored the law regarding individual assessments, issuing instead standardised statements for children with vastly different disabilities; that they have subverted the assessment process by holding informal meetings without parental involvement; that they have withheld information from parents; that the very detailed and cumbersome procedures of assessment for the 2% have proved to be so costly in time and money, that the main intention of the Act – the integration of all children with special educational needs into ordinary schools – has not been fully realised, nor have the needs of the 18% whose learning difficulties do not warrant the protection of a detailed official statement been met; indeed, in some cases the statementing process can take well over a year, and there is evidence in some areas that the multiprofessional teams cannot cope with the burden of work. Additionally, there is still the understandable worry of some parents that their children are not being integrated, rather isolated, pseudo-assimilated or even dis-integrated, and consequently even more disadvantaged, in ordinary schools.

All governors, in all schools, should therefore concern themselves seriously about the challenge of special needs. You will probably find that your LEA gives its governors guidance about special needs. ILEA, for example, instituted a major report, the Fish Report (details at the end of this chapter), which is of help to all governors in any LEA who are keen to consider the problems of special needs in general, and integration in particular. Even though the numbers of children with such needs at any one time may appear insignificant, it must be remembered that cumulatively, over the life of the school, such numbers will be not inconsiderable. Moreover, since much of the 1981 Education Act places clear duties on school governors, they must ensure that their responsibilities are carried out, and that pupils with special needs are given a fair deal, to the benefit of the whole school.

SOME QUESTIONS TO ASK YOURSELF ABOUT SPECIAL EDUCATIONAL NEEDS IN YOUR SCHOOL

Your answers to the following questions will indicate to you how effective you are where this important area is concerned, or how much more thought you, and perhaps your governing body, need to give to special needs.

- Are you aware of the implications of the broader concept of special needs (i.e. 1 in 5 of all pupils) in terms of staffing and resources?
- Are you satisfied with your school's assessment procedures, especially for children from ethnic minorities?
- Does your school prospectus contain sufficient helpful information on special needs?
- Are the pupils with special educational needs really integrated with non-handicapped pupils? Or is integration only token; e.g. are special needs children isolated in special units?
- Do the teachers have whole-hearted commitment to integration? Are they suitably trained? Are there suitable premises, resources?
- Is there a designated special needs teacher, or Head of Department?
- Is the proportion of such children too high so as to damage/change the nature of the school?
- Do the special needs children *feel* isolated; e.g. are there sufficient pupils of similar special needs in the school? (The lone profoundly deaf or Downs Syndrome pupil could feel very vulnerable even though the school paid particular attention to integration.)
- Does your school share links with the local special school? Do you share any facilities, educational programmes, social events?
- Is one of the governors delegated to overseeing special needs?
- Are any of the governors handicapped?
- Does the school encourage close links with parents of special educational needs pupils?
- Does your school have a handicapped teacher?
- Does your school receive sufficient specialist help from the LEA's special educational needs support team?
- Does the school encourage self-help groups? Does it provide information about the variety of voluntary organisations with particular expertise where special needs are concerned?
- Is the school paying sufficient attention to careers guidance?
- Is the curriculum suitable? E.g. is it balanced? Does it allow for integration? Does it include sex and health education? What is the school's examination policy for children with special needs?
- Are there sufficient support staff?
- Are the standards of care adequate, particularly in practical lessons?

- Are the premises safe, from the point of view of a child with special needs, e.g. for partially sighted, epileptic children?
- Have you visited any special classes, units or schools to see the kind of work they do, and to talk to the children and their staff?

FURTHER READING

Advisory Centre for Education	'ACE Special Education Handbook', 1983
Booth T., & Potts P.	'Integrating Special Education', *Basil Blackwell* 1983
Hegarty S. *et al.*	'Educating Pupils with Special Needs in the Ordinary School', *NFER/Nelson* 1982
ILEA	'Educational Opportunties for All?' (commonly known as the Fish Report, after its chairman), 1985
	Special Educational Needs, The Warnock Report, *HMSO* 1978
	1981 Education Act, *HMSO* 1981

Some useful addresses
Advisory Centre for Education (ACE)
18 Victoria Park Square
LONDON E2 9PB

Supplies a range of useful leaflets on special needs. Also has a telephone advice line on all kinds of educational issues (01 980 4596) on weekday afternoons.

Centre for Studies on Integration in Education (CSIE)
16 Fitzroy Square
LONDON W1P 5HQ
(01 387 9571)

Established by the Spastics Society in 1982, the CSIE runs conferences, publishes factsheets and is compiling a national register of successful integration schemes.

Voluntary Council for Handicapped Children
8 Wakley Street
LONDON EC1V 7QE

Has a free information service, booklets and leaflets on all aspects of
disability and special needs and a list of all the organisations concerned
with specific disabilities.

When writing to any such organisation, remember to enclose a
stamped addressed envelope – they are all underresourced!

Additionally, your local information bureau will have addresses for
the many voluntary societies which cater for specific handicaps and
have local branches.

8 Choice, the school prospectus and governors

The school prospectus, handbook or parents' guide is a comparatively recent addition to the education scene. It is a requirement of the 1980 Education Act that schools publish detailed information about themselves. This requirement is based on the fact that although parents have (in theory since 1944) a choice of which school they send their child to, in practice it is difficult for parents to exercise this choice since they do not have the necessary information.

The value of parental interest and involvement in the education of their children being regularly voiced during the 1970s, a government discussion paper in 1977 listed the kinds of information parents could expect from a school; they wanted more information, and had a right to know what was happening in schools. Building on this, the 1980 Education Act imposed a duty on LEAs to publish the following information:

- Address(es) and telephone number(s) of the authority's office(s) to which inquiries should be made.
- Details of all the LEA schools – name, address, telephone number; pupils on roll and their age range.
- Type of school – primary, secondary, middle, county, controlled, aided, special agreement, comprehensive, grammar, secondary modern, co-educational, single sex, etc.
- The authority's admissions policy and criteria, including 'the respective admission functions of the local education authority and the governors'. (Section 8(3) (b))
- The appeals procedure against admission decisions.
- Criteria for offering places at schools not maintained by the LEA.
- A school's religious affiliation.
- In Wales, the policies for the use of the Welsh language.
- The LEA's transfer arrangements, including the governors' role.

- The LEA's transport arrangements.
- The LEA's milk and meals provision.
- The LEA's policy for school clothing, and grant arrangements for those in need of assistance.
- Other LEA grant facilities, e.g. for pupils over compulsory school age.
- Public examination policy.
- The LEA's Special Educational Needs policy and provision, detailing the process by which special needs pupils are identified, schools available, transport, information for advice and guidance.
- Any proposed changes to be made after the start of the school year to which the information relates.

As a governor you ought to have seen your authority's general information booklet, which is available free of charge from your school, the local library or your education office; all governors ought to be aware of the information contained in such a booklet.

As far as parents are concerned, this general information has to be complemented by information about individual schools available in the school prospectus. Having read the authority's general guide, and individual school prospectuses, parents are then able to exercise the right to 'choose' a school for their child – or, in reality, to state their preference under Section 6 of the 1980 Education Act. The LEA is obliged to comply with this preference unless such compliance would prejudice the efficient use of resources and efficient use of education; would be against the admissions policies agreed between the LEA and governors of voluntary schools; or would be incompatible with the child's ability as regards admission to a selective school.

You can see then that unconstrained 'choice' is not really on offer, but at least the onus is on the LEA to prove that the actual stated preference would prejudice the efficient use of resources. In addition, there was provision for an appeals procedure; and parents had to be informed of their rights. These three points, plus the availability of published information about LEAs and schools, were a significant improvement on the 1944 Education Act's general principle that children were to be educated in accordance with parental wishes.

Of course, many parents do not actually state a preference, but seem content to let their child enrol at the local school. Moreover, parents in scattered rural areas will not have as much 'choice' as parents in a densely populated urban area with more local schools to choose from; parents may also not be able to afford the transport costs which attendance at the preferred school would incur.

How can governors help parents to state their preference? What is the governors' role in the provision of information about their school? Section 8, paragraphs 5 and 6, of the 1980 Education Act states:

5) 'Every local education authority shall, as respects each school maintained by them other than an aided or special agreement school, and the governors of every aided or special agreement school shall, as respects that school, publish:–

    (a) such information as may be required by regulations made by the Secretary of State;
    and

    (b) such other information, if any, *as the authority or governors think fit* ...'

6) 'The local education authority by whom an aided or special agreement school is maintained may, *with the agreement of the governors of the school,* publish on their behalf the particulars or information relating to the school referred to in subsection (2) of (5) above'. (My emphasis.) (Subsection (2) refers to the obligation of governors of aided or special agreement schools to publish annually their admission and appeals arrangements).

It seems then that whilst governors of voluntary schools must publish this information, or delegate this responsibility to the LEA, governors of county schools are not mentioned; it is a requirement that the information will be published by the LEA, but no statement is made about who should write that information. What has happened is that heads and their staffs have taken on this task themselves, only rarely involving or consulting their governors. Indeed, there is no legal requirement for schools to publish details of their governors other than the name of the chairman. This omission is curious when it is remembered that this exercise aims to give parents more choice, yet it excludes from them the names and addresses of important people, governors, who they may be able to contact for information on which to base such choice. Of course, now that the 1986 Education Act places an onus on governors to produce an annual report which does list details concerning the governing body (see Section 30 of the Act), more prospectuses may in future contain similar details.

Since governors have oversight of the school curriculum and have a say in the admission of pupils to their school, there is no reasonable argument for excluding governors from consultation and/or active involvement in the writing of the school prospectus, especially since the 1986 Education Act places a duty on governors to publish statements about their curriculum, sex education policies and details about school syllabuses and other educational provision, and to make these available for inspection. The 1980 legislation does, after all, prescribe the *minimum* duties on schools. Sensible schools will seek to involve all those with a legitimate interest in the school in the publication of the school prospectus.

The 1980 Act states that the following minimum information should be included in the school prospectus:

- Name, address and telephone number of the school, and names of the headteacher and chairman of the governors.
- Classification of school (primary, secondary, county, controlled etc.)
- Details of specific arrangements concerning preliminary parental visits.
- Details of school curriculum – particularly curricula for different age groups; subject choices (and procedures for making these) – where applicable; how sex education is taught; the level to which subjects are taught (where applicable); careers education and guidance (where applicable).
- School's religious affiliation – if any.
- Details of the school's religious education teaching, and arrangements it makes where parents seek exclusion of their child from worship or instruction.
- Special educational needs provision.
- How education in the school is organised (mixed ability, setting etc.), and homework requirements.
- Pastoral care arrangements.
- Discipline policy, school rules, corporal punishment.
- School societies and other activities.
- School clothing policy, and details of costs if uniform is required.
- In Wales only: Welsh language policy.
- For schools with pupils over 15 (excepting those in special schools): public examinations policy; examinations usually entered; the following details of the Summer CSE, 'O' or 'A' level examinations: the number of pupils in each year group who, subject by subject, attained each grade in each such examination; the total number of pupils in each age group.

- Any changes in the school to be made after publication of the prospectus.
- The year to which the information relates, with a disclaimer about possible changes.
- The possibility of publishing the prospectus in Welsh or any other language (such prospectuses being freely available, as any others).

These requirements came into operation in May 1981 and related to information to be provided from the 1982 autumn term – such information to be available at least six weeks in advance of the date at which parents may express a preference for a school or in accordance with some special local admission date (this six-week rule does not apply to primary or special schools, although the information must still be available in advance of the school year). Prospectuses should be available at the school on request and without charge, and, in the case of special schools, copies also to be available via LEA offices, again on request and free of charge.

It must be emphasised that the above details for the LEA booklet and school prospectus lay down guidelines for the minimum information – some LEAs and schools have taken the opportunity afforded by this legislation to include much more information in an effort to allow parents to make an informed decision now that they have a statutory right to state a preference.

The school prospectus is both a legal document and a piece of advertising; not all schools appreciate this twofold function of their prospectus. Indeed, some schools fail to provide the necessary legal minimum information, omitting such details as name of chairman of governors, their method of organisation, curriculum policy, sex education details, school clothing policy and so on. That this is so is curious, since LEAs will have given all schools guidance about the content of their prospectus. Some schools seem to offer the information only grudgingly; this can be deduced from the paucity of content and tone of the prospectus. One primary prospectus I examined contained only 506 words. Is this all the school was prepared to say about itself? Such schools fail to appreciate the vital function the prospectus plays as an advertising tool.

If parents are to have a right to state a preference, schools must realise that the school prospectus assumes an important role in parents' eyes. They read it critically; they gather prospectuses from neighbouring 'rival' schools, and they visit only those schools whose prospectus has 'turned them on'. Indeed, similar strategies are employed when we shop around for houses, holidays and other household commodities; perhaps schools and governors would do well to remember this point.

I made a survey of 127 school prospectuses from Leicestershire's 445 schools. Whilst many were admirable documents which would have prompted me to make a visit to the school were I a prospective parent, others were both amateurish and, in part, illegal. Some were poorly produced, rambling documents with no apparent structure or purpose. A few read as if they were extracts from the recent diploma dissertation of the headteacher. Still others are full of the type of educational jargon few parents will understand:

> 'The curriculum is fundamentally common core.'
> 'Our method for teaching reading is a combination of phonics, look and say and sentence method.'
> 'The morning assemblies are regarded as an important part of R.E. These are supplemented with classroom lessons which broadly follow the Durham syllabus.'
> '*Mathematics*. Work is based on the Beta Maths and Hoy books. There is traditional mechanical arithmetic including tables, the four rules and problems, but modern methods involving pattern and shape are extensively used too.'
> 'Physical Education is based on the Bulletin of Physical Education, Vol VI No. 4.'
> 'Class groupings: it is less common to have children in classes divided by academic year. There is usually such a discrepancy in the sizes of year groups that there has to be some sort of vertical grouping to ensure reasonable uniformity of class sizes. However, when such class groupings are arranged they exist for a maximum of one school year.'

The tone of the prospectus is very important; in a fundamental way this document, like any other issued by the school, is part of the school's hidden curriculum. Parents will interpret the following statements in various ways:

> 'There is no formal Parent/Teacher Association. The school looks for the support of all parents at all times in the work we are undertaking.'
> 'Sex education is not taught at this school.'
> '*Ladies Committee*. School functions and fund raising are organised

by the Ladies Committee, which helps the school purchase major equipment.'

Uniform. There is a very simple school uniform ... It helps to give a child a sense of belonging and helps also, and *I think this is of great importance,* to encourage a child to come to school in the right frame of mind. We all know that if we are dressed for the beach that will influence our attitude and behaviour. Leisure clothing puts us into a 'leisure' mood. There is a time and place for everything.' (original emphasis)

If the school sees the prospectus as merely a legal document, then the tone and layout may not be given adequate attention. Many prospectuses carry no illustrations, plans, indexes or headings to help the reader through, whilst others have given such features, along with tone, due consideration so that they are readable, informative documents, as the following examples illustrate:

'*Welcome*
If you are reading this handbook for the first time, it is more than likely that your child will shortly be starting school. If this is the case, may we welcome you and your family to the school where we hope your child will be very happy. Please read through all the handbook and then show it to your relations and friends because we are proud of our village school, and hope you will be too.'

'*The School's aim – a summing-up:*
We want to pass on to the High School a well-balanced confident child, a curious and questioning individual who will have benefited from the close co-operation of parent and school. We try to ensure that each pupil has become aware of his or her potential in academic and non-academic work. The Primary School opens many doors for its children and we try to give our pupils as many relevant experiences as possible.'

'We hope that this handbook will not be taken to be a 'Book of Rules'. This was not our intention. It attempts only to give you some essential information and to show you, briefly, the aims and objectives of the school.'

'I hope this booklet has given you some knowledge of our school and the way we work. The only true way 'to get the feel' of a school, though, is to visit it, and to see it functioning with the children in.'

When you juxtapose the same points from different prospectuses, you appreciate more fully the importance of style and tone, as these extracts from primary school prospectuses show:

'We do not have 'top' children, 'bottom' children, or special prizes to reward those who already have the advantage of particular talents. We aim to help our pupils to improve upon their own previous performance, and to foster the idea that to work well is in itself reward enough.'

'Primary schools, since the demise of the 11+ examination, have so embraced the whole sphere of education that there is a great danger of losing one's way, so rich and varied is the path one can tread. The school therefore is very fortunate in possessing a most impressive number of cups given by parents and friends to reward achievement, endeavour and public service; real awards for which to aim. The Victor and Victrix Ludorum Cups and Endeavour Cup are presented at the Annual Sports. The Castell Trophy for Public Service, the Dudley Trophy for high Academic Achievement, the Dunn Trophy for Perseverance, the Silver Jubilee Cup for Craft, and the Gresley House Shield are presented during the Founder's Thanksgiving Service.'

'Health and Sex Education is regarded as an important part of the school curriculum. I have acquired the services of the School Nurse and Health Education Officer. Together a carefully balanced syllabus has been compiled.'

'Sex education: we believe that this is a subject best left to parents.'

Some schools supplement the legal minimum information contained in the prospectus with lists of staff, teaching and non-teaching, names (and occasionally addresses and phone numbers) of school governors, details of the PTA, School Health Services; a few insert road safety leaflets, Community education information, tips for parents on teaching your child to read. Yet others insert attractively produced 'Starting School' booklets, produced for the children to act as important ice-breakers when they enter the school for the first time. Other schools issue occasional newsletters outlining diary events, sports fixtures, careers conventions, exam results and entry into higher education or the job market, and special achievements. Such schools clearly appreciate the valuable opportunity the prospectus and its supplements affords them of selling themselves to their future clients.

The general conclusion made from my small survey of school prospectuses was that, on the whole, secondary school prospectuses were better produced, more informative, and more aware of their twofold function. A number of reasons may account for this: secondary schools are, generally, considerably larger than primary schools and possess the necessary reprographic facilities – and finances – to produce their own prospectus (it is the duty of the LEA to publish prospectuses generally, and the majority of Leicestershire primary school prospectuses are produced according to a set standard by the local education authority); secondary schools understand that whereas parents may be content to accept the local primary school, though not top of their list, because it is more conveniently situated, they tend to be more selective of their child's secondary education, regarding this as the more important stage of education and are prepared to allow their children to travel greater distances in order to attend the school of their preference; and, by law, secondary schools have to produce more information than primary schools, e.g. on exams and careers guidance. Secondary school prospectuses were more likely to have an introductory letter by the head, staff lists, illustrations, school plans (no primary school prospectus in my sample contained a school plan) and information beyond the legal minimum requirement. Where they tended to be unsatisfactory was in their treatment of the school's exam policy and results.

Parents are, rightly, keenly interested in a school's exam results. They remember that under the old grammar school system, schools took pride in publishing their results in local newspapers. This practice has now generally disappeared, mainly as a result of a policy of headteachers' unions not to publish such information: the trouble is, that raw exam results by themselves do not mean very much, as the following tables show. Look at the tables for School A and School B. Which school has the better results?

SCHOOL A
GCE 'O' Level

Subject	Grades Awarded				
	A	B	C	D	E
Art	6	20	19	5	1
Biology	4	33	36	11	7
Chemistry	1	4	6	5	8
Commerce	–	2	3	5	11
Computer Studies	1	3	5	–	2
Drama	1	4	5	1	2
English Language	20	44	59	62	41
English Literature	7	29	60	29	26
Food and Nutrition	1	11	18	4	11
French	3	15	26	11	27
Geography	2	19	35	19	23
History	1	21	15	21	8
Mathematics	12	42	49	17	28
Music	3	8	3	2	4
Physics	6	19	38	10	29
Religious Studies	2	16	37	28	30
Sociology	–	2	3	14	11
Spanish	–	–	2	1	1
Statistics	17	5	4	1	7

SCHOOL B
GCE 'O' Level

Subject	Grades Awarded						Number taking exam	% pass
	A	B	C	D	E	U		
Art	9	22	20	6	6	2	65	78.3
Biology	9	23	24	–	3	–	59	94.7
Chemistry	10	24	19	4	2	2	61	86.7
Computer Studies	13	9	6	1	–	–	29	96.4
English Language	23	65	86	52	52	23	301	57.6

Subject	Grades Awarded						Number taking exam	% pass
	A	B	C	D	E	U		
English Literature	–	4	6	4	1	6	21	47.5
French	8	18	32	7	12	8	85	68.1
Food and Nutrition	4	9	5	1	–	2	21	85.6
Geography	9	18	29	11	16	20	103	54.2
German	1	2	3	1	2	9	18	33.2
History	2	9	7	6	6	1	31	57.9
Mathematics	22	41	67	18	23	18	189	68.6
Music	–	1	1	2	1	–	5	40.0
Physics	13	27	26	13	12	7	98	67.2
Religious Studies	–	6	12	2	2	4	26	69.0
Sociology	–	4	5	–	10	7	26	34.5
Spanish	1	1	1	1	2	–	6	49.8

Assuming that these results applied to two schools in your area, perhaps one of your own, how would you advise parents over their choice? Both sets of statistics look impressive but what do they tell you? Can you pick out the school's strengths and weaknesses?

We obviously need much more information: what is the school's exam entry policy: does it allow all who want to to sit the exam, or does it rigorously select only those it thinks will pass? What proportion of children in each year take the exam? How do this year's results compare with previous years? How do such results compare with other local schools? What is their comparison with national statistics? What do the various exam grades mean? Many schools publish their 'O' levels according to A–E grades, but fail to mention that D and E grades, though awarded certificates, are not regarded as passes; whilst some schools only record their pass results omitting all mention of the failure rate! You can appreciate the dilemma here; a school without a healthy tradition of exam results, perhaps because it serves a 'disadvantaged' area, may be justly proud of gaining a number of 'E' grades at 'O' level, even though these are deemed to be fail grades. For that school, for those children, this could be seen as an achievement; whereas the local comprehensive which used to be the local grammar school may publish what seem to be infinitely better exam results, even though in reality they compare most unfavourably with its previous results. Indeed, a 1985 research study of 40,000 ILEA

GCE students indicated a considerable variation between exam boards and suggested that personal failure rates varied by as much as one third in some subjects. Furthermore, what is the better result: a 50% pass rate from 120 students, or a 70% pass rate from 80?

In other words, unless you have a great deal of additional information, the raw exam results published by schools should be treated with a pinch of salt. It is because heads realise that such tables may be misleading that there is much evidence nationally that many secondary schools fail to live up to their legal requirements in this respect. In fact, a 1984/5 survey of ILEA secondary school prospectuses showed that not only did most schools not publish their information at the proper time – i.e. at least six weeks before parents had to state their preference – but also that many schools did not make their examination results freely available.

As far as my own survey is concerned, all schools which had to publish information did so, but the majority of them merely published the raw statistics without giving any additional information as to their interpretation. In other words, they were less than helpful. One school gave only information on the number of candidates achieving each grade, accompanied by a statement: 'Full details of these examination results are available to parents on request.' Few schools actually mentioned what the grades for each examination mean. To be able to assess a standard, parents need to know the following information, which was only mentioned by five out of twelve schools which published such information, though rarely in this form:

CSE Grades	1	= 'O' level pass
	2	
	3	
	4	= average attainment of 16 year old
	5	
	U	= unclassified (i.e. fail)
GCE 'O' level	A }	
	B }	= pass
	C }	
	D }	
	E }	= below pass, but certificate awarded
	U	= unclassified (i.e. fail)

GCE 'A' level   A ⎫   ⎫ good pass – usually needed
                 B ⎪   ⎬ for entry into Higher Education
                 C ⎬ = pass   ⎭
                 D ⎪
                 E ⎭

                 O = fails 'A' level, but counts as 'O'
                        level pass

                 F = fail

It is only when parents have this minimum information that they can start to assess what the raw statistics mean. One school gave the following useful information:

'General note on results tables
It is notoriously difficult to draw conclusions from tables of examination results. So many factors are excluded that like can never be compared with like, even within schools, let alone between them. Here are three among many reasons why comparisons can be misleading:

Our results have always been considerably above national averages. It would be satisfying to claim that they were proof of excellent teaching. But we must acknowledge that they can also reflect the College's favourable catchment area.

Results overall are very similar to those of the previous two years with a slight decline in fifth year results and an improvement in those of the sixth and seventh years.

Our policy is to allow all candidates who have followed a course the opportunity of sitting the examination to which it leads, not – as in many schools – only those candidates who are expected to pass. Obviously this can result in tables which appear less favourable.

One way in which we have tried to present a more balanced picture, avoiding excessive emphasis on the successes or failures which will occur in any one year, is to relate percentage passes to a three year period.'

Another school boasted of its consistently high 'A' level results, giving its previous three years' subject pass rates which were between 7% and 10% above the national subject pass rate of 70% at this level. To this important information was added:

'Another method of assessing 'A' level results is to look at the proportion of passes achieved in Grades A, B and C – the three highest grades and therefore those most commonly required for entrance to University degree courses. The percentage of passes nationally in these grades is 35%. For the previous three years ours have been 52%, 52% and 49%.'

Only one prospectus actually quoted the county averages as a comparison. The impression gained is that those schools with the most favourable results reveal the most information. Whilst the dilemma which many schools face about the publication of their exam results is appreciated, there is clearly room for improvement, so that parents can make informed choices.

At the time of writing, plans are well advanced for operating a new single system of examinations for 16-year-olds from the summer of 1988 – the GCSE – such courses starting in the autumn of 1986. Such a system, combining the strengths of the old GCE and CSE, has been long mooted. It will place more emphasis on course assessment (at least 20% of the marks will be awarded according to continual assessment of school work in the preceding two years), and involve more practical work; there will be fewer examinations boards; examination syllabuses will be based on national criteria (thus removing the results bias mentioned on page 164); different papers will be set according to a candidate's ability, and the grades awarded will acknowledge such levels of ability.

A seven-point scale of grades will be used.

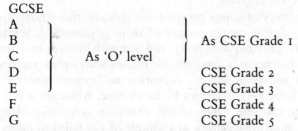

GCSE		
A		
B	}	As CSE Grade 1
C	} As 'O' level	
D		CSE Grade 2
E		CSE Grade 3
F		CSE Grade 4
G		CSE Grade 5

Students who fall off this scale will be 'unclassified'. Since the prime aim of the new system is to increase standards and motivate children by applying learning to experience rather than to the ability to regurgitate theoretical knowledge, it is a sine qua non that schools will need to adjust their curricula to match the different emphasis that future learning will take. Of course, much of this has been done in readiness, although at the time of writing, there is a real worry that, because of the current year-long teachers' dispute, the tight schedule will not be met. Already some governing bodies have written to the

Secretary of State for Education and to the national press expressing their concerns. Such radical changes in curriculum and examinations policy are bound to be of importance to governors and you should ensure that you are kept fully in the picture as the new system develops.

What role do the governors have vis-à-vis the school prospectus? According to the 1980 Education Act, it is only governors of aided or special agreement schools who are legally required to publish the above information; the LEA is the publisher on behalf of all other governors. Does this mean that governors of county and controlled schools should leave it all to their LEA and school? I do not think so. The 1980 legislation merely prescribes a legal minimum; there is no reason why governors should be excluded from the necessary consultations such an annual task places on the school. This is especially so if you accept the Taylor Report's view that there is no area of a school's work which should not be the concern of the governors. Moreover, the school prospectus as a legal document has to contain information with regard to the curriculum, admissions policy, discipline policy over which governors have legal requirements. By placing such information in the public domain, the work of governors becomes, necessarily, more conspicuous; they are made to be more accountable, therefore they have a strong claim to assume responsibility for the presentation and explanation of the information their prospectus contains.

But my survey of school prospectuses indicates that schools are, on the whole, almost contemptuous of their governors. Whereas the PTA (not a legally required body, and one with limited, even though important, functions) is generally mentioned with a paragraph giving details and addresses and an invitation to become involved, the governing body is conspicuous by its absence. Although it is a legal requirement that the name of the chairman is mentioned in the prospectus, nine prospectuses in a sample of 127 failed to do so, and only 30 prospectuses gave governors more space than the minimum requirement. Primary school prospectuses were the worst culprits, only 12½% offering more information about governors than the legal minimum; the detail offered ranged from merely giving a list of the composition of the governing body, but no names, to partial or full lists of names, with only one prospectus actually giving a full list of names and addresses. Additional information about the governing body was often submerged in the text, without a heading, thus:

'The Headmaster is directly responsible to the Governors for the management of the school and is required to report to the Governors each term when they meet at the school. Two governors are elected by the parents, and two from the teaching staff.'

In no prospectus examined did the text give an adequate explanation of the wide-ranging duties and responsibilities of the governing body. The fullest details of the governing body were contained in the following two accounts:

'In accordance with the requirements set down in the 1980 Education Act, the Head Teacher, staff and governors are pleased to present the following information for parents ...' (This is the only reference made in any of the prospectuses sampled of the governors' potential responsibility for the contents of the school prospectus.) 'The Governors normally meet once each term at the school and pay individual visits in addition. They have wide responsibilities connected with the general efficiency and well-being of the school.'

'School Governors are mainly local residents whose contribution to the smooth running of the school helps the welfare and progress of each child. The Governors meet at the school once a term. They visit the school regularly and I am frequently in touch with the Chairman. They share with the Head Teacher a responsibility for ensuring proper maintenance of the school building, for the appointment of staff and for the school's lettings to outside bodies. Their function is important as a part of a system of checks and balances that act as a safeguard against arbitrary decisions made by either the LEA or the Head Teacher. Since my appointment as Head of this school in 1973 I have found their comments, based on a wide range of experience, helpful and positive. They have a role that is both constructively critical and encouraging. They exemplify a cross-section of the views of our community; and among the Governors are two teachers and a parent whose contributions reflect their special and important standpoints.'

However, neither of these prospectuses gave any details of how to contact school governors.

This lack of recognition of governors by their primary schools can be compared with my secondary school sample, almost 50% of which gave their governors more than the legal minimum mention. Again, as in primary prospectuses this additional information varied from partial or full lists of names, to lists of names, addresses and phone numbers. But following primary school practice, little mention was made of the actual duties of governors; one did mention their role in respect of discipline and suspensions, another devoted its back page to a welcoming letter from the chairman of the governors, whilst another stated:

'*The Governors*
The Articles of Government for County Secondary Schools drawn up by the Leicestershire County Council, acting as Local Education Authority, lay down the function of a school's Governing Body. In particular, the Articles state that

'The Governors in consultation with the Headteacher shall have the general direction of the conduct and curriculum of the school'.

'The school has 15 Governors, of which 9 are direct appointments by the Local Education Authority (2 of whom are on the nomination of the Borough Council) and 6 are co-opted.

The Governors meet at least once a term, and pay regular visits to the school. The Chairman of Governors, in particular, has close regular contact with the school and is consulted on all policy matters.'

This is the only prospectus in my sample to mention the crucial phrase in most Articles which states the governors' vital role in connection with the curriculum. All the others shirked away from any such mention. The following table gives a breakdown of the statistics of my survey:

	Primary	Secondary	Special	Total
Legal minimum information (Chairman's name only)	63	20	5	88
More than the minimum (Lists and/or statements about governing body)	8	22	–	30
No mention at all	5	3	1	9
TOTALS	76	45	6	127

Table 11: *The school prospectus and the governing body*

Since a wealth of research evidence has shown that parental attitudes towards their children's education are vitally important for educational success, and since it is the parents' legal duty to cause their children to receive 'efficient full-time education' – which means, except in rare cases, attendance at school – it is fortuitous that parents now have available to them more information on which to express their preference. However, some of this information, in the form of the school prospectus, is of dubious quality, and the verdict for many schools is: 'tries hard, but could do better'. This is the age of increasing parental power; they are consumers of the educational service; they have a right to be involved and they have a right to accurate and detailed information. Without this information, it is difficult for parents to know how particular schools operate, and whether their children will benefit from attendance. Moreover, there is much evidence that parents are keen to find out more about their local schools and that, contrary to some teachers' views, parents do care about their children's education. Some research evidence, however, shows that parents are not very efficient at exercising choice. Michael Rutter's 'Fifteen Thousand Hours', a detailed study of twelve inner city comprehensives, found that parents were not good at selecting schools which maximised their children's performance; Rutter's study found that the 'best' schools (i.e. schools with good exam results, low truancy rates, good discipline) were not always the most popular with parents.

The onset of falling school rolls and increase in parental rights have altered the status of the school prospectus. Where parents are concerned, it is an important document. If parents are not offered the school of their choice, they have the right of appeal; although the appeals procedure is intimidating, more and more parents take their grievances to appeals committees, on which sit selected school governors. It seems that while 92% of parents get the school of their 'choice', or accept the school they are offered, a significant proportion of parents is disappointed every year, and makes an appeal. Only a few of these appeals eventually reaches the appeal committee stage, an accommodation between parents and LEA having been reached meanwhile. However, in the first three years of admission appeals, 1982–84, 26,000 cases were heard, complaints were made to the ombudsman on 175 of them (most of which subsequently secured their preferred school) and 40 formal ombudsman reports were issued. It was found that there was confusion in the appeals committees concerning their powers, where the onus of proof lay, biased membership, dubious use of evidence and failure to communicate decisions adequately. Whilst some LEAs are generous in eventually submitting to the parents' wishes (in 1982 67% of Leicestershire's 80 appeals were successful, compared to the fairly steady national average over the past three years of only a 33% success rate), many feel that the appeals procedure is too lengthy, loaded in the LEA's favour, and disproportionately costly in money and time. A 1983 study estimated that the 9000 appeals in 1982/3 cost around £2 million and resulted in only 3000 successful appeals. Is this too heavy a price to pay to ensure parental preference, and/or does it highlight the fiction surrounding the notion of 'choice'? Governors would do well to monitor the appeals procedure in their own LEA to see whether it is loaded in favour of the LEA or the parents.

Parents do have the right to appeal to the Secretary of State for Education if they feel that the LEA's rejection of their appeal was unreasonable. However, in 1982, every one of the 313 such appeals made to the Education Secretary was rejected; it is difficult to prove that an LEA has acted unreasonably. Nevertheless, in 1984 a High Court appeal decided that the LEA could no longer hide behind the argument that to admit a child would prejudice 'efficient use of resources'; the decision was that the LEA would have to give specific reasons to back up this claim. As a result of this decision, parents may find it easier to challenge future LEA decisions.

Although there is much force in the argument that the 1980 Education Act has caused much dissatisfaction by raising expectations that cannot be satisfied, governors should appreciate the importance of 'choice' to parents, and the role of the school prospectus in enabling this choice.

It is only proper, then, that governors should be consulted about the contents and presentation of the school prospectus, which should no longer be allowed to gather dust in some school cupboard, but should be elevated to its central place in the education system.

FURTHER READING

ACE	'School Choice Appeals', *Advisory Centre for Education* 1982
Taylor F. and Rogers R.	'ACE School Prospectus Planning Kit', *Advisory Centre for Education* 1980
Taylor F.	'Choosing a School', *Advisory Centre for Education* 1983

9 Suspensions from school – the case of the obscene graffiti

'The power of suspension should be used with great caution, it should be used only in the interests of the pupil concerned or those of the school as a whole, it must be firmly rooted in facts which can be established, and it must be exercised strictly in accordance with the ... articles of government.'

Such is the excellent advice given to governors if they are ever involved in a suspension case, in G. Barrell's authoritative book, 'Teachers and the Law'.

There can be little doubt that teaching today has changed out of all recognition from the picture which many governors may carry with them about their own school days. Evidence shows that teachers are increasingly suffering from classroom stress, with as many as 10% of an LEA's teaching force being absent from school every day. Headteacher unions are concerned about the worrying trend of early retirement amongst headteachers caused by the growing stress of their jobs; much of this stress is caused by what heads see as continued underresourcing of the education system; by the effects of the long-running teachers' dispute in the early 1980s; and by the general feeling of demoralisation connected with the two preceding points. There is no doubt that in the mid-1980s, we find our education system at a low ebb. On top of this, it is clear that some of this stress is due to growing discipline problems in schools which have been particularly exacerbated since many LEAs abolished the administration of corporal punishment in their schools (such LEA directives did not affect voluntary schools, many of which continue to allow corporal punishment). So bad has become the problem of indiscipline that at least one teachers' union has called for the presence of security guards in inner city schools because of the increase of classroom violence.

Whatever a governor's own feelings about corporal punishment are, it is worth wondering why Great Britain remained one of the decreasing number of western nations still to retain corporal punishment in its schools until it was banned by only one vote in the House of Commons in July 1986; schools have until summer 1987 to phase out this practice and to make alternative arrangements. Such a close decision remains controversial, and you may find governors and teachers who find it difficult to support. It does, however, indicate that public pressure and an orchestrated campaign can have an effect, and that schools are dynamic organisations which have to move with the times. No doubt the anti-caning pressure group, STOPP, which found in a 1983 survey that 238,688 'beatings' were administered in schools in England and Wales (about one every 19 seconds) will take some of the credit for the decision to abolish corporal punishment. Moreover, the decision is likely to have been influenced by the cases brought before the European Commission on Human Rights in Strasbourg by over 40 English parents to date which have shown that in certain circumstances corporal punishment could amount to 'degrading treatment or punishment' and consequently constitute a breach of the Human Rights convention (one English complainant was awarded £1200 damages).

If a school cannot resort to corporal punishment in dealing with its recalcitrant members, then it is more likely to resort to suspension, in which case the school governors will be involved. It seems no coincidence that the number of suspensions appears to have increased in the past few years. There are no national figures about suspensions from schools, and it is probable that many cases go unreported. You may find it interesting to search out your own school's or LEA's figures over the past three years, and to keep such figures under review.

WHAT IS THE GOVERNOR'S ROLE?

LEAs vary in their involvement of governors in suspensions, so you should check carefully the guidance your LEA gives its governors in the comparatively rare eventuality of their being involved in a suspension case. Three examples from the early 1980s (and before the provisions of the 1986 Education Act) are cited for illustration:

Cambridgeshire LEA's advice to its governors where suspension is concerned was as follows:

'Under Authority derived from the Articles of Government, the Head has the power of suspending pupils from attendance for any cause which he considers adequate ... The Governing Body's responsibilities in this matter are generally carried by the Head, who is responsible to them for the conduct of the school and for the control of the discipline of the school.'

By contrast, Berkshire LEA was more detailed in its advice to governors, outlining their role in the appeals process:

'Parents of suspended pupils have a right of appeal to governors ... The usual procedure is for the Chairman to appoint a panel of Governors (usually three in number) to whom the parents may state their case in person. This panel is entitled to the advice of a representative of the Director of Education and may also invite any other person (e.g. the Head) whose views may be helpful in reaching a decision.'

Birmingham Education Committee's Governors' manual was even more detailed in its commentary on suspension, not only outlining the agreed procedures and the governors' role, but also adding a word of caution:

'Several points need to be made ... First, there is no power of expulsion whatsoever given under the law to Heads, to Governors, or even to the Authority itself. Suspension from attendance at school is not the same as expulsion and the decision may well be taken to return him to his school after suspension (whether confirmed or not). Second, even when a child is required to attend a special centre, he remains on the roll of his original school and the decision may be taken to return him there. Third, there is no *automatic* transfer of a suspended pupil to another school. There may be no room in another school anyway, and a Headteacher will naturally be cautious about agreeing to take a child into his school if there is a record of bad behaviour. Governors should not therefore assume that a transfer to another school can always be arranged.

Suspension of pupils, and the action to deal with their cases, will be reported to the Governors at each meeting. Governors will obviously consider these cases carefully, as they will provide an indication of the kinds of problem the school is facing, as well as the effectiveness of the measures being adopted by the Headteacher and his staff to deal with them. It should be remembered that suspensions are relatively rare – less than one pupil per thousand of the school population is involved in a suspension each year – and Governors of many schools will never encounter a suspension case throughout the whole of their period of office.'

These three extracts show the range of LEA views concerning governors' involvement in the suspension process. Whereas Cambridge-shire seemed to be telling its governors they had no role, not even at the appeal stage – 'The Governing Body's responsibilities in this matter are generally carried by the Head' – Birmingham gave much more prominence to the role of the governors, giving them details of the agreed procedures (not quoted here), and explaining to them the necessity for caution. (Birmingham seemed to rule out any possibility at all of expulsion, presumably because it implied a failure of the LEA to fulfil its duty in providing an education, even though this was clearly an option.)

Such LEA statements are likely to have been changed following the detailed, and complex, provisions of sections 22–28 of the 1986 Education Act as summarised on pages 36–38 of this book. You should refer to these pages, and to the advice given to you locally, since the procedures are currently evolving and are unlikely to resemble those you may have been used to up to 1987. The major effect of this legislation is that whereas the governors used to have the ultimate power to reinstate a suspended pupil, this has now been given to the LEA in most cases, although the governing body can appeal against such an LEA directive.

It must be emphasised that generally a suspension is only resorted to when a series of other possibilities (parental consultation, guidance from the educational welfare officer, help from the child guidance clinic, the possibility of transfer to another school) have been tried and that suspension is not (as it is in independent schools), or should not be, considered a punishment, but merely a period of 'cooling off', a 'breathing space' so that a fruitful solution to the problem may be found. It is unfortunate that many see suspensions as a punishment; it is a funny kind of punishment which gives pupils an additional 'holiday' from school.

In fact, the term 'suspension' is often applied to two other forms of action – exclusion and expulsion – and it is important that you understand the different applications of each term.

Exclusion refers to the temporary debarment of children from school on medical grounds usually because pupils may be suffering from an infectious or contagious disease: AIDs caused a stir in some of our nation's schools in 1985 with the subsequent exclusion of a few children; more usually, such serious infectious illnesses as tuberculosis, dysentry, diphtheria, cholera or poliomyelitis prompt an exclusion in accordance with the LEA's regulations. Very occasionally, verminous children are excluded as are children with some serious psychological disturbance. Governors would have no role in such exclusions, but could expect to be informed at a subsequent meeting. In the unlikely event of a school being closed because of an epidemic, then governors would of course learn of the event much earlier.

You will often find the term 'exclusion' used euphemistically for suspension and/or expulsion.

Expulsion refers to the *permanent* debarment of a pupil from school. *Suspension* refers to the *temporary* debarment of a pupil for a fixed period of time – usually a matter of days – because of the serious infraction by the pupil of some school rule.

The headteacher is responsible for the day-to-day management of the school and for maintaining discipline, having regard to any guidance from the governing body. In this respect it is recognised that there will occasionally be disciplinary incidents which so undermine the smooth running of the school that the usual range of school disciplinary measures are quite unsuitable. In such cases the head has the power to suspend the culprit(s) from school, provided he informs the governors and the local authority (the precise procedure varies, and you need to consult your local rules for this). Such suspensions cover a wide range of disciplinary infractions; e.g. in recent years pupils have been suspended for the following reasons:

- violence against teachers, e.g. stabbing a teacher
- violence against other pupils
- damage of school property
- being continually disruptive in class
- being abusive to a teacher
- firing an air pistol in class during a lesson
- bullying
- extortion
- because a child's parents refused to allow him to be caned for smoking in school
- for attempting to kiss a young woman teacher
- for persistently wearing to school clothes deemed unsuitable by the head

- the wearing to school by a Sikh boy of his kirpan (ceremonial dagger), which was deemed by the boy to be an indispensable item according to his religion, but to be a dangerous weapon by his headteacher and governors.

Sometimes, as in the graffiti case to be examined later in this chapter, heads will recommend to their governors expulsion of the offender, on the grounds that to have him back would damage the smooth running of the school.

Governors must satisfy themselves that the head does not use these ultimate sanctions 'arbitrarily, wantonly or capriciously'. There is sometimes the suspicion that certain heads use their powers to suspend over-enthusiastically, and governors must ensure that any suspension is not the school's easy way out of a tricky situation, but also has regard to the welfare of the offender. It is important to remember that the grounds for the suspension are not seen to be unreasonable since it has been established in law since 1959 that 'a pupil shall not be refused admission to or excluded from a school on other than reasonable grounds'. If parents feel that their child has received unreasonable treatment, they may exercise their right to appeal to the governors. Additionally, cases of suspension are often picked up by the local and national press, resulting in bad publicity not only for the pupil, but also for the school, and sometimes the governors; this is bound to be an unwelcome event and in the interests of none of the parties concerned.

If an expulsion is recommended, a number of tricky problems arise both for the LEA and parents, as the following case of Poundswick High School illustrates. Since this became something of a cause célèbre in 1985/86, and since it constitutes a useful case history for governors, the remainder of the chapter offers a detailed account and commentary of the notorious Poundswick High School graffiti row.

THE CASE OF THE OBSCENE GRAFFITI

The Poundswick graffiti row concerns a large Manchester Comprehensive school which found itself in the national limelight when the headteacher, supported by his governors, recommended for 'exclusion on a permanent basis', i.e. expulsion, five fifth form boys for allegedly covering a 100 yard section of an outside school wall and windows with obscene and racist remarks about ten members of the school staff and their spouses. Whatever the rights and wrongs of the various participants – and you can be the judge of this yourselves when you examine the details which follow – this case ended up the way no suspension/expulsion should: the dirty washing was hung up in public over many months and a stalemate was reached early on during the row from which none of the parties was willing to move. It is hoped that other governors, should they ever find themselves in the comparatively rare position of presiding over a suspension case in their school, will learn the lessons which the Poundswick graffiti row reveals.

The chronology of the case was as follows;

1985

17 June –	Graffiti appeared on school walls (presumably following a weekend escapade).
18 June –	Suspects interviewed by the head teacher.
19 June –	Five boys, who had allegedly used spray cans and felt-tip pens, suspended for serious misconduct.
1 July –	The Poundswick High School Governors confirmed the Headteacher's 19 June action, and made a recommendation to the City Council that the five boys should be permanently excluded (i.e. expelled) from the school. The boys' parents were present at this meeting.
13 September –	(A Friday) A sub-committee of the Education Committee met to hear the case; this sub-committee was delegated by the City Council to hear all such cases and to decide the issue. After a six and a half hour meeting at which all the parties concerned presented their case – one of the parents with the aid of a barrister – the sub-committee, 'only on a fine balance of long argument, and in no way reflecting any lack of concern about the seriousness of the pupils' misbehaviour or the views of Governors and teachers', determined on a 4–2 vote that the five boys should be readmitted to Poundswick High School subject to reassurances as to their future behaviour.
18 September –	The Poundswick Headteacher informed the Chief Education Officer that the teachers, supported by their unions, refused to teach the boys – i.e. they found themselves effectively excluded (suspended) by the teachers.

24 September – The Chief Education Officer visited the school and told the teachers they were obliged to teach the boys.

26 September – After eight working days during which the teachers refused to teach the boys, the Council decided to send those teachers home for breach of contract. However, before this could happen, some 35 staff out of a total of 60 had walked out, leaving only some 300–400 pupils from a total of 1000 receiving any lessons.

27 September – More teachers joined their colleagues, only a few remaining on duty.

Subsequently, 47 teachers were suspended by the LEA for refusing to teach the five boys: 18 members of NAS/UWT were suspended without pay, 29 members of NUT and AMMA were sent warning notices and went on strike, rather than teach the boys. Teachers of other schools were prepared to stop work to support their colleagues.

30 September – A small deputation of some 50 parents, Poundswick teachers, and children handed in a 1000 signature petition at Council Offices calling for the teachers' reinstatement and the boys' expulsion.

4 October – A larger demonstration of some 200 teachers from other Manchester schools – the first-ever joint strike action by teachers in Manchester – and parents marched to Town Hall in support of the suspended teachers. An estimated 25,000 pupils missed lessons.

Manchester secondary school heads voted to strike in support of Poundswick staff. Meanwhile, Poundswick's lower school was closed; only a handful of staff and pupils remained at work in the upper school. By this stage, other schools had offered to take the boys, and home tuition was available.

10 October – A half-day strike by Secondary Heads Association members in Manchester.

16 October – A Special Meeting – the third such – of councillors, union officials and education officers found no solution, reached deadlock, and adjourned.

Lord Mayor of Manchester called a special Council meeting to debate the case.

21 October – 4,500 Manchester teachers staged a half-day strike,

closing 350 schools and affecting up to 80,000 pupils. After a rally and march, they handed in a petition to the council leader. All five teacher unions united, and support was claimed throughout Great Britain.

'The dispute had touched a nerve in Manchester and the whole country' (Guardian 22.10.85).

Some Poundswick parents prepared to seek an injunction in the High Court to compel the City Council to accept the boys' expulsion.

22 October – Parents of one of the expelled boys threatened to take the union to court if no settlement was reached within a week.

Meanwhile, the Education Committee offered a compromise: the teachers named in the the graffiti would not have to teach the reinstated boys, who would be educated both on and off the school site. The unions would not accept this compromise.

The General Secretary of the National Association of Head Teachers wrote to the Education Minister to seek discussions clarifying the governors' role regarding suspensions and expulsions.

23 October – Manchester's local authority unions backed the LEA position and told teacher unions to accept the LEA decision which followed the correct procedures and was in no position to reverse the sub-committee decision.

25 October – Manchester's Liberal councillors, supported by Conservative councillors, proposed a peace formula – a revision of the evidence.

This was deemed unacceptable by Labour councillors, who instead offered conciliation process, either by the Arbitration, Conciliation and Advisory Service (ACAS), T.U. or religious leaders. Teachers were willing to consider this.

30 October – Further meeting between the five teacher unions and Education Policy Sub-Committee failed to reach agreement; ACAS unacceptable. Each side of dispute maintained its position. Teachers willing to accept a conciliation process provided the five boys were not readmitted during the conciliation; the LEA unwilling to accept this condition.

A Poundswick parents' pressure group accepted £1000 from the right-wing 'Freedom Association' to start legal action against Manchester LEA for allegedly failing in its legal obligation to educate the 1000 Poundswick pupils during the dispute.

5 November – Teachers agreed to a conciliator, the Dean of Manchester, a C. of E. education expert (11 days after the idea of conciliation was first mooted!).

12 November – A meeting of ACAS broke down and adjourned indefinitely.

15 November – Meeting of the teachers' unions and boys' parents, under the guidance of the Dean of Manchester.

18 November – A re-airing of the evidence at a special public meeting of the education policy sub-committee, in a bid to get the governors to reconsider their expulsion. It was alleged that 18 youths had been involved in the 17 June graffiti incident; did the governors have the full evidence in June?

AMMA considered legal action against the LEA over three of its suspended teachers.

25 November – Headteacher unions sought a meeting with the Secretary of State for Education to clarify powers of LEA over governors and teachers. NAHT claimed LEA powers to be excessive.

26 November – Governors put forward a peace plan which entailed the five boys receiving their education in a Further Education College, or being taught in a Poundswick annexe, not by existing staff but by eight extra staff.

This peace plan was rejected by the LEA, which maintained that the boys were entitled by law to be taught in the school of their choice, 'except in exceptional circumstances'.

4 December – Chairman of the Poundswick PTA initiated a meeting in consultation with ACAS between unions and LEA.

13 December – It is learnt that six MPs and 26 members of the public had complained to the Secretary of State for Education during the dispute. He asked the LEA to find a solution, but did not consider it necessary to intervene directly. In other words, he did not find the LEA to be in default, and the LEA took this to be a vindication of their position.

18 December – NUT offered to end strike action by its members at Poundswick if LEA suspended its action on 29 NUT teachers, and to limit its strike action to classes involving the five boys.

20 December – By this time ACAS, which had been involved since November, held a further meeting with unions and LEA; the Education Secretary asked to be kept informed.

Up to this time, the LEA had held 13 meetings with the unions.

27 December – NUT and AMMA (but not NAS/UWT) agreed that their staff could return to work in January with normal education for the pupils of the first few years, but with their action continuing to disrupt the classes of 150 fifth year pupils whose classes included the five boys. Although far from satisfactory, this was at least a partial settlement.

1986

7 January – A partial re-opening of Poundswick School, with first and third year pupils returning.

13 January – The remaining class returned, but fifth formers miss many of their lessons since NUT and AMMA members refused to teach such classes. Meanwhile, 18 of the 26 NAS/UWT teachers were still suspended, and the original 'dirty five' were off the premises, working from home.

24 January – Another peace plan suggested that all the fifth year pupils should be taught elsewhere by volunteer tutors; this was rejected.

NAS/UWT still being sent home for refusing to teach these boys. At this stage, after seven months of dispute, it seemed an impasse had been reached: no progress had been made, no further major initiatives were forthcoming. The graffiti row finally fizzled out in May 1986 when the five suspended boys officially left school, and the Poundswick NAS/UWT teachers returned to their duties.

Such, then, are the bare bones of the 'graffiti row'. It need hardly be said that this case highlights not only the crucial role governors can play in the suspension/expulsion process but also the confusing legal position of the parties involved. Additionally, the 'graffiti row' gives much ammunition to those who argue that the time for a review of suspension procedures is long overdue.

What is the legal position of the parties involved? A statement issued on 25 September 1985 on behalf of the Education Committee and City Council stated:

'The City Council are required by law to educate all young people up to the age of 16 and are further required by law to have regard to the wishes of parents. It is an important 'right' of parents to choose the school they wish their children to attend, and the City Council cannot disregard the wishes of parents other than for the most serious of reasons, such as lack of space or unreasonable additional public expenditure.'

This position was stated early on in the dispute, and stuck to throughout. Is the LEA correct in its interpretation of the law? The 1944 Education Act places a duty on parents, not on the LEA, to 'cause their children to be educated at school, or otherwise'. The LEA's duty is merely to provide the necessary facilities, that is, suitable school places, 'sufficient for their area', so that if a child is expelled after due process, it is the parent who has failed in his duty, not the LEA. As far as Manchester LEA's interpretation of the 1980 Education Act's 'choice' provisions are concerned, it is extremely generous to parents. Their statement of 25 September reads: 'the City Council cannot disregard the wishes of parents other than for the most serious of reasons, such as lack of space, or unreasonable expenditure'. A similar statement of 26 November maintained that the boys were entitled by law to be taught in the school of their choice, 'except in exceptional circumstances'. Is Manchester LEA arguing that a serious infringement of school discipline, i.e. grossly obscene graffiti naming teachers, does not constitute a serious reason or exceptional circumstance in which the LEA can deny parental preference?

Although Manchester LEA's interpretation of the relevant law is debatable, what of its policy as far as suspensions are concerned? Were the boys suspended after due process? The 25 September statement made the following point:

'Once parents' wishes have been met and a pupil is enrolled at a school, the pupil cannot be permanently excluded from school other than by the City Council, although s(he) may be temporarily 'suspended' for misconduct or other good cause by the school governors. While in attendance at school, all pupils must be taught without discrimination.'

A sub-committee of the Schools Sub-committee of Education is delegated to hear all such 'permanent exclusion' cases. Consequently, Manchester's position is clear: heads can recommend suspension to their governors; governors can confirm this, or go further and recommend 'permanent exclusion' to the LEA; the LEA alone, through its appropriate sub-committee, can recommend 'permanent exclusion.'

The case seems to rest on whether the due process was followed by head, governors, and LEA. Manchester LEA maintains that every year 'a few exclusion cases' are heard, of which roughly two thirds are upheld and one third are not and the pupils are returned to school, 'without difficulty'. The LEA position rests on the action of the head, governors and teachers. Clearly, the gross nature of the graffiti was upsetting and demanded prompt action by the head. The LEA and parents maintain that the five boys alone were not the cause of the 100 yards of graffiti, that at least thirteen other youths, some not at the school, were involved, and that at the time the head and governors made their decision, they were not in full possession of the facts. Moreover, the LEA maintains that the headteacher wrote to the chairman of the governors recommending the boys' exclusion *before* he had interviewed them. The governors subsequently held their special meeting and had a clear majority for 'exclusion'.

We have already referred to the governors' position in relation to suspensions: they have an important role. The question is: is this role adequately defined, and could it be improved? Governors need to convince themselves in any case of suspension that they are in possession of all the facts, and that they do not merely rubber stamp a headteacher's decision. Some suspension cases are indeed brought about on flimsy ground, and too many governors support their head almost unthinkingly because they defer to his authority and seek the quiet life. But suspension cases can have serious effects on pupils: expulsion cases even more so – especially if they occur in an exam year, as in the case at Poundswick. Governors must ensure that pupils are given a fair, unbiased hearing. Was this the case at Poundswick? It seems that the composition of the governing body was loaded towards teachers' interests; the chairman of the governors was a teacher at another school, an NAS/UWT member on the governing body was a representative of the Education Committee, and the majority of other governors were either teachers or those co-opted at the request of teachers. Was this an impartial body?

What of the appeals procedure? It must surely be a sine qua non of any such procedure that its decision will be final and binding – otherwise there is no point in having a procedure. In this case, the duly elected South District Sub-Committee investigated the case for six and a half hours. Full presentations were made by all parties, including a solicitor acting on behalf of one of the parents. This committee concluded that there was insufficient evidence to merit permanent exclusion, and decided on reinstatement of the five boys. The 25 September Statement said that this decision 'was reached only on a fine balance of long argument, and in no way reflected any lack of concern about the seriousness of the pupils' misbehaviour or the views of governors and teachers'.

What do we make of this extract from the Statement? It appears to acknowledge that there was some case for the boys to answer because it talks of 'the seriousness of the pupils' misbehaviour'. But was appropriate weight given to the views of the governors and teachers by the LEA? It must have realised that this case had already achieved national notoriety, and that to reinstate would undermine the head and governors and would be seen by them to make their job of ensuring adequate discipline throughout the school much more difficult in the future. Did the reinstatement decision also take into account the feelings of the many teachers slurred by the graffiti?

The LEA took a clear line in support of their own power, and of parental rights, and hence against the power and rights of the head and governors. As they stated in their Statement of 2 October:

'In 1980 Parliament gave legal rights to all parents, and new draft legislation shortly to be presented to Parliament will strengthen those rights, particularly in the area of suspensions and exclusions. The Committee are concerned that parents should have their legal rights on school attendance as fully enforceable as their duties. They are greatly concerned that many young people are, for reasons beyond their control, out of school – in some cases for long periods. Some parents find it difficult to obtain support, whether legal or otherwise, in defending their rights against the 'authorities'. The overall position is that, at any one time, an unacceptable number of pupils are being denied their rights in law to full-time education. It is against this background that the Education Committee and City Council are now acting.'

Given that very early on during this dispute a number of schools were willing to accept the boys, it must be asked who was advising the boys' parents to persist in their desire for their sons to be educated at Poundswick, especially since the teachers were unanimous in their determination not to accept the five. What of the rights of the many hundreds of Poundswick pupils who were denied many weeks education during the dispute? Should not the LEA have considered *their* rights in law to a full-time education? The dispute seriously affected the 'O' Level chances of many of the fifth form pupils, and the January interim settlement resulted in the situation that whereas the five boys had access to 'home tutors' or 'counsellors' – the LEA claiming that they were being assessed, not taught – a number of innocent fifth formers were receiving no schooling at all and many were receiving a severely disrupted schooling, since the NAS/UWT teachers were still suspended. In other words, while the five boys were being assessed for the educational effects of the dispute, many other innocent pupils caught up in the dispute were receiving no similar 'assessment' or 'tuition'.

What of the teachers' position? Understandably they were incensed at the scurrilous graffiti since it attacked in grossly offensive sexual and racial tones ten of their colleagues and their spouses. If they were to be able to uphold standards of discipline and decency, they were looking to the head to deal effectively with the miscreants. Did he act too hastily with the boys, even though they were, on their own admission, involved in writing the graffiti? (According to evidence supplied by the NAHT, and by the father of one of the boys, the boys each admitted involvement in the graffiti episode – though denied they wrote the most obscene bits. There is conflicting evidence as to the amount of graffiti they admit to having written – the boys deny they wrote the vast majority of it, whereas the NAHT claims the boys admit to a 'significant proportion'.) However, following the boys' reinstatement after their appeal, did the teachers have any right to refuse to teach the boys? Legally, no. Since only headteachers can be involved in suspension procedures, it follows that teachers have to accept any decision which results. Notwithstanding the unprecedented inter-union solidarity over the issue, teachers cannot pick and choose whom to teach. Manchester LEA saw this as the crux of the issue: the unions are not to be allowed to decide who they will teach; this is for the LEA to decide, just as is its policy on disciplinary action over its teachers. But should not the LEA have taken into account this teacher solidarity? This was no ordinary suspension case. Relationships had broken down; the named teachers in the graffiti could not be expected to want to teach the boys again, and their colleagues could reasonably be expected to support them: the return of the boys was made almost impossible, as subsequent events proved. This is highlighted by the various peace plans which were put forward by the various parties during the dispute:

(a)   the governors proposed that the boys should receive education in a Poundswick annexe, taught not by existing staff, but by eight additional staff (was this an affordable solution?).

(b)   the NAHT proposed that the boys should remain on the Poundswick High School register, but be taught elsewhere, or at home!

(c)   there was a proposal for removing the entire fifth form to another building and staffing it with volunteer teachers.

Although the NUT and AMMA eventually agreed to a de-escalation of the dispute in January 1986, and to return to normal working except as far as the five boys' classes were concerned, the NAS/UWT remained firm in its stance. Remember the NAS/UWT affiliation of the chairman of the governors. Whilst this dispute was in progress, NAS/UWT members in Manchester schools twice attempted to refuse to teach pupils who had been before governing bodies for 'exclusion' where the governing bodies decided to readmit; in both cases the parents involved removed their children from the school before the NAS/UWT members took industrial action.

Obviously this was a case where the simple solution could not be found. Was the head's decision to suspend hasty? Did it take into account all the facts? Was the governing body impartial? Did the teachers, although seriously provoked, overstep their powers? Were the parents ill-advised in the circumstances, considering their wishes to secure an efficient 'O' level education for their sons? Did the LEA, although not unreasonable in retaining its power to review a school's decision, seriously undermine the head, governors and teachers, whilst seeking to protect the rights of a few pupils? This unfortunate mix resulted in a case from which none of the parties emerged untarnished.

You must judge from the facts yourselves. There are many important lessons to be learnt from the Poundswick graffiti case and there is no doubt that the relevant sections of the 1986 Education Act were drawn up with the events at Poundswick very much in mind.

Whether the provisions for suspension and reinstatement in the 1986 Education Act, outlined in Chapter 3, have sufficiently tightened up the previous loose system remains to be seen.

Perhaps the most sensible advice comes from the Advisory Centre for Education. For a number of years it has campaigned for an overhaul of suspension procedures and a redefinition of the governors' role. Any overhaul of the existing procedures rests on the simple premise that the governors of the school involved in a suspension case cannot be neutral, and that neutrality is a prerequisite of any appeals procedure; such neutrality is already recognised in the appeals procedure connected with parental choice of schools under the 1980 Education Act. Independent appeals panels, as advocated by ACE, would be fairer for the suspended pupil and would allow for neutral governors to be more critical and constructive since they would not be placed in a position of conflict of interest as they are under the present system. This is the position adopted by the Taylor Report in its discussion of suspensions. Moreover, this is the procedure which operates in Manchester: appeals are heard by a neutral, independent sub-committee. Indeed, the advice of ACE, the Taylor Report's recommendations and appeals procedures like Manchester's seem to have been taken into account by the legislators, since this is the system by which all suspension appeals must be heard by 1989 as a result of the 1986 Education Act. Some governors may feel that a central appeals panel erodes their responsibilities, but ACE's argument is that 'released from the role of arbiter, governors may more energetically work towards internal solutions to the problems that lead to suspension; ... a centralised and impartial appeal system ... will inevitably open to wider scrutiny the suspension records of individual schools – an encouragement to governors, staff and the authority to engage in frequent reviews of school performance in this respect.' ('Where', March 1984, p. 29).

Many LEAs and schools have explored a number of imaginative schemes to cope with pupils as an alternative to suspension and corporal punishment; these include various types of centres for truants, disaffected and/or disruptive pupils, special units attached to schools, home tuition – some of the teaching in such schemes comes under the aegis of the Special Needs Unit of the LEA, and is a recognition that the LEA has a duty to provide a suitable education for all its pupils. Now that corporal punishment has been banned, it is likely that other imaginative schemes will be tried, and governors should inform themselves of these; for example, do you know what educational provision your LEA makes for pregnant school girls? Do you know whether your school has accepted an excluded pupil from another school? If so, do you know whether special provisions were made, and whether the transfer proved successful for the pupil, or problematic for the school?

ACE's advice to governors is that they should concern themselves more in reviewing their school's internal discipline policy, review the reasonableness of any action taken, and concern themselves more than heretofore about the individual welfare of pupils in trouble at the school; rather than wishing to wash their hands of troublesome children, governors should satisfy themselves that any solution is in the child's best interests, even when transfer to another school or learning situation is seen to be the solution.

Since governors have an important role to play in a school's discipline policy and procedures, and since no governors wish to see their school hit the headlines like Poundswick did, this chapter has dealt at length with this distressing period in a school's life in the hope that governors will be able to spot warning signs in their own schools and, along with the head and staff, will be able to defuse any potential Poundswick situation. Forewarned is forearmed.

FURTHER READING

Ackroyd C.	'Suspensions: Improving procedures to make them fairer', *'Where' (Advisory Centre for Education)* March 1981, No. 166
Advisory Centre for Education	'Suspensions Survey', *'Where'* March 1981, No. 166
Advisory Centre for Education	'Re-thinking the governor's role', *'Where'* March 1984, No 196
Barrell G.R.	'Teachers and the Law', *Methuen* 1978 (More recent editions may be found under Barrell G. and Partington R.)
Monck E.	'Are governors taking suspensions seriously?', *'Where'* January 1984, No. 194
NAGM	'The Suspension of Pupils from School', Paper No. 12
NAGM	'Governors and Suspensions: a dramatised governors' meeting', Paper No. 21

10 To dismiss or not to dismiss? The case of a headteacher's right to 'freedom of speech'

We have dealt with governors' rarely-used powers in the removal of pupils from a school, seeing how all the procedures need to be followed to the letter and noting the relative functions of governors, headteacher and LEA. We have seen, too, how suspension cases can flare up into national issues if handled without due care.

This chapter deals with the even rarer and even more sensitive situation where the removal or dismissal of teaching staff is concerned. It is often assumed that teachers cannot be dismissed once in post. Such an assumption is false: as employees – of the LEA, or in the case of voluntary aided schools, of the governing body – teachers are subject to the conditions of their contract, and can, like any employee, be legally dismissed. However, it is true to say that in the case of teachers, breaches of contract are notoriously hard to prove, so it is unlikely that governors will ever be in the difficult position of having to deliberate over a case of dismissal in their school.

However, it is in no-one's interest if unsatisfactory or incompetent teachers are allowed to stay in school, and governors must not shirk their responsibilities if such a rare event confronts them.

This chapter briefly outlines the procedures involved, gives examples of recent dismissals, then presents a case study which it is hoped will alert governors to the issues involved. The procedure for the dismissal of staff takes a slightly different direction as a result of Section 41 of the 1986 Education Act, which will come into effect by 1 September 1988 for county and maintained special schools, and by 1 September 1989 for voluntary schools. Up to this time, the general rule was that teachers and headteachers could not be dismissed except on the recommendation of the governors, 'except when otherwise determined by the local education authority'. This procedure worked well until, as the following case study reveals, the LEA wanted to dismiss a headteacher it thought unsuitable, whereas the governing body were not prepared to recommend dismissal. The problems this impasse caused can be seen later.

When Section 41 of the 1986 Education Act comes into force, the procedure will be as follows:

For all schools other than aided or special agreement, a duty is placed on the LEA to consult the governing body and headteacher (unless he is the person to be dismissed) before dismissal. (Foundation governors can still require the LEA to dismiss a reserved teacher, i.e. a teacher specially appointed to teach R.E. according to the principles of the voluntary body.) Governors can recommend dismissal and the LEA has a duty to consider the recommendation. Governors and/or headteacher have the power to suspend any staff member if they consider 'his exclusion from the school is required', in which case the LEA must be informed, as well as the head or governing body as appropriate. Such a suspension must be ended if the LEA so directs. Because the procedures are changing/have changed it is vitally important that you seek expert advice in any such case and that you follow your authority's disciplinary procedures to the letter; these procedures are contained in what is commonly known as 'the burgundy book' and are available for inspection. Additionally, it will be understood that any allegations must be substantiated if dismissal procedures are to be initiated. A teacher facing such allegations would be suspended on full pay pending any investigation in order to protect the safety of the pupils or members of staff, or because his very presence on the premises would inhibit investigation of the allegations. Paramount in governors' minds in such cases must be the welfare of the pupils, and the requirements of natural justice for the teacher.

Dismissal for 'misconduct or other urgent cause', which includes criminal offences, indiscipline, or incompetence, has been successful in the following types of instances:

- Misappropriating school funds. For example, in 1984 a special school headteacher was jailed for three months for stealing £1500 from his school – £600 from the school fund, and £900 from the capitation allowance; he also asked for 32 similar offences to be taken into account.

- Sexual offences. For example, a teacher was jailed for 12 months in 1984 for indecently assaulting his school children, while in 1983 a deputy headteacher of a primary school was jailed for six months after admitting a series of indecent assaults on girls at his school.

- In 1983 a music teacher was dismissed for 'gross professional misconduct' when he wrote these words on a pupil's 'A' Level music exam paper: 'Associated Board Arnold Goldborough'. It transpired that part of the syllabus was a study of five Scarlatti sonatas, and that soon after the exam began, the music teacher realised that the pupil would not know the particular edition of Scarlatti's work used, so he approached his pupil's desk, and wrote the four offending words on it. He was 'shopped' by a colleague, and compounded his 'crime' by refusing to admit his indiscretion immediately, necessitating the headteacher to subject the pupil concerned to a lengthy and stressful interview in which she tried to protect her teacher.

- Mismanagement of the school curriculum. The famous William Tyndale Primary School case in the mid-1970s is well known, but there are many similar, less publicised cases, which come to a head when relationships at a school have broken down. Such allegations have been known to be initiated by teachers themselves, by governors, and by parents, and dismissals have followed.

- Extreme political views and actions. This relates to teachers who have had active and well-publicised links with such groups as the National Front and Animal Liberation Front, especially if such involvement is linked to law-breaking activities.

- Around the general area of 'indiscipline' there have been many cases of dismissal. For example, poor timekeeping and failure to control a class – a case of indiscipline and incompetence led to a teacher's dismissal in 1973; as did a teacher's refusal in 1980 to teach a class deemed by her union to be too large – seen to be a case of refusing to obey a headteacher's reasonable instructions. In 1978 a Muslim teacher who regularly attended his mosque on Friday afternoons to observe his religion was dismissed; in 1977, a teacher with fundamentalist religious beliefs refused to give an undertaking to teach R.E. according to his authority's Agreed Syllabus and was dismissed – the subsequent industrial tribunal judged this to be a failure to carry out a reasonable request and to obey a lawfully-imposed policy. In 1983 a teacher was dismissed for leaking details of his school's corporal punishment incidents to the anti-caning organisation, STOPP (the Society of Teachers Opposed to Physical Punishment); it is also alleged that this teacher threatened his colleagues, preached Communism in the classroom, and failed to reveal details of his past criminal record at the time of his appointment; teachers have also been dismissed for drug offences, including taking and/or growing cannabis, for falsely declaring superior academic qualifications, and for a variety of other misdemeanours too numerous to mention here. What governors will appreciate from the above is that in cases involving criminal offences, dismissal is generally clear cut. Indeed, teachers guilty of gross misconduct (e.g. sexual offences against children, supplying drugs) are generally deemed to be unfit to teach, and their name is entered on the DES List 99 which is circulated to LEAs so that such teachers do not receive employment elsewhere. It is estimated that there are currently some 1000 names on List 99 and that some 50 names are added annually; teachers can actually 'serve their term' on this list and be recommended for future employment in the profession. Of course, most disciplinary offences do not find their way to List 99; indeed, in many cases, teachers resign before dismissal procedures can be put into effect. It is for this reason that we have no reliable figures for the number of teachers who leave the profession 'in disgrace', and why the general public perceive teachers to be unassailable.

What is clearly true, however, is that few of the cases revolve around the issue of incompetence, which is the subject of much public concern. 'Incompetent' teachers need much support from the head and authority advisory staff; if, however, after repeated attempts (e.g. in-service training, decreased work-load, constant support from other teaching staff), incompetence is still an issue and can be proved, dismissal is an option – if the correct procedures have been followed.

It is hoped that governors will never be involved in any such cases. However, if they do occur, governors have an important role to play, as the following case study seeks to show. As you read through the following, what do you think the governors' response should be? Is this a case for dismissal?

THE CASE OF FREEDOM OF SPEECH

The school in question is situated in a large industrial town in the North with a population of some 464,00 inhabitants. From the 1960s,

Asian immigration was encouraged as a source of cheap labour; in 1961 there were 7000 Asians in the town, in 1986 there were 60,000 – mainly of Pakistani, Indian or Bangladeshi origin (there were also some 14,500 white immigrants of Irish and European origin). The town has 27 mosques, and a growing school population, much of it in inadequate facilities. Some 16,000 pupils are Muslims, out of a school population of 85,000. The town used to adopt a bussing policy to keep proportions of black children under 20% in any one school, but this policy was deemed discriminatory in 1980 under the Race Relations Act. In some schools at least two-thirds of the pupils are black, in others, over 90%.

The Asian community is politically active; in 1974, when 1 in 10 pupils in the town's schools was Muslim, the Muslim Parents Association was formed in the town. In 1983 the town's Asian Youth Movement made allegations about racial attacks, graffiti, and recruitment to the National Front and British Movement in local secondary schools. The Education Committee accepted the nature of the problem, and issued guidelines to heads on racial harrassment and the need to keep records. Indeed, in November 1982, the Education Committee published a policy statement sent to all heads, which stated that the town had:

> 'both a multiracial and multicultural population and all sections of the community have an equal right to the maintenance of their distinctive identities and loyalties of culture, language, religion and custom.'

The town had already mounted an enquiry into racism amongst the staff of one particular school. The LEA, recognising that it was a multiracial community, held the view, supported by all 3 parties in a hung Council (43 Tory, 41 Labour and 6 Alliance in 1985), that it had a duty to provide a service tailored to local needs.

The town had one black (Afro-Caribbean) headteacher. In 1983, whereas 33% of its white fifth-formers found jobs within three months of leaving school, only 7% of 'black' fifth-formers were similarly fortunate. In 1985 the town elected its first Asian Lord Mayor (indeed, Britain's first), a Pakistani.

The school in question, a middle school (9–13) of 550 pupils, appointed a new headteacher in 1980. At the time of his appointment the school contained 49% Asians, the LEA having pursued its bussing policy until 1980. Once this policy ceased, the percentage of black children rose rapidly, so that by 1985, 95% of the pupils were black; out of 123 new pupils admitted in 1985, only one was white. The school building was an old building, ill-suited to modern educational developments, but it had a waiting list of Asians wanting to send their children there. The children were well-behaved and hardworking, and staff/pupil relationships were friendly and positive. Most of the pupils were bilingual and many had problems with English, the medium of instruction. The school had accepted the LEA's policy of single-sex P.E. with Muslim girls being allowed to wear concealing clothing; halal meat was served; and the school's 27 white teachers were encouraged to take the advice of their two Asian colleagues concerning the pupils' cultural traditions and the appropriateness of teaching materials. In common with similar schools, there was hardly any extra-curricular activity, and little inter-ethnic pupil friendship carried on beyond the school gate. Urdu classes were organised, which parents could attend, and, in an effort to break down communication barriers, the new headteacher adopted a policy of visiting parents' homes once a week with an interpreter, hoping to involve them more in the life of the school. Parents' evenings were well attended, the school laying on a creche for the children.

All the indications were that the school was on the whole a reasonably successful one, and that the head was able.

However, within two years of his appointment, the headteacher started to run foul of his LEA. In 1982 he wrote a letter on school headed notepaper to the local newspaper criticising a grant to a 'West Indian' association for a new community centre. He was disciplined for voicing his views in this way.

In 1982 he published an article, 'Multiracial Myths?', in the 'Times Educational Supplement', in which he criticised multiracial education, and proposed a 'non-interventionist approach' to the education of 'the strangers in our midst'. The under-achievement of Afro-Caribbean children was explained by 'lack of support for the school and its values amongst West Indian parents and the support given by some teachers to the idea of a multiracial education'; while vetting textbooks for racial bias was termed 'cultural revisionism' and 'literary McCarthyism'. As far as this head was concerned, for the 'settler child... in a pretty ruthless meritocracy, ... the emotional and psychological price to be paid for emigration is the pain of change and adaptation'.

His next article, 'Multi-ethnic intolerance', appeared in June 1983 in the Salisbury Review, an obscure far-right journal 'of conservative thought' with a circulation of around 1000. In this article he talked of Afro-Asian 'settler children in our schools', 'a volatile Sikh', 'multi-ethnic nightmare', the 'malign quango (The 'Commission for Racial Equality')', and advanced one of his main themes, an attack on 'the multi-ethnic brigade' which consists of 'well-meaning liberals and clergymen suffering from a rapidly dating post-Imperial guilt; teachers building a career by jumping onto the latest educational bandwaggon; a small but increasing group of 'professional' Asian or West Indian intellectuals; and a hard-core of left-wing political extremists... They are united by two false and subversive notions: that we all ought to sentimentalise and patronise ethnic minorities, and that society has a duty to impose racial tolerance by government dictat. The same people often welcome race riots as signs of healthy revolt...'

In September 1983, his second 'TES' article, 'When East is West', appeared describing a week in the life of his school. Although his school toed the LEA's line on halal food and Muslim girls' P.E., he was clearly dismissive of these accommodations, putting their presence down to 'a combination of religious fanaticism, official timidity and the misguided race relations lobby. I have been ordered to concede by the office – and I disobey at my peril'. In this article he mentioned the visit of a 'troubled' parent of poor English whom he had never before met:

> 'A figure straight out of Kipling is bearing down on me... He wears white baggy trousers, long black coat buttoned, military-style, up the front, and a white hat; and he sports a beard dyed orange. His English sounds like that of Peter Sellers' Indian doctor on an off day.'

In Spring 1984 a further article, 'Teacher and Social Worker – an inevitable conflict', appeared in the Salisbury Review. In this he espoused his criticisms of working class culture as opposed to middle class, or 'high culture'. To him, 'the curriculum of the proletariat' consisted of 'bingo... the football pools and earnest study of the tabloids... stories of broken marriages, unmarried mothers, hire purchases, debts and evictions; of big brother in prison and sister eloped with a black man. And all must be transmitted in appropriate language – the argot of the gutter.'

His next and subsequently much-quoted article, 'Education and Race – an Alternative View', appeared in the Salisbury Review's winter edition in 1984. His previous views were reiterated, and he wrote:

> "Cultural enrichment' is the approved term for the West Indian's right to create an ear-splitting cacophony for most of the night to the detriment of his neighbour's sanity, or for the Notting Hill Festival whose success or failure is judged by the level of street crime which accompanies it. At the schools' level the term refers to such things as the Muslim parent's insistence on banning his daughter from drama, dance and sport, i.e. imposing a purdah mentality in schools committed to the principle of sexual equality...'

Introduced into the debate were his negative views on multilingualism, and, more significant, his crusade against the habit of a 'high proportion of Asian immigrants' dispatching their children to the Indian sub-continent during term time, and exceeding the legally permitted absence of ten school days in a year for such trips, which he fervently believed led to 'obvious deleterious educational consequences'; he was indignant both that he could not dissuade Asian families from this practice, nor could he persuade his LEA to enforce parental responsibility regarding school attendance.

Pakistan was described as 'a country which cannot cope with democracy... A country ... which, despite disproportionate western aid because of its strategic position, remains for most of its people obstinately backward. Corruption at every level combines with unspeakable treatment not only of criminals, but of those who dare to question Islamic orthodoxy as interpreted by a despot ... Pakistan, too, is the heroin capital of the world. (A fact which is now reflected in the drug problems of English cities with Asian populations.) It is not surprising that such a country loses more of its citizens voluntarily to other countries than any state on earth. How could the denizens of such a country so wildly and implacably resent the simple British requirement on all parents to send children to school regularly?'

In this article he talked of being 'accused of trying to deprive negroes of their welfare benefits'. Finally, he sought to champion the white children who constituted the 'ethnic minority', whom he argued to be educationally disadvantaged:

> 'It is no more than common sense that if a school contains a disproportionate number of children for whom English is a second language (true of all Asian children, even those born here), or children from homes where educational ambition and the values to

support it are conspicuously absent (i.e. the vast majority of West Indian homes – a disproportionate number of which are fatherless) then academic standards are bound to suffer.'

This article was quickly followed by another Salisbury Review article, 'The Right Education', in January 1985. In this he propounded arguments against comprehensive schools, the abolition of streaming, the introduction of mixed-ability teaching; he questioned 'non-subjects' such as Peace Studies, Anti-Sexism, Multiracial Education, Black Studies, Life Skills. His political colours were nailed to the mast – every educational idea and writer of the left was scorned, whilst those of the right, who made 'enormously refreshing and intellectually coherent statements' were applauded, as were independent schools, 'the comforting alternative which provides the aspiring parent with an answer to the unacceptable face of the state system'.

It can be argued that potted summaries of articles distort the views of the writer, and that in this country we all have freedom of speech. Full references are given at the end of this chapter so that readers can judge for themselves the fairness, or otherwise, of the summaries. As to freedom of speech, has any headteacher the right to express the kinds of views quoted? You may feel that in a free society the answer is 'yes'. Now pose the question differently: has the headmaster of a multi-ethnic comprehensive school with a black proportion of over 90%, in a working class area, in a multiracial town like Bradford, with a declared multiracial and anti-racist policy, the right so to speak and write? This was the issue which kept Ray Honeyford, the Bradford headmaster of the Drummond Middle School, and the author of the articles quoted, in the national limelight between 1982–1985. Furthermore, following the theme of this chapter, is there a case for dismissal for a headteacher who publicly airs such views in such an area?

The LEA thought there were grounds for dismissal, not just for publishing these articles and in so doing bringing the authority into disrepute, but also for failing to carry out council policy. Remember that this same headteacher was mildly disciplined in 1982 for sending a letter on school notepaper to the local newspaper critical of plans for a 'West Indian' community centre. The education committee took the view that he was at odds with a multicultural policy which had received all-party support and that headteachers were expected to comply; as far as they were concerned, if heads had personal doubts these were to be discussed with colleagues and officers of the authority and were not matters for the press.

It would be useful to know the backgound of events upon which the issue was eventually settled. Following the publication of his 1982 letter to the local press, relations with his LEA were not good. He had wanted to introduce school uniform 'to try to improve morale, and to affirm the school's essential and traditional authority', but his LEA refused to support him. He was 'urged' (his word) by LEA advisors to subject his textbooks to the sort of analysis outlined on page 136, but refused. He was 'ordered' (his word) to check story books for relevance to a multicultural society, but refused. He was 'ordered' (his word) to produce an anti-racist policy, monitor and keep records of racist incidents, discuss such issues in staff meetings, and involve parents. Again he refused, arguing that it was for the headteacher, not LEA officers or politicians, to be responsible for discipline.

Not surprisingly, in March 1984 his articles had come to the attention both of his employers and of some of the parents of the children at his school who formed the Drummond Parents' Action Committee, the leading member of which was a parent governor. The headteacher was subsequently ordered to appear before an education sub-committee for propounding his assimilationist and offensive views and for refusing to carry out council policy. Part of that policy, agreed in 1982 by the three parties and applicable to all the city's schools, was that schools should aim:

- to seek ways of preparing all children and young people for life in a multiracial society;
- to counter racism and racist attitudes, and the inequalities and discrimination which result from them;
- to build on and develop the strengths of cultural and linguistic diversity;
- to respond sensitively to the special needs of minority groups.

The Parents' Action Group organised demonstrations, a march to the council offices, a boycott of the school in which some three out of four pupils stayed away from school, or attended an 'alternative school' for a week. Because of the antagonism that had resulted thus far, the LEA decided to investigate Honeyford's school which was subjected to a week-long inspection by eight authority advisers and two educational psychologists in June 1984. Honeyford wrote an article in the local paper criticising the LEA's motives for the inspection. Although the summer holidays afforded some respite, the Parents' Action Committee kept up their momentum of demonstrations, half-day strikes and even orchestrated some 230 of the parents to write (identical) letters to the Chief Education Officer asking for their children to be transferred to other schools. Meanwhile, the advisers' report on the school was published; like many such reports it praised some aspects of the school, and damned others: particularly damning were its comments regarding Honeyford's commitment to Bradford's multicultural education policy and the obvious point that by that time he had lost the confidence of the parents. The governors met to discuss the advisers' report at a noisy public meeting; they simply noted the contents and called on the authority for more resources, trying also to pass a vote of confidence in the head, which was ruled out of order by the clerk to the meeting. This was followed by a further public schools' sub-committee meeting at which Honeyford was asked to produce six reports concerning aspects of his school by March 1985. He was also given extra support by multicultural advisers from the authority.

When these reports were submitted, Honeyford still had the support of his governors, but after a long meeting of the schools' sub-committee, a vote of no-confidence in him was narrowly passed, 8–7, and he was subsequently suspended in April 1985 pending a full enquiry. The Chief Education Officer considered him unsuitable as a head for any of the authority's schools, and he was called to face a disciplinary hearing of the governing body in June 1985. This meeting was yet another very bitter one at which only 11 of the 18 governors were present; the absentees were anti-Honeyford governors, including the parent governor, who refused to take part in 'the charade'. After hearing the evidence for three days and deliberating for eight hours, the governing body recommended that Honeyford should be reinstated since he was not guilty of the accusation of racism made against him. However, he remained suspended while Bradford's Assistant Director of Education, who was responsible for the authority's disciplinary procedures, reviewed the governors' verdict.

Meanwhile, Mr Honeyford, backed by his Union, the NAHT, sought a High Court ruling that the governors' decision to reinstate was binding on the authority which had no right to continue his suspension. In September 1985 he won his appeal and returned to the school to renewed hostile demonstrations, boycotts and half-day strikes. Bradford Council appealed against this High Court ruling.

As part of the Parents' Action Group campaign, the following 'Pupils Charter' was issued to the pupils:

PUPILS' CHARTER

Pupils you are engaged in a heroic struggle to remove Ray Honeyford, your headmaster. Why? Because he has insulted your religion and your culture. He has insulted your parents. That's why you have been on strike. On Monday you will be back at school, but the fight goes on. You have a part to play.

1 Do not be intimidated by the strike breakers.
2 Do not be intimidated by Mr Honeyford. If he attempts to punish you, report it to your parents or someone from the Action Committee. We will prosecute him.
3 We have no argument with your teachers, respect them. But if you see Mr Honeyford, let your views be known. Honeyford out!
4 There will be further half day strikes.
5 Knock! Knock!
  Q   Whose (*sic*) There?
  A   Ray
  Q   Ray Who
  A   Ray Cist.

Ironically, and moving into line with governing bodies all over the country in order to meet the requirements of the 1980 Education Act which became enforceable in September 1985, Drummond Middle School had to have its *own* governing body, and not one shared with four other schools as hitherto (the knowledge that Drummond School had a grouped governing body may help explain to readers some of its actions up to this point). As headteacher, Honeyford had to arrange an election for three parent governors; predictably, three Asian, anti-Honeyford governors were elected. But this governing body was not complete without the election of three community governors. Twenty-one nominations were received – most unknown to the school – and at yet another stormy governors' meeting in October 1985, at which hundreds of demonstrators converged on the school and at which the press and TV were well represented – the election took place; fury erupted when three pro-Honeyford community governors were elected. This meant that the governing body was evenly split between pro- and anti-Honeyford supporters; the elected chairman was pro-Honeyford, and, again ironically, Honeyford as headteacher was now accorded full voting rights (something he did not have on his previous grouped governing body). At this meeting a vote in support of Honeyford as head was passed narrowly,

Honeyford using his vote. The community rage which ensued, the increased hostility at the school gates, the death threats, meant that Honeyford had to have police protection; behind-the-scenes negotiations were in hand to offer Honeyford early retirement, if acceptable terms could be found.

In November 1985, the Court of Appeal *reversed* the High Court's ruling, giving Bradford Council the final power to discipline or dismiss, and not the school governing body. Honeyford's union urged him to make an appeal to the House of Lords. However, in the face of increasing pressure, Honeyford decided to resign his post, his union having secured a generous financial settlement and pension rights of £161,900. Since he was on 'sick leave' anyway, he never returned to the school.

What are the lessons to be learnt from this most bitter dispute? Did it revolve around the issue of free speech? Was it a case for dismissal? How would your governing body have reacted if it were your school?

As an issue it illustrated as never before the curious balance of power between governors and the local education authority where the dismissal of staff was concerned. This is because Bradford's Articles, like those of most authorities, stated that it was only when the governors recommended dismissal that the LEA had power to act, and in this instance, the governors did not recommend dismissal. The LEA not unnaturally wished to assert its rights as employer, claiming that it had a right to review any decision of the governors and that in any case the Articles of Government for its schools not only state that a headteacher cannot be dismissed unless recommended by the governors, but also add a crucial clause 'except when otherwise determined by the council.' The Court of Appeal clearly favoured the LEA's case.

What of the protagonists in this case? Was Honeyford in order to write such articles? Were they offensive, racist, accurate? If they were, did this matter, since we have freedom of speech? But does not freedom of speech carry with it certain responsibilities such as obeying laws concerning defamation and inciting racial hatred? Interviewed on television, Honeyford declared 'Britain is not a racist society, it is a remarkably tolerant society.' He was appalled that the charge of racism was made against him. He added: 'I am not a racist, and on the other hand not an anti-racist; most people are neither – they are non-racists, and that's what I am'. Is such a view supported by his writings? Indeed, in one article he wrote that 'racism is not a specially heinous or isolated human failing.' Is such a contention borne out by the facts of racism in this country? Although Honeyford claimed much support nationwide – he was even voted the fourth most popular man in England in a radio poll in the autumn of 1985 – you may consider that all this does is to point to the amount of racism which is a feature of Great Britain in the 1980s. And where facts are concerned, could we not expect a headteacher with research degrees in education to produce the supporting evidence to bolster his 'commonsense' view (outlined on page 198) that standards were bound to fall when white children were in the minority at school? He did not produce any statistical evidence, even though he had been in office long enough to collect it; the headteacher of a school which shared the same site as his dissociated himself from such a contention; the advisers could find no such evidence; Bradford Education Committee knew of no such evidence in any of its schools; up and down the country other headteachers with similar ethnic mixes disputed his 'commonsense' observation; and nationally-produced figures in a DES statistical Bulletin 13/84, 'School Standards and Spending: Statistical Analysis', found that different degrees of exam success in different LEAs were mainly a result of differences in home background, making the point that when other social factors were discounted, high proportions of non-white children were associated with slightly better results.

What of the governing body? It supported the head throughout the dispute. Did it bother to read the offending articles? Did it give enough weight to the effect this dispute was having on the smooth running of the school? Was it a representative body? Clearly not in the early stages of the dispute when it was a grouped body with other schools under its wing. Did the seven governors, including the parent governor who led the Parents' Action Group, act sensibly in withdrawing from the crucial meeting in June 1985? Did the governing body support the Council's multiracial policy? What should a governing body do if it does not support a council policy?

What of the Parents' Action Committee and the parent governors who were members of it? There can be no dispute that they ran an effective campaign which they sustained over a period of time. But were their tactics fair and appropriate? They were accused of circulating incorrect, distorted translations of Honeyford's articles to parents to inflame them. Furthermore, were they in order to involve the pupils as they did, especially in the manner suggested by the Pupils' Charter?

What of the LEA? Should it have taken a stance regarding Asian pupils missing large chunks of schooling on visits abroad? Politically, it was saddled with a hung council which could not make up its mind what to do with Honeyford (the Labour and Liberal groups wanted to dismiss him, the Tories to keep him); did this council proceed too quickly with its anti-discriminatory policies, or (given the nature of the area) not quickly enough? Was the authority correct in disciplining Honeyford because of his articles? Remember the verdict passed against the fundamentalist teacher as detailed on page 193. If an LEA has a policy which conforms to its obligations under the law (in this case the Race Relations Act), can it not expect its heads to carry out reasonable requests (e.g. monitor racist incidents, submit text books to multicultural analysis), to follow that policy, not to contravene it openly and not to publish critical and offensive articles?

Is not an LEA entitled to expect that its employees will implement its policies which have been negotiated over a period of time and which have all-party support, failing which appropriate action will be taken? But were its disciplinary procedures suitable? The Assistant Director of Education had the power to suspend a teacher; if the governors subsequently supported this decision, the Assistant Director could then recommend dismissal, in which case the teacher concerned could request a hearing before an education sub-committee. In Honeyford's case, not only was the governors' role ambiguous (after a three day hearing and eight hour deliberation they did not recommend dismissal, but this decision was challenged by the Assistant Director who kept Honeyford under suspension), but he was put in a position of having to appeal to the same sub-committee which had previously passed a vote of no confidence against him.

In this case, as in the Poundswick case, the point to emerge is that in any national cause célèbre surrounding a school there are no winners, only losers; race relations in Bradford were set back years with an increase in racist attacks; the case for multicultural education was damaged as people's prejudices were fuelled; and the principal losers were the children themselves whose education was severely disrupted during the dispute. This is why a governing body always needs to know its school, its headteacher, its teachers, its pupils, the school curriculum, local and national educational policies, and why the governing body needs to act at all times with knowledge, tact, fairness and firmness in the best interests of the children concerned.

In her book, 'School Managers and Governors: Taylor and After', Joan Sallis mentions the notice which every school should have prominently displayed:

'PLEASE EXAMINE YOUR CHILD BEFORE LEAVING AS
MISTAKES CANNOT BE RECTIFIED AFTERWARDS.'

Governors would do well to remind their colleagues and teaching staff
of the implications of this notice and of the consequences of insensitive
behaviour, especially in schools with children from a wide range of
ethnic backgrounds.

FURTHER READING

Regarding dismissal of teachers, including actual cases (some of which
used in this chapter):

Barrell G.R.	'Teachers and the Law', *Methuen* 1978
Partington J.	'Law and the New Teacher', *Holt, Rinehart and Winston* 1984

Regarding the Honeyford Case:

Honeyford R.	'Multiracial Myths?, *Times Educational Supplement* 19.11.82
Honeyford R.	'Multi-ethnic Intolerance', *The Salisbury Review* Summer 1983
Honeyford R.	'When East is West', *Times Educational Supplement* 2.9.83
Honeyford R.	'Teacher and Social Worker – an inevitable conflict', *The Salisbury Review* Spring 1984
Honeyford R.	'Education and Race – an Alternative View', *The Salisbury Review* Winter 1984
Honeyford R.	'The Right Education', *The Salisbury Review* January 1985
Lee-Potter L.	'The Hounding of Ray Honeyford', *Daily Mail* 16.12.85
Honeyford R.	'The Race Meddlers who ruined my school', *Daily Mail* 17.12.85
Honeyford R.	'Ordeal by Violence as the Militants Move in', *Daily Mail* 18.12.85
Honeyford R.	'The sad, sad lessons in Life!', *Daily Mail* 19.12.85
Brown A.	'Trials of Honeyford; problems in multicultural education', *Centre for Policy Studies* December 1985

Enquiries regarding The Salisbury Review:
7 Lord North Street,
London SW1.

11 Governor training and support: 'You're not going to teach them their rights, are you?'

Nationally, the provision of training for school governors is patchy and far from satisfactory. LEAs seem reluctant to provide the necessary information, but surveys by NAGM in 1982 and the National Consumer Council in 1984 indicate that fewer than half of the 104 English and Welsh LEAs offer their governors any training. Moreover, it appears that much of the 'training' on offer is unco-ordinated, consisting of occasional one-off meetings; whether a public meeting can be considered 'training' is highly debatable. Indeed, barring a few notable exceptions, it is true to say that most LEAs have sold their governors short where training is concerned. The reason may be adduced from the comment of a senior LEA official who, when discussing course proposals for training from one course provider, queried: 'You're not going to teach them their rights, are you?'

When we consider that holders of other voluntary positions such as magistrates, marriage guidance counsellors, Citizens Advice workers and Samaritans are obliged to receive training, then you can appreciate the low esteem in which many governors appear to be held by their LEA. But is the work done by governors any less valuable than that done by the trained volunteers in other fields? Clearly not.

There have been a number of calls for governor training, principally from the 1977 Taylor Report and the 1984 Green Paper 'Parental Influence at School'; both these reports sought to extend the influence and activity of governing bodies, as earlier chapters have shown.

As far as the Taylor Report is concerned, it stated, in its shortest but possibly most important chapter on 'Training the new Governors', that:

> 'In our view all governors should be given the opportunity to inform themselves on matters of educational theory and practice which will play a more central part in their deliberations. In addition to this basic need, we believe that there are a number of difficulties faced by governors today which a basic training programme could help to overcome:
>   (i) many are uncertain of the nature and extent of their powers and unfamiliar with committee procedures;
> (ii) they are sometimes confused by the complexities of laws and regulations and puzzled by educational terminology;
> (iii) they do not always understand how the administrative machine works or the process by which educational policy decisions are reached;
> (iv) some feel isolated because there are few opportunities for exchanges of views with other governors.'

These four points – uncertainty, unfamiliarity, lack of knowledge, isolation – were also found by the Open University when it researched its 'Governing Schools' course in the late seventies, and are commonly voiced by new governors attending training courses.

This need for training was echoed in the 1984 Green Paper 'Parental Influence at School', which pointed to the inadequacy of most existing training opportunities, arguing:

> 'The responsibilities ... for governing bodies are so important and complex that a governor cannot be expected to discharge them effectively without some training going beyond the normal process of picking up the job by doing it. That process is by itself relatively slow to act, and could in this case serve to perpetuate unsatisfactory practice.'

Consequently, Section 57 of the 1986 Education Act requiring every LEA to secure free information and training for its governors can be seen as something of a landmark. No LEA can escape its training and support obligations after 1 September 1987 when this section comes into force.

What form does this training take? Up to 1986, a number of agencies were involved, the principal ones being LEAs, NAGM, Workers' Educational Association (WEA), Open University, National Consumer Council, Advisory Centre for Education, some University

Extra-mural departments and Diocesan Boards of Education, but there is no uniform pattern of provision across the country. The Open University was quick to respond to a clear plea in the Taylor Report for initiative and enterprise by LEAs and national and local agencies interested in adult education where training was concerned. The OU secured DES funding for a four-year project, 1979–1983, to produce and evaluate distance learning material. In April 1981 it launched its excellent 'Governing Schools' short course which consisted of a lengthy training manual, four videos concerning the governing body of a middle school, and two audio cassettes; students who completed the fifty hours or so of study and computer-marked assignments received a 'Letter of Completion' recognising their efforts. In the absence of any concerted national work in training, the response from governors to this course was very healthy. By 1984 over 6000 individual governors enrolled, at their own expense, most of them new governors. Such a response indicates that governors are serious in their intentions, will seek out courses where none exist locally, and are prepared to give up even more of their spare time in an effort to make themselves more effective.

In addition to these individual students, the Open University sold over 1200 course sets to organisations which used the material as resources for their own training. For example, in West Sussex the LEA purchased 150 course sets which it loaned out to its adult education service to stimulate training; the entire governing body of a Derbyshire school used the material as a training resource; some governors formed small self-help groups; and there is evidence that various adult education agencies capitalised on the availability of this material to stimulate local initiatives. The WEA in Leicestershire, for instance, has successfully used the OU course as the basis for its training courses in that county since 1982, as the following discussion highlights. Although the OU videos are no longer broadcast, they can be borrowed from the OU, along with its excellent, though expensive, training manual, 'Governing Schools' (P970) – see address at end of this chapter. Additionally, the OU has produced a short, reasonably priced 'Starter Pack' which is available separately and gives governors an elementary introduction to their role. The OU was even approached in 1985 by Birmingham LEA which wanted to adapt the longer 'Governing Schools' course to its local needs. The result was a training package 'Governing Schools in Birmingham' which was the basis for a four-week course for governors. (A special 'Guide for Course Tutors' is also available with this course.) This package is available from the OU for governors outside Birmingham and is an indication of what an imaginative and committed LEA can do for its governors. The main weakness of such material is that it has failed to keep up with recent changes in legislation, based as it is on the OU's 1981 text.

The excuse given by many LEAs for their lack of involvement in training was not lack of commitment to the idea of training, but lack of resources. It is understandable then that many projects are collaborative, organisations pooling their resources and expertise. As the Taylor Report stated:

> 'There is positive advantage, from the point of view of effectiveness as well as economic sense, in the local education authority's sharing the task with other agencies.'

One such collaborative exercise is the Governor Training Scheme in Leicestershire with which the writer has been centrally involved. The initiation of this training scheme and its subsequent development is interesting because of the underlying political tensions about the issue of training courses for governors which it reveals.

At a meeting of the Leicestershire County Council in July 1981, the Education Committee and its Sub-Committees were instructed to discuss proposals concerning training courses for members of school and college governing bodies. The Director of Education produced a Report for the September 1981 meeting of the Schools Committee in which he outlined the various constituent groups which composed Leicestershire's 4000 governors. He wrote:

> 'There can be no rigid 'job description' for a governor but their role is, of course, an important one carrying as it does responsibility, with the Principal/Head, for the general direction of the conduct and curriculum of the school. Even more important, it may be thought, is the direct or indirect support which governors can give to a school or college by enhancing and protecting the good name of the institution they serve.'

The report acknowledged that governors had the help of a Handbook of Guidance which was being updated (this updating took four more years!), and their Instruments and Articles. It was recognised that a county-wide organisation of training courses would be difficult because of staffing reasons, but attention was drawn to the LEA's 1979 governor training plans (shelved because of financial stringency and 'a straitened office staff') which proposed holding 15 meetings throughout the county. The 1981 training course would follow the 1979 proposals, consisting of 15 public meetings, chaired by the Chairman or Vice-Chairman of the Education or Schools Committee and addressed by the Director or one of his senior colleagues who would speak for some 15–20 minutes 'on the general duties and powers of governors before throwing the meeting open for questions and discussion.' This, then, would be the 'training' offered to Leicestershire school governors, which it was envisaged would be supplemented by the help and guidance of governors' colleagues and clerks to the governors. After some discussion this 'training' scheme was turned down, and the Labour-controlled Schools Committee instructed the Director to write to the East Midlands District of the Workers' Educational Association about the feasibility of the WEA organising training courses for school governors. The WEA is a national adult education association, funded by the DES and LEA, and independent of any political or religious ties. Its main aim is to provide stimulating adult education classes in the broad field of liberal studies which enable people to further their own development and to play a more active part in a democratic society. It is assumed that the approach was made because the WEA is an organisation with no axe to grind and with an expertise built up over 80 years of working with adult groups.

It so happened that not only had the OU had collaborative meetings with the WEA at a national level about the possibility of using the OU course, but also the local WEA organiser had been wanting to use this OU material and had enrolled on the 'Governing Schools' short course. It was, therefore, quite straightforward for the WEA to propose a pilot scheme of six courses of eight weekly sessions based at venues throughout Leicestershire using OU materials, and to supply relevant costings.

It is here that local authority politics enters the scenario once more. The Tory group was not happy that the Director's previous plan had been rejected, and that the WEA had been asked to furnish a scheme, so when this issue was again discussed at the November Schools Committee meeting, the local newspaper carried an article with the heading 'Row over plan to train governors'. However, the WEA scheme was accepted, and the WEA organiser made immediate contact with the OU Governing Schools team for their help and advice. This was generously given and in December a small group of part-time WEA tutors was briefed by the OU team on the best ways of using their material. The tutors held two subsequent briefing sessions. Meanwhile, a course leaflet had been designed and circulated by the LEA to all its school governors. The first courses were scheduled for April 1982 and over 300 students applied for the 104 places on offer.

Since this was a pilot course it was very carefully evaluated by the WEA and OU courses evaluator, who was later to write that
    'Such a model could quite easily be transferred to other areas.'
    (*Education*)

This scheme was clearly successful, and further courses were funded by the LEA on an annual basis so that by the summer of 1984 over 500 Leicestershire governors had received training. At this stage we re-enter the political scenario. Government spending cuts were affecting LEA budgets, and Leicestershire's Director of Education was being asked to make cuts of ½% on 'non-essential' items in his budget; that is, he had to propose savings of £800,000 on his £160,000,000 budget. He therefore proposed that the Governing Schools courses (which were allowed £3000 p.a.) should be axed, stating that:

'When finance is reasonably plentiful it is desirable to run courses for governors but in the present circumstances I believe savings will have to be made in areas like this which do not directly affect the education of students and children.'

The WEA had been\forewarned that this was the LEA's intention and mounted a local campaign of protest from its current governors on training courses and previous governor trainees. Letters were sent, phone calls were made, and councillors were made well aware of the depth of feeling there was about this proposal and governors' support for the courses. During the June 1984 Schools Committee meeting, councillors acknowledged that governors felt strongly about the proposed axing of the courses. However, since the last political squabble about these courses two years previously, County Hall had changed politically, the Labour group losing overall control with the Tory group in the driving seat. The Director admitted that his proposals were a 'delicate subject', but maintained that savings had to be made. Tory councillors wholeheartedly supported the proposals, one stating that she had not wanted a governors' course, had not attended one, therefore they were not needed. 'You don't need instruction, commonsense comes into it. Why go on a course? They probably go on till midnight and are full of intellectual hotch-potch'! The Director argued that whilst it was recognised that the courses were 'excellent', Leicestershire governors were effective before the courses started, and had recourse to their handbooks and their clerks. It was therefore decided to suspend the courses and to review the position in the Autumn of 1984, the decision being taken on the casting vote of the chairman. Those who supported the courses were of the opinion that the courses were the victims of their own success: governors were becoming too assertive and too effective.

However, local party politics is a curious beast, and in the Autumn of 1984 the courses were resurrected, some wheeler-dealing being done behind the scenes between meetings. It seemed, then, that the local campaign had been successful and the potential political damage was not worth enduring for the sake of a trifling £3000. Since then, the courses have been continued, so that by Summer 1987 over 1500 Leicestershire governors from some three-quarters of all Leicestershire schools had enrolled.

What do the courses consist of? An eight-week scheme of two hourly sessions – morning, afternoon, evening, and weekend – has emerged, dealing with the following:

- Governors' rules and responsibilities: their historical and legal status; an updating of the relevant educational legislation.
- Governors and school visits: how to make a school visit; the visitors' report; formal and informal visits.
- Governors and meetings: committee procedures; how to be effective in a meeting.
- Governors and the curriculum: what are the curriculum issues; how to exercise oversight; the hidden curriculum; equal opportunities.
- Governors and interviews: the interview panel; interviewing techniques; a school's staffing structure; conditions of service.
- Governors and the community; the impact the school makes on its community; how to deal with problems.

The above skeleton is brought to life by the use of four OU videos, case studies, small group tasks, simulations. It is found that 18 governors per course is the ideal number, governors gaining greatly from the sharing of experiences of one another's schools and governing bodies. Some groups even invite outside experts like HMIs, headteachers, County Hall education department staff to contribute, while others arrange trips to County Hall to see their councillors at work in the Education or Schools Committees.

Governors' comments about these initial courses are overwhelmingly enthusiastic and complementary. As well as many comments which cluster around the following:

- it has increased my awareness/confidence
- I shall be more active
- it has broadened my knowledge
- it has sharpened up my approach to the role
- it has made me more enthusiastic about being a governor

there were such comments as:

- I shall pay more attention to the school curriculum and have already spoken to the head who is to present governors with a series of papers on the subject.
- Prior to this course I had really very little knowledge of what was expected of me and what I could contribute towards my school.
- I find it quite alarming to think that there is no compulsion on governors to become better informed on educational matters.
- The course has made me realise that I need not be afraid to air my views.
- I have been elected as chairman, and feel far more confident about accepting.
- I have appreciated how much more governors can do to support the school in arguments for resources.
- I was encouraged to make a controversial (not over-critical) report of my school visit, at the last governors' meeting. I raised many questions, including the actual purpose of school visits and whether they were of any value, when not followed up by frequent repeat visits. As a result, I have been invited by a teacher-governor to sit in at Staff Council meetings. (This from a *retired* teacher.)
- The tutor has transformed me from a struggling amateur to a more knowledgeable, confident and determined school governor. I no longer feel I am walking through a minefield. (This from someone who had been a governor for more than five years.)

Many governors even make the point that such courses should be compulsory.

These initial courses have been supplemented by further updating courses to try to meet the demand from governors for more opportunities for training. It is recognised that busy people like governors may not be able to commit themselves to lengthy initial training courses – some governors had said that they would not have attended any course of more than eight meetings – and that initial courses tended to be be very much like Cook's tours for governors. These updating courses of ten two-hourly meetings can operate at a more leisurely pace, and study more fully topics like educational finance, educational decision-making, governors and the law, sexism, racism, governors' problems and schools of the future. One governor who enrolled on such a course wrote on the back of his enrolment form:

> 'You may be interested to know that since the last course with you the High School governors now inspect one department of the school and the Head of Department comes and gives a report on it. The governors now give a written report with the minutes and we discuss education and not fabric: we are now curriculum orientated.'

It does indeed appear that many governors are soon able to put into practice many of the ideas they glean from such training sessions, to the ultimate good of their school.

You may be lucky to be in an LEA area like Leicestershire which offers a county-wide scheme either run by its own education department staff or in association with a body like the WEA or NAGM. ILEA, for example, has for many years paid much attention to its governor training and gives additional support via a regular governors' newsletter and the production of appropriate materials. Sheffield and more recently Cambridgeshire LEAs are similarly keen to train their governors. One of the big drawbacks with these LEA schemes is that they are generally underresourced and can train only a small proportion of their governors.

One way round this is to arrange a large-scale training event, which is the approach of some LEAs and is particularly favoured by such organisations as NAGM and the NCC. These one-day events tend to be oversubscribed, with upwards of 200 governors attending; a series organised by NAGM in 1985 for parent governors attracted |over 1000 applications for 700 places. Although governors respond enthusiastically to such training days, these are surely not as effective as the longer progressive course. A mixture of the two would seem to be the ideal combination. Additionally, there is a limit to the amount of training a small voluntary group like NAGM can undertake (it has just over 1000 members in just six branches). Its main strength is as a pressure group; it produces excellent guidance for governors and produces good training materials. Their latest (1985) Training Package, acknowledging that only limited time is available and that adults learn better by practice and through participation, is based on simulation and role play. Four sessions of 2½ hours each are recommended around the themes of the Governors' Meeting and the Appointment of a Deputy Head. These components are important on any training course, but they are to be seen as 'starter packs' only.

Similar role play material is available to governors who may not have access to any LEA or other scheme. The Advisory Centre for Education issues much campaigning literature for governors through its magazine 'Where' and its many publications, available from your library. It also produces two training booklets – 'Working Together', one for primary, one for secondary schools – which are recommended for use on LEA schemes, but which can, like the NAGM material, be used on a self-help basis. ACE recognises that public simulation exercises, though they can be immensely valuable, are counter-productive for groups who have not had time to get to know each other. The ACE material therefore consists of a series of Case Studies and role play exercises, which cover a wider range of themes than the NAGM package, including:

- problems which emerge when a school changes heads, and styles
- the school budget
- a proposed amalgamation
- headteachers' reports
- a headteacher's diary
- the introduction of Greek into the curriculum
- an LEA request for the school to introduce social education into its curriculum.

ACE's approach to training is 'that it is unnecessary to think in terms of covering *all* the tasks which governors may have to undertake – to attempt to do so would lead to despair among trainers and indigestion among those trained – but simply to select carefully the kind of material which will provide 'windows on the school' '.

It is encouraging to note that the mid-1980s have seen a growth in the development of this type of training material for governors. Cambridgeshire LEA, for example, has produced two Case Studies – Pegworth Primary and Bafton Comprehensive, devised by Cambridge University staff. The Pegworth case study concerns a role-play exercise of a meeting in which governors have to deal with:

- the threat of closure
- a burglary
- the ethics of fund-raising

- sex education
- sexism in the curriculum
- the case of a 10 year old who has tinted her hair
- a parent's complaint against a teacher.

Whilst it is acknowledged that this is not the typical fare of a governors' meeting, the availability of such training material is to be welcomed. An interesting addition to the training materials now available is the arrival on the scene in 1986 of a package of material produced by the Society of Education Officers and the National Association of Head Teachers. Their 15-hour package of six sessions on school finance, interviewing, discipline, everyday problems, a simulated meeting and agenda, mirrors the core material provided by many of the agencies outlined above.

Hence we find ourselves at the end of 1987 in the curious position of having an enormous amount of widely scattered and excellent training material available, not matched by the resources or by the commitment to put training into effect in any but a few of the LEA areas. How LEAs will respond to their governor training obligations under the 1986 Education Act remains to be seen. To stimulate more LEAs into action, the government put up £100,000 in 1985 in special Educational Support grants for governor training. Only a few LEAs, Leicestershire included, profited from such a small sum, and at the time of writing these ESG-funded courses have still to be run and evaluated. The logistics for an LEA to train effectively its army of governors are vast. Most schemes, however well-meaning, will only scratch the surface unless much more money is released. Although attempts by the various bodies like NAGM, ACE, the WEA and so on are valuable, governor training can only be really effective when schemes available to governors are progressive and county-wide; governors need access to the components recommended by Taylor – initial; advanced; in-service – anything else will remain merely piecemeal, however valuable the particular training event. Indeed, contrary to ACE's view, it is the one-off training events which are likely to give governors indigestion, because of the temptation to pack too much in (although the occasional bout of indigestion is infinitely preferable to starvation); the more leisurely structured, modular, progressive scheme – the smorgasbord approach – will be better able to afford governors a balanced training diet.

Whilst it is clear that untrained governors are a liability to their school and LEA, it is interesting to ask yourself why training has never featured high on the agenda. Does it signify governors' lowly status in the educational world? Are LEAs and heads fearful of the 'trained' governor? Whilst from a governor's point of view, knowledge is power, from some heads' point of view, a little knowledge is a dangerous thing. Many heads and teachers are nervous of the 'trained' governor – with good cause in some instances. Just as many governors can relate horror stories concerning individual teachers or schools, so, too, many heads and teachers can relate horror stories of governors: those who always get the wrong end of the stick; those who always seem to be in the wrong place at the wrong time; those whose motives seem to be questionable (the 'wreckers' who are mentioned in the concluding chapter); those who are obviously uninterested in schools or the maintained system of education. 'Training' for such governors can indeed be dangerous; if you substitute the word 'governor' for the word 'woman' in the following quotation, (the sentiments of which reflect a former age), you will appreciate the fears of some of the 'professionals':

'To educate a woman is to put a knife in the hand of a monkey'
(Indian proverb)

I was once asked to address a group of primary headteachers about governor training. Although I appreciate that such a group cannot be considered typical, I was struck by their antipathy towards governors. At least two-thirds of them were of the opinion that governors were forced upon the school; that they were the local tinkers, tailors, and candle-stick makers without whom the school would get on perfectly well. These heads were aghast when they heard that governors were allowed to have a say in curriculum issues. I received the 'we're the professionals', 'we've been to college', 'we're the experts' type of argument often heard concerning professional versus lay involvement in schools. When this group heard that we also offered 'advanced' courses in governor training, one head guffawed:

'They'll be getting degrees in it soon – and expect to be paid'(!)

Obviously, not all heads and teachers feel similarly; some heads actually phone me up to enrol their governors on training courses, and a few heads and teachers actually enrol on the courses themselves. Would that such a situation were more common! It is to be hoped that, as more heads and teachers see the value of the 'trained' governor to the school, the doubts of the 'professionals' will be erased.

If you are a governor who wants 'training' but it is not on offer by your LEA, then do your best to persuade the LEA to initiate training, pointing out its obligations under the 1986 Education Act; additionally you will find a very sympathetic ear if you approach organisations like NAGM, the WEA, ACE or AGIT (details below) to help you. The existing piecemeal provision is far from satisfactory, but there are good materials available and the keen governor or group of governors should be able to profit from the available expertise. NAGM has even started, in 1985, a consultancy service to help governors to get going. The only problem with this is that whilst it is felt that governor training should be free and supplied by the LEA, organisations like the WEA, NAGM and ACE have to charge fees if LEA sponsorship is unavailable. But now that there is commitment from central government for small amounts of cash to stimulate local initiatives, it seems as if Taylor's plea for national resources is starting to be heard.

Following calls for a national development centre for the training of school governors there was launched, in October 1986, an umbrella organisation, Action on Governors' Information and Training (AGIT). This is a consortium of those individuals and organisations which have been active in meeting the training needs of school governors. Its aim is to co-ordinate the provision already available, to spread good practice, to provide information and to develop governor training nationally – details at the end of this chapter.

Alan George, arguing for a national scheme of training for school governors, wrote of them that:

'... the quality of their voluntary service provides some measure of the health of our communities. Good experience in school governing can release energy for contributions in other areas of civic and rural life. Ignoring the training needs this substantial body of volunteers leads at best to a moribund system and at worst to alienation. Surely the nation's governors deserve something better? (*Education*)'

Although governors now have a right to free training and support, this is not the time for complacency. Few LEAs have shown themselves to be committed to governor training in the past and some LEAs may be less than generous in their interpretation of Section 57(b) of the 1986 Education Act which states that every LEA shall secure

'that there is made available to every such governor (free of charge) such training as the authority consider necessary ...'

Governors may well have to campaign to ensure that their free training provision is of the sustained, high quality they deserve.

FURTHER READING

Burgess T. and Sofer A.	'The School Governor's Handbook and Training Guide', *Kogan Page* 1986 (Revised edition)
George A.	'Resource Based Learning for School Governors', *Croom Helm* 1985
Open University	'Governing Schools' (P970) 1981 'Parental Influence at School' *HMSO* 1984 The Taylor Report

Further information on the range of training material available

ACTION ON GOVERNORS INFORMATION AND TRAINING
c/o The Community Education Development Centre,
Briton Road,
Coventry

Aims to supply information, maintain a resource bank, offer support to trainers, and arrange occasional conferences.

ADVISORY CENTRE FOR EDUCATION (ACE)
18 Victoria Park Square,
London E2 9PB

Among its many excellent publications it publishes 'Working Together', training exercises for governors, heads and teachers, which are handbooks (one for primary, one for secondary) specially written for ACE by Joan Sallis. Lively and recommended.

CAMBRIDGESHIRE LEA
Education Department,
Shire Hall,
Castle Hill,
Cambridge CB3 OAP.

For the Pegworth and Bafton simulated case studies and for the Society of Education Officers and National Association of Head Teachers 'Page One Training Package: Assisting Governor Education'.

FOCUS IN EDUCATION LTD
65 High Street,
Hampton Hill,
Middlesex.
01 783 0338

An enterprise advised by leading educationists, FIE produces a range of video training materials, including three video tapes and supporting materials, 'On being a school governor'.

NATIONAL ASSOCIATION OF GOVERNORS AND MANAGERS (NAGM)
Membership Secretary,
125 Beresford Road,
Birkenhead L43 2JD.

The national body representing governors' interests. Welcomes new members, publishes up-to-date sensible material, issues a newsletter, publishes training material, and arranges a regional training programme. Highly recommended.

NATIONAL CONSUMER COUNCIL
18 Queen Anne's Gate,
London, SW1H 9AA.

OPEN UNIVERSITY
Contact the Learning Materials Service, Centre for Continuing Education, The Open University, P.O. Box 188, Milton Keynes, MK7 6DH.

SOCIALIST EDUCATIONAL ASSOCIATION
110 Humberstone Road,
London E13 9NJ.

An organisation affiliated to the Labour Party, SEA produce a range of publications, including a 'Handbook for Labour Governors'; this handbook is of use to governors of all, or no, political persuasions. It is merely quoted since, as far as the author knows, no similar material has been published by other political parties or groups.

WORKERS' EDUCATIONAL ASSOCIATION
National Office:
Temple House,
9 Upper Berkeley Street,
London W1H 8BY.

Tel. 01 402 5608/9

The WEA is a nationwide, democratic, voluntary adult education
provider, independent of party or religious ties, founded in 1903; it is
grant-aided by the DES and works in partnership with LEAs and
University Extra-mural departments. There are 21 regional offices (or
Districts) throughout the UK putting on over 8000 adult classes
annually and recruiting some 180,000 students. Your local WEA
branch would respond positively for a request for help in Governor
training, or any other adult education request. The WEA's main
purpose is to interest adults in their own continued education and in
education generally. The WEA believes that education is not merely a
means to personal development but also vital to the health of a
democratic society.

12 Conclusion – governors: slaves or sleeping beauties?

The essential functions of governing bodies are to promote and protect the interests of the school and to be a link between the school and the community it serves: this was the message of the Taylor Report, reflecting what had been the intention for over one hundred years. Whilst governors have been given ever-increasing powers in recent years, they have not been given the guidance to use such powers: this has been the aim of this book.

This concluding chapter seeks to underline some of the main themes of this book and to direct governors to areas which need active consideration in the future. This book will gradually become out of date; there will be other Education Acts, yet more initiatives, local and national, for schools and governors to come to terms with.

It should be patently clear that the writer holds various positions in relation to a number of educational issues, and it is accepted that many readers will disagree with some of the points made. Such disagreements are healthy: education is a vastly complex subject and many people – professional and lay – consider themselves to be experts when discussing the subject. Since our children's schooling is, understandably, precious to us, we hold strong views about it. Such views, however firmly held, need not be fixed, and it is the duty of everyone with a stake in the education service to subject their views to regular scrutiny, acknowledging that the only constant in our education system is change. You have been asked in this book to examine your motives for wanting to be a governor; indeed, one training manual for school governors puts it bluntly; 'Why do you want to be a governor? Have you the time to do all the jobs entailed?' ('Handbook for Labour Governors').

The position you take on a whole range of issues affects your actions, and your decisions, in the governing body. Where do you stand on the following education issues?

- Should schools be allowed to retain corporal punishment, even though in 1987 it will be against the law?
- What about school uniform? Are schools which encourage its use doing their pupils a favour?
- Do today's teachers come up to the mark in terms of standards of dress?
- Is it acceptable for pupils to address teachers by their first name?
- Should the education service be more selective than it has been in recent years? Should there be more streaming and/or a reintroduction of the 11+ and grammar schools?
- Should we perpetuate a system of independent ('public') schools alongside the maintained ('state') schools? Should governors who send their own children to independent schools be allowed to be governors in the maintained sector?
- Are schools which abolish competitive sports doing their pupils a disservice?
- Has R.E. a place in today's schools?
- Should schools have a legal requirement to provide sex education?
- What is the main aim of schooling: to bring out the best in a child for his or her individual development, or to mould the child for the industrial needs of a competitive society?
- Should there be more central governmental control of education – a national curriculum – or should power be devolved to the consumers – the parents and children?
- Do governing bodies really serve a useful function, or should they be abolished?

Each of these questions reveals the tensions which exist concerning educational issues, and you may prefer to sit on the fence over some of them. But they are the type of important questions which governors have to confront, and, in the final analysis, ought to be able to take an informed stand on.

The major criticism of governing bodies over the years has been their political nature: 'It's all about politics', 'There's too much politicking' are the kinds of comments voiced. Indeed there is a substantial amount of truth in this. All the reforms since the Taylor Report have been aimed at removing the unacceptable face of politics in school governing bodies, but we still, in the mid-1980s, read newspaper headlines like:

'The art of governing by dirty tricks'
'Fury over governors' guide'

'Relationship with school governors sours'
'Governors bid to solve school row'
'School row splits village'
'MP to intervene in school row'
'Councillor hits out over school sign'
'Parents fight to regain school choice'
'Fight begins to keep school open'
'Clear-out at crisis school: head and five staff go in 'left-wing' row'
'LEA 'unfair to parents''
'Court fight over parent governors'
'Parents take on LEA over intake'
'Prison warning by DES to school governors'

Such headlines remind us that schooling is a political issue and that passions are quickly aroused when problems occur, as the Poundswick and Honeyford cases revealed.

You may feel that the Tory Government was correct in removing the LEA majority on governing bodies in the 1986 Education Act and in transferring 'power' to the parents at the school level. But have you considered the motives for such a political decision? Why should central government wish to make the LEAs weaker where the government of schools is concerned? Has not our educational system developed for over one hundred years as a decentralised, locally administered one? By weakening the powers of the LEAs, is not central government strengthening its own position whilst maintaining that 'power' remains at the local level, in the hands of the governors, particularly the parent governors? As they stand, LEAs are powerful conglomerations and can resist, and have resisted, central diktats. Once their power is diminished, where is the voice of opposition? School governing bodies, though influential at the local level, are rarely organised at district or even county level (after 16 years of formation, NAGM still has only 6 branches nationally). Consequently, although it seems that governing bodies have grown more powerful, has this been at a price we are willing to pay? Has all the manoeuvring been merely a case of divide and rule?

Understandably, the LEAs have protested that their autonomy has been slowly whittled away by the government's increasingly centralist policies in recent years; this tendency has been most evident in the government's tighter financial controls which have entailed, annually, different rules to follow, and impositions such as 'rate-capping', so that local authorities have found it difficult to plan ahead. Along with the ever-increasing financial squeeze on local authorities which, in a very real sense, has left them little room for manoeuvre, central government has taken greater control over what is taught and how it is assessed through its various initiatives towards a 'core curriculum' and national guidelines as to examination criteria; nor has teacher education escaped this centralist influence, so that, for example, students with a first degree in sociology, psychology or philosophy have been deemed 'unsuitable' for receiving post-graduate courses of primary teacher education, and colleges have been dissuaded from recruiting them.

Additionally, various financial devices such as Educational Support Grants for initiatives such as Governor Training, the provision of services to support parents of pre-school age children with special needs, and the provision of computerised learning aids in FE colleges for students with special educational needs, mean that the DES exercises even more influence over the education system nationally. (It can be argued that all the Secretary of State for Education is doing by these devices is using powers which have always been there, and that he is simply exercising positive leadership to an education service that has lost its way; and that it is not unreasonable for a government which spends some ten billion pounds annually on schools yet controls only 1% of this spending to seek to increase such a low proportion.) Whilst this may in some respects be a reasonable argument to pursue, we must not lose sight of the increasing influence which the Manpower Services Commission (MSC) – accountable to no local democracy – has wielded over vocational education for the 14+ age range in recent years, the power here lying not with the DES, but with the Department of Industry and Employment. Although the MSC has capitalised on an acknowledged weakness in our education service – vocational education – and with massive injections of cash and an ever-increasing number of initiatives has sought to improve and to reform, schools, governing bodies and LEAs have had little influence, and the same is true of the DES. Indeed, there is a certain irony that while schools have been starved of money for books and essential repairs, the MSC *underspent* by some £200 million in 1985.

When you ponder over the above centralist trends, the statement by a DES official in 1984 that 'People must be educated once more to know their place' takes on a particular meaning.

This insidious trend towards centralisation has come too fast and furiously to be appreciated by most schools and LEAs. They feel themselves to be hectored, harangued, hassled. Change – however meritorious – is difficult to accept if you do not feel loved and cossetted, which teachers and schools have not felt for years. Understandably, teachers feel suspicious about the motives behind recent changes. Although we hear regular complaints of declining standards, all the evidence shows more and more children leaving schools with more and better qualifications, and fewer leaving without any form of qualification, than ever before; so the motives behind the various reforms cannot be due to any such oft-quoted decline. Teachers worry about both the increased power of central government and of governing bodies – they are worried about their status at the middle. Coincidentally, such concern is compounded when survey after survey outlines the under-resourcing of the education system, whatever the protestations of government to the contrary. Schools are growing increasingly dilapidated, and reports show headteachers having to spend significant proportions of their time on the care and upkeep of buildings whilst at the same time trying to respond to the overwhelming variety of initiatives aimed at them; all this with an under-resourcing of the curriculum and increasing efforts to raise cash via PTAs and miscellaneous fundraising events for the essentials of education – one 1985 survey found that in primary schools PTAs were raising 30% of the capitation allowance, and secondary schools 9% and that this was still not sufficient. Indeed, one head ruefully said, 'Some of us wonder at times whether we are running a school or an amusement arcade', whilst another wrote to a national paper, 'It will be a great day when our schools get all the money they need and the air force has to hold a cake stall to buy a bomber'.

No wonder, then, that the mid-1980s saw a breakdown of relationships between the DES and the teaching profession with a long, damaging period of industrial action which sorely stretched the capabilities of headteachers and had a damaging effect on relationships between parents and teachers. Arguably, the education service has never been through such a rapid period of change and stress. Unfortunately, the teachers' industrial dispute also resulted, in some instances, in strained relationships between teachers and governors. From a teacher's point of view, not only has central government interfered in the classroom, but to cap it all teachers have to be even more accountable to non-professional, lay governors at the school level. Consequently, effective school governors need to be conscious of the changing educational scenario so that they can best deal with their range of new powers and duties whilst remembering the impact these have on the teaching staff. There are, unfortunately, too many accounts of uneasy relationships between governors and teachers, some of them the result of governors learning more about their role: a little learning is a dangerous thing/knowledge is power – it depends on one's perspective. There are tales of governors fresh from training courses ('training' is surely not the appropriate word; we need to find a better one) returning to their schools which have been described by Alan George as 'combat zones, dominated by obstructive headteachers, obstructive chairpersons, political hack governors, unsympathetic LEA officers, and internecine warfare on the governing body'.

It is hoped that this does not describe your governing body, although there have been isolated accounts of such bodies being infiltrated by people whose main motive has been to further their own political careers rather than the education of the children. That this has been the case in a number of schools as far apart as Avon and Merseyside has been illustrated by the circulation of what John Izbicki, the Daily Telegraph's former education writer (now its chief Paris correspondent) has called the 'Wreckers' Charter', a four-page duplicated set of 'guidelines' aimed at governors with Militant Tendency or similar Trotskyist political inclinations. These 'guidelines' give directions on a number if issues such as corporal punishment, school uniform, peace studies, minority ethnic groups, mixed ability teaching, religious instruction and nationalist groups on a school's staff, and propose various courses of action at governors' meetings, depending on 'whether members are in a majority or not'. The tips for meeting procedures include the following:

- When in the majority, ensure Chair and Vice are members and continually press to a vote.
- When in a minority, interpose frequently on points of order, and prevent a vote.
- Use 'filibustering' on important matters or on unimportant matters until non-members are exasperated, then produce the proposals you want at the *end* of the meeting.
- Constantly refer to 'the Governors' in respect of previous meetings although an individual put forward points.
- Always have unfinished business when meetings end, requiring further (extra) meetings.

- Increase number of meetings to two – three per term: if members find attendance difficult, so much the better.
- Prolong meetings by prevaricating ... and insist on being heard out.
- Pick awkward times for meetings – 5.30 pm, 9 am.
- Seek to annoy non-members.
- Seek to discredit the clerk – question accuracy, put in a member to clerk.

The 'guidelines' suggest a number of ways of undermining the headteacher to 'make staff, parents and students suspicious of Head's motives and create tension in and around Head', among which are the following:

- Constantly question statements made by Head.
- Imply concealment of information.
- Seek to isolate Head from staff and governors.
- Visit school unannounced: find out when Head is away and visit then.
- Ring up and question Head on any and all matters.
- Suggest unrest among parents, teachers, students. Imply low morale, low opinion of school locally.
- Continually question fundamental educational practice.
- Ignore good exam results – concentrate on weak areas.
- Quote articles of Government for schools and imply Head's ignorance of them.

The teaching and non-teaching staff are subject to such tactics, too. 'Members' are told to infiltrate the staffroom and 'seek out Union Representatives, Chairpersons of Staff Committee etc.' The advice the 'guidelines' offers them includes:

- Always show willingness to help.
- Hint at unfairness, awkwardness, lack of communication of Head, of some Governors, of LEA.
- Request chance to meet out of school, home telephone etc.
- Always support grievance procedure, whatever the grievance.
- Avoid being asked to address the staff as a whole.
- Seek to join splinter groups.
- Hint at unfairness in Head's promotion policy.

'Members' are exhorted to find out 'other likely sympathisers. Concentrate to begin with on teachers of Humanities, Social Studies, Religious Instruction, Political Studies, etc. Find out any nationalist groups – Welsh, Irish. Ignore P.E., Music, Classics'; and when appointing new staff 'look for *good* track record: chairing of staff groups, social clubs Treasurer, Secretary – similarly University groups etc. Look for foreign travel especially S. America, E. Europe ... Note that teachers trained in the late sixties are often suitable.'

The 'guidelines' also offer advice as to how to champion the interests of students and parents against the Head. Where parents are concerned, 'members' are told: 'Always bring up parents' complaints at Governors meetings, use AOB regularly, say 'some parents' even if only one. Infiltrate PTA committees ... Question whether Head should attend PTA meetings.'

All this advice ends with the statement:

'REMEMBER: FOUR YEARS IS NOT LONG.'

No-one knows the true circulation of the 'Wreckers' Charter' or the impact it may have made, or will make, on governing bodies. It is to be hoped that the 'guidelines' have been, and will be, treated with the contempt they deserve since they fundamentally oppose the very basis upon which a successful governing body should seek to operate: that of partnership. However, they should be a warning to governors that although LEA representation on the governing body has lessened as a result of the 1986 Education Act, the role of politics will not necessarily decrease since it is often the politically active and conscious parents who stand for such positions. This is not to say that politics has no place in school government, rather that it should be used to the advantage of the pupils; what governors should beware of its politicking for its own sake.

Much of this book has documented the various legislative changes which have been made since 1944 in an attempt to spell out more clearly the various rights and responsibilities of the partners in the education service, but principally those of the school governors, so that they can no longer be described in John Sayer's words, 'a communal democracy of slaves'.

An unfortunate trend in recent years has been the use of the courts to settle educational disputes, as some of the headlines on pages 224–225 illustrate; this is due partly to the increased consumerism which has been encouraged in the education service (think of the various appeals procedures), partly to an increased knowledge – and its accompanying trait: assertiveness – of groups like parents and governors, and partly to the increased tension which has been a feature of the education service in recent years. It would be pleasant to think that a period of calm lay ahead as a result of the 1986 Education Act, but the early indications are that this piece of legislation, like its predecessors, has not been tightly enough drawn, leaving too much confusion as to powers and responsibilities in such areas as control of the curriculum, so that there is still scope for tension and uncertainty.

As governors help steer their schools towards the year 2000, they would be wise to remind themselves that the education service is going through a period of great change: traditional conceptions of schools as apprenticeship factories for the 5–16 year olds, with a period of post-16 and higher education for the few, are changing; different methods of assessment, different curricula, different rules and regulations, are new ingredients in the education cake. Governors, with their new-found powers and responsibilities, occupy an elevated status in the education kitchen. Nevertheless, it should be abundantly clear that governors who cannot stand the heat have no place in this kitchen: today's governorship is no sinecure.

Some research by Kogan on governing bodies in 1984 concluded that governors were 'sleeping beauties still waiting for the kiss of politics.' This book has sought to provide that embrace, so that, armed with the appropriate information, governors can support their schools with knowledge, commitment, tact and understanding.

Appendix A

'Parental Influence at School: A new framework for school government in England and Wales' – Green Paper 1984
A brief summary of the main conclusions.
(See pages 53–55.)

- Three-yearly appointments were recommended, which would entail a continuous rolling programme, with frequent by-elections, held annually. Co-options would not be allowed. If insufficient parents stand for election, the LEA would make appointments.

- Where the curriculum is concerned, the respective functions of the LEA, headteacher and governing body were outlined, and the Green Paper called for increased governing body curricular powers: the governing body would have a duty to *determine* the statement of the school's curricular aims and objectives, but not its organisation and delivery, which would continue to be the head's duty.

- Governors should be responsible for the general direction of the conduct of the school, i.e. 'the ... appearance of the school; the rules and conventions which govern the behaviour of pupils; the relationship between pupil and teacher, between pupils and between teachers; the attitudes towards the school, and the support for and understanding of its work, of parents, pupils and the local community; and the school's success in explaining its work to those whom it serves and in consulting them effectively about it.'

- Discipline was seen to be a matter for headteachers, but the governing body 'should have responsibility for establishing guiding principles within which the headteacher operates'. It was proposed to tighten up procedures concerning 'debarment' (i.e. suspension) – see Chapter 9 of this book for a full discussion of this.

- Governors to be given slightly more responsibility regarding *appointment* of staff, but less regarding *dismissal*.
- Governors to be given more understanding of school finance; 'the governing body ought to be aware of what is actually being spent on the school. The Government therefore proposes that the LEA should be required annually to provide the governing body with an itemised statement of its recurrent expenditure on the school so as to enable the governing body to form a judgement on whether that expenditure was providing value for money.' Capitation, i.e. money spent in the main on books, equipment and stationery, to be allocated to the governing body as of right, but this expenditure could be delegated to the head.
- The use of school buildings *outside* school hours to be the responsibility of the governors.
- Governors to be consulted by LEA on admissions.
- Governors to prepare an annual report and to hold an annual parents' meeting to discuss the report, hold elections, pass resolutions; such measures designed to strengthen accountability of governing body to parents.
- Governors to receive more information, and to be trained.
- Governors to hold *at least* four meetings annually.
- LEAs to be empowered (not obliged) to pay travelling and subsistence allowances to governors.
- Governors of voluntary aided and special agreement schools not affected by above proposals, but asked to consider them.

The appearance of this Green Paper certainly accomplished what it set out to do: it stimulated much discussion nationally and drew an enormous amount of written responses, some 470. Consequently, the role of governing bodies again assumed centre stage. However, the Green Paper somewhat backfired on the Government, being generally universally criticised; only 33 of the written submissions were supportive.

All the teachers' unions, LEA organisations, most parents' groups, and organisations like NAGM, the National Consumer Council, the General Synod Board of Education and the National Federation of Women's Institutes, were critical, especially about the Green Paper's central aim to give parents a majority of seats on the governing body. Those bodies which had originally opposed the Taylor formula of equal shares for all constituent groups now realised the reasonableness of the concept of partnership and supported this.

There was much criticism that the Green Paper proposals were misleading and ill-informed. It was generally felt that the proposals would lengthen administrative procedures, and that elections, annual reports, more meetings, governors' allowances and training would all, however valuable, increase costs to the LEA who were not to be given any additional resources in a period of growing central demands, but declining central financial support. Moreover, no LEA would welcome spending this extra money when the intention of the proposals was to lessen the LEA's control by moving power across to the governing body. Additionally, three-yearly appointments were seen to be too short for most governors to be able to learn how to do the job effectively. Authorities such as Cornwall and Northumberland with dozens of rural schools with under 50 pupils also pointed to the difficulty of recruiting five parents, and it was pointed out that the occasional school would have more governors than pupils!

However, not many submissions criticised those proposals which dealt with discipline and curriculum, which could in many respects be seen to be even more controversial than parental majority. For example, the Government had been wanting to legislate to give parents a choice about corporal punishment for their children, and had met much opposition. But in this Green Paper it was stated that the Government did not feel that LEAs should have 'unspecified and broad powers to override governing bodies and headteachers in matters of discipline'; in other words, the Government had begun to manoeuvre itself into a position where it could frustrate those LEAs which had imposed a blanket ban on corporal punishment by giving individual governing bodies the power to override such bans.

One curious feature of this Green Paper was that it appeared to have united two bodies at opposite ends of the political spectrum who both wrote in support of the proposals: one was the right-wing Centre for Policy Studies, a think-tank established by the then Secretary of State for Education, and therefore not a surprising ally; the other was the Advisory Centre for Education, which claimed that electing more parents would 'galvanise' school governing bodies and stimulate more communication between homes and school. There was, however, widespread support for the proposal that the powers and functions of governing bodies should be more clearly defined.

Appendix B

'Better Schools' – White Paper 1985
A brief summary of the main conclusions.
(See page 55.)

Size of school:	Elected by and from parents[b]	Appointed by LEA	Head-teachers[c]	Elected by and from teachers	Co-opted[d] or, for controlled schools:		Total
					Foundation	Co-opted[d]	
fewer than 100 pupils	2	2	1	1	3		9
					2	1	
100 – 299 pupils	3	3	1	1	4		12
					3	1	
300 pupils or more[a]	4	4	1	2	5		16
					4	1	
600 pupils or more[a]	5	5	1	2	6		19
					4	2	

Table 12: *The proposed composition of governing bodies for county, voluntary controlled and maintained special schools*

Notes (a) the LEA would be free to choose either composition for schools with 600 or more pupils.

(b) where insufficient parents stood for election (or, in any case, for schools with at least 50 per cent boarders) the LEA would appoint parent proxies to fill vacancies. LEA members and employees and co-opted members of the Education Committee would be ineligible for such proxy appointments.

(c) the headteacher would be able to choose not to be a governor.

(d) the number of co-optees would be reduced by one to allow for the addition shown in the following mutually exclusive circumstances:–

(i) one representative of the minor authority (or minor authorities, acting jointly) in the case of a county or controlled primary school serving an area in which there is one or more minor authorities;

(ii) one representative of the District Health Authority in the case of a hospital special school;

(iii) one representative of a relevant voluntary organisation in the case of any other maintained special school.

It can be seen that although more parent governors were proposed than under the 1980 Education Act, they would not predominate, nor would any other group; co-options would be allowed, as would parent proxies if insufficient interest was shown (compare this with the 1984 Green Paper proposals, page 54 and Appendix A; the above table, of course, is identical to that on page 30. *Four*-yearly appointments were suggested, parents being allowed to serve on the board *even if* their children had left the school. The proposal for four annual meetings was dropped 'in the interest of flexibility; the current minimum of three termly meetings to continue. But, as now, governing bodies will be expected to hold additional meetings if the proper discharge of their functions requires this.'

As far as functions and powers of the LEA, headteacher, and governing body were concerned, these followed the Green Paper proposals on curriculum, discipline, appointment and dismissal of staff (although the proposed appointing panel consisted of three, not two governors), finance and annual meetings and reports.

The importance of these changes was underlined by the statement:

'As a result of the intended legislation, statute law will, for the first time, specify in considerable detail the composition of governing bodies and their functions for all categories of maintained school.'

The powers and responsibilities of governors of aided and special agreement schools were similar to those of maintained school governors in respect of discipline, finance, annual meetings and reports, information and training; they were to consult the LEA before publishing their admission arrangements. Governors of aided primary schools would have control of the curriculum, just as their colleagues in aided secondary schools had. Proposals were also made to allow governors of controlled schools to seek aided status, up to that time not allowable.

It was estimated that the extra costs for the implementation of these changes – including those of training, for which the government subsequently offered Educational Support Grants of £100,000 for pilot projects in 1986–87 – would amount to £10 million in a full year, to be found by the LEAs.

Appendix C

THE APPOINTMENT OF TEACHERS: THEIR PAY AND CONDITIONS

Elsewhere in this book it has been stated that the only constant in education is change, and this applies no less to teachers' pay and conditions. Since 1919 teachers have used collective bargaining to determine their salaries through the Burnham Committee. The bitter and lengthy teachers' dispute in the mid 1980s, which had not been resolved at the time of writing this appendix, had revealed in the then Conservative government's view the inadequacies of the old system. Consequently, there was imposed a legal 'settlement' of the dispute over pay and conditions – the 'Teachers' Pay and Conditions Act 1987'. The removal of teachers' negotiating rights was not well received by teachers in general, and the ripples will continue to be felt for some time to come.

THE APPOINTMENT OF TEACHERS

A school is only as good as its staff, both teaching and non-teaching, but there is much evidence that where the appointment of staff is concerned governors are, as in most other areas of their responsibility, in the dark.

However, if you consult your Articles of Government you will find in them a statement very much on the lines of:

> 'The appointment of teachers is made to the service of the local education authority by the governors in consultation with the head.'

The important words here are that the teachers are *appointed by the governors* in consultation with the head. Many governors find this wording a revelation, having been used to a situation where appointments were made by the headteacher, governors being informed at a subsequent meeting. There may be some good reason why this should occasionally be the case, but this section, by seeking to outline the case for more governor involvement, hopes to alert governors to their legal obligations where staffing is concerned: this is particularly relevant in the field of equal opportunities.

Each local education authority approves its individual complement of teaching staff, full-time and part-time, on a permanent or temporary basis, and fixes the number of teachers each school is allowed on the basis of its pupil/teacher ratio, which, as illustrated on page 68, varies between LEAs. Generally, any vacancy is advertised locally and nationally, although recently, because of falling school rolls, LEAs have had to redeploy existing staff to vacant posts, with a consequent reduction of advertising. A contracting teaching force, and the use by LEAs of an increasing number of temporary appointments, have meant that opportunities for governors to be involved in staff selection have dwindled.

In county and controlled schools, it is the LEA who is the employer, so it is obvious that officers of the LEA will want some role in the appointment process. Teachers in aided schools are employed by the governors, although salaries are paid by the LEA, who will rightly expect to be involved in any appointment.

In all schools, then, it can be seen that both the governors and the LEA jointly have an interest in the appointment of staff. It follows that both groups – governors and LEA officers – should ideally be involved in the appointment of all new teaching staff, as the 1986 Education Act confirms.

However, the involvement of governors varies throughout the country. In some cases they are involved not only in the shortlisting process, but also in the interviews, in other places in the interviews only, and in some, neither at shortlisting nor interviews (the provisions of the 1986 Education Act give governors a more prominent role). Generally, their involvement has been greatest where the appointment of senior staff was concerned, or if the school is an aided school. For the less senior posts, it has in many areas become 'accepted practice' for governors to delegate appointments to the head, whilst retaining some occasional involvement.

Since it is the responsibility of the governors either to make the appointment (in aided schools), or to recommend the appointment to their LEA, it is worth considering why it has become 'accepted practice' for governors to delegate their responsibility to the head. Are junior teachers any less important than more senior staff? Is the appointment procedure of such staff any less rigorous, or mentally and emotionally any less demanding? Is it sensible, or fair, to leave the appointment procedure to just one person, as happens in some appointments? If your governing body takes little or no part in the appointment of staff, are you satisfied with this?

Recent research which focused on the appointment of headteachers showed how amateurish and hit and miss such procedures were. The important point was made that the head will be responsible in the course of the headship for some millions of pounds worth of educational spending; the educational careers of hundreds, or thousands, of children; and be in receipt, cumulatively, of a salary of up to half a million pounds, or more. The main thrust of this research was that we should be more professional in the appointment of our headteachers, appropriate training playing an important part for all concerned, including governors. Whilst there can be no disputing this evidence, it is curious that similar arguments have not been voiced for all appointments. Remember that any member of staff could be in post for up to forty years, affecting the educational career of hundreds of pupils, and also consuming over a lifetime vast sums in terms of salary and resources.

It is for this reason that governors should welcome the provisions of the 1986 Education Act which restate the important role governors have to play in *all* appointments. Does your governing body ensure that it takes part in all appointments? Or does it still take the easy option, and delegate to the headteacher – a practice still allowed under the 1986 Education Act?

Staff selection is a difficult business and, ideally, every member of an interview panel should have received some form of training, or at least been given sound advice from more experienced colleagues. Helping to appoint a new member of staff is perhaps a governor's most significant and important act: you owe it to yourself and to your school to prepare yourself adequately for what is, generally, an onerous duty. (A book such as this cannot supply the A–Z of interview techniques. If specialist training is not available or feasible, the inexperienced governor may find that learning the ropes gradually by playing a minor part on a panel and being guided by an experienced governor colleague – perhaps the Chair – is one way to gain the necessary insights, experience and confidence. Some governing bodies have an appointments sub-committee which oversees the whole selection process, involving those governors who express an interest in taking their part in this vital aspect of a governor's role.)

TEACHERS' PAY AND CONDITIONS

From October 1987 teachers will be paid according to a completely new system and governors need to have some understanding of this, and the old one, if they are to be effective in future appointments.

Contrary to popular opinion, teachers do not just work for the love of the job: their remuneration is important to them. Until October 1987 teachers were paid according to the scale point system. There were five scales – 1, 2, 3, 4 and Senior Teacher, plus deputy head and headteacher scales, each of which allowed the teacher to progress annually to a maximum. A new teacher was appointed to scale 1, her/his salary increasing incrementally on this scale unless promoted. Promotion to the higher scales was related to the expertise and responsibility attached to the new post. Once on top of the scale, the teacher remained there unless further promoted.

In April 1986 the scales ranged from £6425 – £10,533 in fifteen increments for teachers on Scale 1, to £11,349 – £15,330 in eight increments for Senior Teachers. There were separate scales for teachers in special schools. Headteachers and deputy heads received salaries according to the size of school on a range from £7905 – £11,163 for deputies of the smallest schools, to £17,592 – £19,104 for deputies of the largest schools, and £10,959 – £12,195 for heads of the smallest schools to £24,795 – £26,259 for heads of the largest schools.

The size of the school and the age ranges taught influenced the staffing structure and the salaries paid by determining:
- the number of teachers on scales above scale 1
- the highest scale upon which an assistant teacher could be placed
- the salary of the head and deputy.

Each school worked out its 'unit total' according to a national formula, and the unit total determined the school's *group* and its *point score*. Put simply, the smaller the school and younger the children, the lower the unit total, the smaller the group of school on a range 1–14, and consequently the fewer promotional scale points that could be offered to teachers; a small village school had only a handful of scale points compared to a large comprehensive with over 100 scale points. These scale points were meant to be awarded by the governors on the recommendation of the headteacher, and it is for this reason that governors ought to have had some understanding of the system. However, since many teachers themselves never mastered the intricacies of the scale point system, it is understandable that many school governors were left in the dark. Nevertheless, it will be appreciated that in financial and promotional terms progression through the scales was important to teachers. Therefore, the operation of the scale point system by the head and governors was an important motivational and managerial function. Staff, not unreasonably, formed their own judgements as to the fairness and effectiveness of this system.

The bitter teachers' dispute of the mid 1980s highlighted the weaknesses in this complicated scale points system, which had the effect of trapping some 245,000 teachers, over one half of the profession, at the top of scales 1 and 2 with a maximum salary of £10,986 (at 1986 levels). Indeed teachers were aggrieved that only 2% of their number earned over £14,500. After a protracted period of unsuccessful negotiations between the teachers' unions and the government there was imposed, in March 1987, the 'Teachers' Pay and Conditions Act', which removed the teachers' negotiating rights, and established an interim Advisory Committee on teachers' pay and conditions.

How does this affect governors? As people who play an important part in staff appointments, clearly governors need to be aware of the system operating currently, just as they need to have an understanding when they scrutinise application forms for a new staff member of the difference between a scale 2 teacher and a deputy head of a group 9 school. Governors are involved in appointing to their schools teachers of the appropriate qualifications and experience, and this is what the old scale point system helped signify.

Under the new conditions, operative from October 1987, teachers have received an average increase in their pay of 16.4%, but the old scale point system has been abolished. In its place is a single *basic scale* for all teachers, other than heads and deputies, ranging from £7600 – £13,300 in 11 increments, graduates starting higher up the scale. Heads and deputies are paid spot salaries (according to the size of their school), i.e. they no longer have an incremental scale.

For teachers on the basic scale there are now five *incentive allowances,* ranging from £500 – £4200 which are paid in respect of one or more of the following reasons:

- responsibilities beyond those common to the majority of teachers

- outstanding classroom teaching
- shortage skills
- recruitment to posts deemed 'difficult to fill'.

The new salary scales and incentive allowances are as follows:

THE PROPOSED PAY STRUCTURE FROM 1 OCTOBER 1987

TEACHERS
OTHER THAN HEADS AND DEPUTIES
BASIC SCALE

Scale £	
7,600	Entry point for non-graduates
7,900	Entry point for graduates
8,200	
8,500	Entry point for good honours graduates
9,200	
10,000	
10,600	
11,200	
11,850	
12,600 (12,800)★	
13,300	

Progression up the scale is by annual increments on
1 September.

★*Teachers on Point 12 of Scale 2 at 30 September 1987 would be paid*
£12,800 from 1 October 1987

FIVE INCENTIVE ALLOWANCES

Ordinary Schools	Special Schools and Classes
£500	£1,000
£1,000	£2,000
£2,000	£3,000
£3,000	£4,200
£4,200	

HEADS AND DEPUTIES

SPOT SALARIES

DEPUTIES SCHOOL GROUP	£	HEADS SCHOOL GROUP	£
		1	15,500
		2	16,000
Below 4	14,750	3	16,500
4 and 3(S)	15,000	4 and 3(S)	17,000
5 and 4(S)	15,375	5 and 4(S)	17,750
6 and 5(S)	15,750	6 and 5(S)	19,000
7 and 6(S)	16,250	7 and 6(S)	20,000
8 and 7(S)	17,000	8 and 7(S)	21,250
9 and 8(S)	18,000	9 and 8(S)	22,750
10 and 9(S)	19,000	10 and 9(S)	24,250
11 and 10(S)	19,750	11 and 10(S)	26,000
12	20,750	12	27,750
13	21,500	13	29,000
14	22,250	14	30,500

S = Special Schools

London allowances and social priority allowances will continue to be paid. Teachers in special schools receive enhanced salaries in the range of £8,600 – £15,300, according to their scale.

Teachers on scales 3 and 4 and Senior Teachers automatically received allowances of £1000, £3000 and £4200 respectively. Not all scale 2 teachers received the £500 incentive allowance, which caused some understandable grievance. In ordinary schools, the number of incentive allowances is as follows:

Primary

	OCTOBER 1987	SEPTEMBER 1990
£2,000	—	4,000
£1,000	16,000	17,000
£500	14,000	34,000
	30,000	55,000

Secondary

OCTOBER *1987* SEPTEMBER *1990*

£4,200	6,500	11,000
£3,000	28,500	24,000
£2,000	—	24,000
£1,000	53,000	24,000
£500	11,000	27,000
	99,000	110,000
Grand totals:	129,000	165,000

Progression from the 1987 figures to the 1990 figures will be in three equal steps at September 1988, 1989 and 1990. The government will provide rules about the range of allowances available in different sizes of school, and governors should check with their clerks about how the new arrangements affect their schools.

In *special* schools, some 1500 teachers are on scale 3 (S) or the Senior Teacher scale. By 1990 it is intended to allow a further 1500 promotions, additional to the £1000 basic special school allowance, at the £2000, £3000 and £4200 allowances.

Some questions, however, remain. Although in ordinary schools there is an expansion of incentive allowances so that only 45% of all teachers will remain on the basic scale in 1990, compared to 60% of teachers on the old scales 1 and 2 in 1986, teachers are far from happy; primary school numbers are due to increase in the transition period, and secondary school numbers are due to decrease. How is the diminution of four and a half thousand £3000 allowances, and twenty-nine thousand £1000 allowances going to be managed in the secondary schools without upsetting some staff? Who will decide what 'outstanding classroom performance' is? Will teachers in non-shortage subjects or those who take non-exam classes suffer a loss of status?

Attached to the new pay structure are detailed conditions of service. Since these will have important implications where the smooth running of the school is concerned, the relevant sections of the government's draft order are reproduced.

PROPOSED CONDITIONS OF EMPLOYMENT

TEACHERS

Reproduced below are relevant extracts from the draft order on which the Government is now consulting. These apply to teachers other than Head Teachers.

EXERCISE OF GENERAL PROFESSIONAL DUTIES

1. A teacher who is not a head teacher shall carry out the professional duties of a school teacher as circumstances may require –

    (a) if he is employed as a teacher in a school. under the reasonable direction of the head teacher of that school;

    (b) if he is employed by an authority on terms under which he is not assigned to any one school, under the reasonable direction of that authority and of the head teacher of any school in which he may for the time being be required to work as a teacher.

EXERCISE OF PARTICULAR DUTIES

2. (a) A teacher employed as a teacher (other than a head teacher) in a school shall perform, in accordance with any directions which may reasonably be given to him by the head teacher from time to time, such particular duties as may reasonably be assigned to him.

    (b) A teacher employed by an authority on terms such as those described in paragraph 1(b) above shall perform, in accordance with any direction which may reasonably be given to him from time to time by the authority or by the head teacher of any school in which he may for the time being be required to work as a teacher, such particular duties as may reasonably be assigned to him.

PROFESSIONAL DUTIES

3. The following duties shall be deemed to be included in the professional duties which a school teacher may be required to perform –

Teaching (1) (a) Planning and preparing courses and lessons.

    (b) Teaching, according to their educational needs, the pupils assigned to him, including the setting and marking of work to be carried out by the pupil in school and elsewhere.

    (c) Assessing, recording and reporting on the development, progress and attainment of pupils.

Other activities (2) (a) Promoting the general progress and well-being of individual pupils and of any class or group of pupils assigned to him.

    (b) Providing guidance and advice to pupils on educational and social matters and on their further education and future careers including information about sources of more expert advice on specific questions; making relevant records and reports.

    (c) Making records of and reports on the personal and social needs of pupils.

    (d) Communicating and consulting with the parents of pupils

    (e) Communicating and co-operating with persons or bodies outside the school.

    (f) Participating in meetings arranged for any of the purposes described above.

Assessments and reports (3) Providing or contributing to oral and written assessments, reports and references relating to individual pupils and groups of pupils.

Appraisal (4) Participating in any arrangements within an agreed national framework for the appraisal of his performance and that of other teachers.

Review: Further training and development (5) (a) Reviewing from time to time his methods of teaching and programmes of work.

    (b) Participating in arrangements for his further training and professional development as a teacher.

Educational methods (6) Advising and co-operating with the head teacher and other teachers (or any one or more of them) on the preparation and development of courses of study, teaching materials, teaching programmes, methods of teaching and assessment and pastoral arrangements.

Discipline, health and safety (7) Maintaining good order and discipline among pupils and safeguarding their health and safety.

Staff meetings (8) Participating in meetings at the school which relate to the curriculum for the school or the administration or organisation of the school, including pastoral arrangements.

Cover (9) Supervising and so far as practicable teaching any pupils whose teacher is absent:

Provided that no teacher shall be required to provide such cover –

    (a) after the teacher who is absent has been absent for three or more consecutive working days; or

(b) where the fact that the teacher would be absent for a period exceeding three consecutive working days was known to the maintaining authority not less than two working days before the absence commenced.

unless –

(i) he is a teacher employed wholly or mainly for the purpose of providing such cover (a 'supply teacher'): or

(ii) the services of a supply teacher to provide cover for the absent teacher are not available; or

(iii) the teacher required to provide cover is a full-time teacher at the school but has been assigned by the head teacher in the timetable to teach or carry out other specified duties (except cover) for less than 75% of the hours covered by the school timetable.

Public examinations (10) Participating in arrangements for preparing pupils for public examinations and in assessing pupils for the purposes of such examinations; recording and reporting such assessments; and participating in arrangements for pupils' presentation for and supervision during such examinations.

Selection etc of staff (11) Contributing to the selection for appointment and professional development of other teachers, including the assessment of probationary teachers.

Management (12) (a) Co-ordinating or managing the work of other teachers.

(b) Taking such part as may be required of him in the review, development and management of activities relating to the curriculum, organisation and pastoral functions of the school.

Administration (13) (a) Participating in administrative and organisational tasks related to such duties as are described above, including the management or supervision of persons providing support for the teachers in the school and the ordering and allocation of equipment and materials.

(b) Attending assemblies, registering the attendance of pupils and supervising pupils, whether these duties are to be performed before, during or after school sessions.

WORKING TIME

(1) After 1 August 1987 –

(a) subject to subparagraph (c), a teacher employed full-time may be required to work on not more than 195 days in any year, of which 190 days shall be days on which he may be required to teach pupils in addition to carrying out other duties:

(b) a teacher may be required to work at specified times and places at the direction of the head teacher or the authority as the case may be for not more than 1,265 hours in any year, to be allocated reasonably throughout those days in the year on which the teacher is required to work;

(c) subparagraphs (a) and (b) do not apply to a teacher employed to teach or perform other functions in relation to pupils in a residential establishment;

(d) time spent in travelling to or from the place of work shall not count against the 1,265 hours referred to in subparagraph (b);

(e) unless employed under a separate contract as a midday supervisor, a teacher shall not be required to undertake midday supervision, and shall be allowed a break of reasonable length either between school sessions or between the hours of 12 noon and 2 pm;

(f) a teacher shall, in addition to the requirements set out in subparagraphs (a) and (b) above, work such additional hours as may be needed to enable him to discharge effectively his professional duties, including, in particular the marking of pupils' work and the preparation of lessons, teaching material and teaching programmes. The amount of time required for this purpose beyond the 1,265 hours referred to in subparagraph (b) and the times outside the 1,265 specified hours at which duties shall be performed shall not be defined by the employer but shall depend upon the work needed to discharge the teacher's duties.

(2) In this paragraph, "year" means a period of 12 months commencing on 1 September unless the school's academic year begins in August in which case it means a period of 12 months commencing on 1 August.

PROPOSED CONDITIONS OF EMPLOYMENT

HEAD TEACHERS

Reproduced below are relevant extracts from the draft Order on which the Government is now consulting.

Overriding requirements (1) A head teacher shall carry out his professional duties in accordance with and subject to –

(a) the provisions of the Education Acts 1944 to 1986;

(b) any orders and regulations having effect thereunder;

(c) the articles of government of the school of which he is head teacher, to the extent to which their content is prescribed by statute;

and, to the extent to which they are not inconsistent with these conditions,

(i) any provisions of the articles of government the content of which is not so prescribed;

(ii) any rules, regulations or policies laid down by the employing authority or governing body; and

(iii) the terms of his appointment.

General functions (2) A head teacher shall be the leader of the school community, and shall be the principal representative of the school in its relationships with the authority that maintains it, the governing body, the local community and the parents of its pupils. Subject to paragraph 1 above, he shall be responsible for the internal organisation, management and control of the school.

Consultation (3) In carrying out his duties he shall consult, where this is appropriate, with the authority, the governing body and the staff of the school.

Professional duties (4) The professional duties of a head teacher shall include –

School aims (1) Formulating the overall aims and objectives of the school and policies for their implementation.

Appointment of staff (2) Participating in the selection and appointment of the staff of the school.

Management of staff (3) (a) Deploying and managing all teaching and non-teaching staff of the school and allocating particular duties to them (including such duties of the head teacher as may properly be delegated to the deputy head teacher or other members of the staff), in a manner consistent with their conditions of employment, maintaining a reasonable balance for each teacher between work carried out in school and work carried out elsewhere.

(b) Ensuring that the duty of providing cover for absent teachers, as prescribed in paragraph 3(9) of Schedule 3, is shared equitably among all teachers in the school, taking account of their teaching and other duties.

Liaison with staff unions and associations (4) Maintaining relationships with organisations representing teachers and other persons on the staff of the school.

Curriculum (5) Determining, organising and implementing an appropriate secular curriculum for the school, having regard to the needs, experience, interests, aptitudes and stage of development of the pupils and the resources available to the school.

Review (6) Keeping under review the work and organisation of the school.

Standards of teaching and learning (7) Evaluating the standards of teaching and learning in the school, and ensuring that proper standards of professional performance are established and maintained.

Appraisal of staff (8) (a) Providing information about the work and performance of the staff employed at the school where this is relevant to their future employment.

(b) Supervising and participating in any arrangements within an agreed national framework for the appraisal of the performance of teachers who teach in the school.

Training and development of staff (9) Ensuring that all staff in the school have access to advice and training appropriate to their needs, in accordance with the policies of the maintaining authority for the development of staff.

Pupil progress	(10)	Ensuring that the progress of the pupils of the school is monitored and recorded.	*Relations with other educational establishments*	(18) Maintaining liaison with other schools and further education establishments with which the school has a relationship.
Pastoral care	(11)	Determining and ensuring the implementation of a policy for the pastoral care of the pupils.	*Resources*	(19) Allocating, controlling and accounting for those financial and material resources of the school which are under the control of the head teacher.
Discipline	(12)	Determining, in accordance with any written statement of general principles provided for him by the governing body, measures to be taken with a view to promoting, among the pupils, self-discipline and proper regard for authority, encouraging good behaviour on the part of the pupils, securing that the standard of behaviour of the pupils is acceptable, and otherwise regulating the conduct of the pupils; making such measures generally known within the school, and ensuring that they are implemented.	*Premises*	(20) Making provision, if so required by the governing body or the maintaining authority, for the security and effective supervision of the school buildings and their contents and of the school grounds; and ensuring (if so required) that any lack of maintenance is promptly reported to the maintaining authority or, if appropriate, the governing body.
	(13)	Ensuring the maintenance of good order and discipline on the school premises whenever pupils are present, including the midday break.	*Appraisal of head teacher*	(21) (a) Participating in any arrangements within an agreed national framework for the appraisal of his performance as head teacher.
Relations with parents	(14)	Making arrangements for parents to be consulted and given regular information about the school curriculum, the progress of their children and other matters affecting the school, so as to promote common understanding of its aims.		(b) Participating in the identification of areas in which he would benefit from further training and undergoing such training.
			Absence	(22) Arranging for a deputy head teacher or other suitable person to assume responsibility for the discharge of his functions as head teacher at any time when he is absent from the school.
Relations with other bodies	(15)	Promoting effective relationships with persons and bodies outside the school.		
Relations with governing body	(16)	Advising and assisting the governing body of the school in the exercise of its functions, including (without prejudice to any rights he may have as a governor of the school) attending meetings of the governing body and making such reports to it in connection with the discharge of his functions as it may properly require either on a regular basis or from time to time.	*Teaching*	(23) Participating to such extent as may be appropriate in the teaching of the pupils at the school.
			Midday break	(5) Without prejudice to his duties under paragraph 4(13) and (22) above, a head teacher shall be allowed a break of reasonable length in the course of each school day.
Relations with authority	(17)	Maintaining liaison and ensuring co-operation with the officers of the maintaining authority: making such reports to the authority in connection with the discharge of his functions as it may properly require either on a regular basis or from time to time.		

It is fair to say that teachers in general felt 'aggrieved at the imposition of these detailed conditions. For teachers, particular points of contention are the cover arrangements, which appear open-ended, and working time arrangements. The specification of annual working hours of 1265, added to which is a subclause that a teacher shall work 'such additional hours as may be needed to enable him to discharge effectively his professional duties' was seen as insulting to a hardworking profession. Who is to define this open commitment is unclear. Furthermore, since independent research studies have shown that teachers work on average some 500–600 hours more than the designated 1265, it is not understood why the contractual hours have been set so low. Appraisal, too, is a worry to many teachers, especially as it appears to be linked to financial rewards via the incentive allowances. Governors need to be sensitive to such teacher responses.

Headteachers will have to evolve a system of time management for their staff to ensure that the 1265 hours are spread reasonably throughout the year; no easy task when there has evolved over many years on open-ended commitment in time by most teachers, especially where extra-curricular activities are concerned. And since teachers are no longer required to undertake midday supervision, governors will wish to ensure that suitable arrangements have been made for the midday break, without imposing too great a burden on the head.

An additional feature of the 1987 Act, and one not much debated, is that it enables the Secretary of State for Education to make different provision for different cases, including different geographical and subject areas. Does this mean that our national system of pay scales is eventually threatened?

It has been stated that it is the intention to renew teachers' negotiating rights in 1990 when the Teachers' Pay and Conditions Act expires – unless extended, on an annual basis, on the approval of both Houses of Parliament. The indications are that until teachers' negotiating rights are reinstated they will continue to be in dispute and life in the classroom will be disrupted.

Any transition from one system to another is bound to meet with teething problems. Governors will appreciate that in this fluid interim state, no good advice can be given, except the need to keep up to date and informed.

Glossary

Articles of Government – these are a legal statement of a governing body's powers and duties which delineate the relationship between the LEA, governing body and headteacher. All governors, and all teachers, must be given a copy of the school's Articles on appointment – see also **Instruments of Government**.

Assessment of Performance Unit – APU: established by the DES in 1975 to monitor levels of performance in a range of subject areas and to see how these change over time. The APU conducts surveys in England, Wales and Northern Ireland, details of which can be had free by writing to the address on page 259.

Banding – a device for dividing a year group into a number of bands differentiated by ability (hence similar to streaming), each band containing a number of classes not necessarily of equal size or ability – see **mixed ability grouping** and **setting.**

County schools – are LEA owned and funded primary and secondary schools of a non-denominational nature. Over two-thirds of our schools are county schools.

Department of Education and Science – commonly known as the DES, is a government department, headed by the Secretary of State for Education (a senior government minister with a seat in the cabinet). The DES enables the Secretary of State to fulfil his/her statutory duty under the 1944 Education Act 'to promote the education of the people of England and Wales'; in spite of this wording, Wales has its own Secretary of State for certain educational functions: Scotland and Northern Ireland have their own Secretary of State. Although the government does not employ teachers, does not control the curriculum and does not own any educational buildings, it does influence, control and direct the education service by various legislative means – especially Acts of Parliament – and through its control of resources for teachers, buildings and educational spending. The DES ensures that the LEAs provide efficient education.

Examination system – currently subject to a major overhaul. Up to 1987 the main secondary exams in England, Wales and Northern Ireland have been the General Certificate of Education (GCE) which was introduced in 1951 and the Certificate of Secondary Education (CSE), introduced in 1965. GCEs could be taken at Ordinary ('O') or Advanced ('A') levels and were aimed at the top 20% of the ability range, whereas CSEs, intended for 16 year old pupils, catered for the next 40% of the ability range.

GCE 'O' levels and CSE examinations are to be replaced by the General Certificate of Secondary Education (GCSE) for which courses started in the autumn of 1986 for examination in the summer of 1988.

'A' level examinations will continue, but a new level, Advanced Supplementary, or AS levels will be introduced in 1987 for examination in 1989. These can be regarded as half an 'A' level, and are an attempt to broaden the sixth form curriculum, being taken alongside 'A' levels.

The Certificate of Pre-Vocational Education (CPVE) is a one year course taken at 17 available in schools and colleges. It was introduced in 1985/6 and is aimed at those who wish to remain in school after 16 years of age, but do not wish to take 'A' levels.

Students who attend Further Education Colleges have access to a more extensive range of vocationally-oriented examinations.

Foundation governors – are the group of a voluntary school's governing body appointed by the voluntary body to ensure that the school's voluntary nature is preserved and that it is run in accordance with any trust deed.

Her Majesty's Inspectorate – commonly known as HMI – is an independent body of some 500 Inspectors, HMIs, in England and Wales which reports to the Secretary of State for Education and Science about the work of our schools and colleges, and offers advice. HMIs conduct in-service courses for teachers and publish various reports, surveys and discussion papers. Since January 1983 all their reports on formal inspections have been available free of charge, as have periodic reviews of these reports – see further information section page 259, for the address. All schools and colleges are subject to inspection.

Instruments of Government – these detail the composition of the governing body for each school and specify the procedures by which the governors are appointed – see also **Articles of Government**

Local Education Authority – commonly known as the LEA. England and Wales are divided into 104 LEAs. Each LEA is headed by a Chief Education Officer (CEO) or Director of Education whose job is to carry out the policy of the education committee which consists of local elected councillors and selected representatives of groups such as teachers and church organisations. LEAs ensure that our national educational system is locally administered, having a statutory duty under the 1944 Education Act to contribute towards the local community's spiritual, moral, mental and physical development by ensuring that 'efficient education ... shall be available to meet the needs of the population in their area'. LEAs receive their finances partly from central government via the Rate Support Grant (RSG), specific grants including in-service training of teachers, Educational Support Grants (ESG) and Section 11 funding; the remaining finance is met through the rates and income from letting charges and adult education classes.

Maintained schools – contrary to popular usage, we do not have a system of state schools in this country. Rather, most schools are maintained schools, so-called because their running costs are met by the LEA: all county *and* voluntary schools are maintained schools. The exception to this rule is that small group of schools which cater for some 7% of the total pupil population: these exist alongside the maintained schools and are known as independent (or 'private' or 'public') schools. Independent schools rely on fees, some of which are met under the government's Assisted Places Scheme.

Maintained special schools – are similar to county schools although they cater exclusively for children with special educational needs as a result of some physical or mental handicap. As a result of the 1981 Education Act children with such handicaps are being integrated into 'ordinary' schools where possible. *Hospital schools* are included in this category.

Minor authority – districts within an authority such as district councils or parish councils have a right to have a minor authority representative on the governing body of a primary school. In the ILEA (Inner London Education Authority) the minor authority is the council of a particular Inner London borough; in Wales it is the community or district council.

Mixed ability grouping – a system of class groups of wide range of pupil ability. Requires individual teaching and very skilful, well-organised teachers. (A governing body is a mixed ability group, which may be seen as a strength or a weakness, depending on the skill of the chair in bringing out individual talents and strengths) – see **banding** and **setting.**

Pupil Teacher Ratio – or PTR – a very misleading statistic which has the effect of establishing that a school contains say, one teacher for every 19 pupils, whereas class sizes may exceed 30. The PTR calculation takes the total number of pupils in a school (or LEA) and divides this by the number of full-time teachers, while taking no account of teaching staff who do little or no teaching (e.g. some heads, deputy heads, heads of department) nor of peripatetic teachers who have small groups of pupils.

Records of achievement – going hand in hand with curriculum changes and a reformed examination system are a number of pilot schemes to document secondary pupils' record of achievement. Since our system is so geared to success in public examinations, most pupils leave school with no measure of their success, capabilities or achievements in the range of experiences to which they are exposed at school. Records of achievement, which will be the result of close consultation between the students and their teachers throughout their secondary school careers, are an exciting innovation in our education system. One major pilot scheme is known as the Oxford Certificate of Educational Achievement, known as OCEA (being piloted in Somerset, Leicestershire, Coventry and Oxford); another scheme is EMRAP (being piloted in Derby, Lincolnshire, Nottinghamshire and Northamptonshire.)

It is the government's intention that by 1990 all pupils who leave school will take with them a record of achievement.

Reserved teacher – is a teacher appointed to controlled or special agreement schools according to his/her fitness to provide religious education which conforms to the provisions of the voluntary body. The foundation governors are consulted by the LEA over such appointments, and can require the LEA to dismiss a reserved teacher they deem to be incompetent in giving religious education. Schools with fewer than three staff may or may not have a reserved teacher.

Setting – a system in which pupils are grouped according to their prowess in individual subjects. A flexible system which can be incorporated in **banding** or **mixed ability** systems of classroom organisation. For example, a year group may have 210 children in seven classes and ten sets if staff are available. Setting is common in languages, maths or science subjects. This system recognises that a child has a range of talents, and may be placed in the bottom set for languages, but at the top for maths.

Technical and Vocational Education Initiative – TVEI – an MSC (Manpower Services Commission) funded and directed curriculum project piloted since 1983 in certain LEAs which aims to provide pupils of 14+ with a more relevant preparation for the transition from school to adult working life. As its name implies, the emphasis is on vocational preparation for work in a technological society. Although in 1986 only 3% of pupils eligible for the scheme participated, TVEI is set for rapid expansion. Not all pupils in a school will necessarily be on TVEI courses.

Voluntary Schools – were founded by voluntary bodies, usually churches or educational trusts who provided the premises. They constitute roughly one third of all our primary and secondary schools and they work in partnership with the LEA which is responsible for most of their running costs. Church voluntary schools have denominational religious education.

There are three groups of voluntary school:

(i) Aided schools – the largest group; the governors are required to meet 15% of certain building costs (with government grants contributing the remaining 85%). As a consequence of this, such schools are not subject to total LEA control: the governing body employs the teachers (not the LEA, although it pays their salaries) and has greater say over curriculum, admissions and finance.

(ii) Controlled schools – the LEA meets all their financial obligations. In recognition of the voluntary foundation, the governing body controls religious education.

(iii) Special Agreement – a very small group of schools, not likely to increase. They are very similar to aided schools, with slightly less independence from the LEA.

Youth Training Scheme – YTS – an MSC funded scheme of training which began in 1983 for all 16 year olds who choose the training and work experience on offer. Most training takes place with an employer and involves a period of college-based work. Initially a one-year scheme, it has now been extended to two years.

FURTHER READING

A BOOKS ABOUT GOVERNING SCHOOLS

Bacon W.	'Public accountability and the schooling system'★, *Harper and Row* 1978
Baron G.	'The Politics of School Government'★, *Pergamon* 1981
Baron G. & Howell D.	'The government and management of schools'★, *Athlone Press* 1974
Brooksbank K. & Revell J.	'School Governors'★★, *Councils and Education Press* 1981
Bullivant B.	'The Governor's Guide'★★, *Home and School Council Publications* 1979
Burgess T. & Sofer A.	'The School Governors' Handbook and Training Guide'★★★, *Kogan Page* 1986 (2nd edition)
Kogan M. *et al*	'School Governing Bodies'★, *Heinemann* 1984
Sallis J.	'The Effective School Governor'★★★, *ACE* 1980
Wragg E. & Partington J.	'A Handbook for School Governors'★★★, *Methuen* 1980

NB as general rule, the more recently the book was published, the more valuable it is to consult.

★   – academic
★★   – more readable
★★★   – recommended

B Other books of a more general nature on wider educational issues, and not quoted in other reading lists in this book, but still of interest to school governors include:

ACE	'Education A–Z: where to look things up', *ACE* 1986
Brooksbank K. (ed.)	'Educational Administration', *Councils and Educational Press* 1980
Harrison G. & Bloy D.	'Essential Law for Teachers', *Oyez Publishing* 1980

Itzin C.	'How to choose a school', *Methuen* 1985
O'Connor M.	'A Parents' Guide to Education', *Fontana* 1986
Rogers R.	'Schools under Threat', *ACE* 1979
Rutter M. *et al.*	'Fifteen Thousand Hours: Secondary Schools and their Effects on Children', *Open Books* 1979
Sallis J.	'The School in its Setting', *ACE* 1980
Sayer J.	'What Future for Secondary Schools?', *Falmer Press* 1985
Shipman M.	'Education as a Public Service', *Harper & Row* 1984

This is only a brief selection of a comprehensive and growing list of books on education available from your bookseller. The only way to keep up to date is to read those newspapers and magazines which have an education column, particularly the Guardian, Telegraph, Independent and Times: specialist papers and journals like 'The Times Educational Supplement' and 'Education' are extremely valuable sources of up-to-date information. Ask your librarian for details, and keep your ear to the ground for the latest developments!

USEFUL ADDRESSES

ADVISORY CENTRE FOR EDUCATION (ACE)
8 Victoria Park Square,
London E2 9PB.
Tel. 01 980 4596

An independent watchdog body which publishes a monthly magazine 'Where' dealing with all educational issues of interest to governors and parents; also produces many excellent publications of direct interest to governors and operates a free advice service. Well worth contacting.

CAMPAIGN FOR THE ADVANCEMENT OF STATE EDUCATION
25 Leyborne Park,
Kew Gardens,
Richmond,
Surrey.

A campaigning pressure group aiming to improve educational standards; has local groups, and publishes helpful leaflets.

DEPARTMENT OF EDUCATION AND SCIENCE (DES)
Elizabeth House,
York Road,
London SE1 7PH.
Tel. 01 928 9222.

Has overall responsibility for the administration of the education service in England – the LEAs being responsible for local administration. The DES's main concern is with national policy; it provides information and statistics; arbitrates in disputes; controls educational building and supply and training of teachers; houses H.M. Inspectorate; responsible for the administration of *Great Britain's* universities.

In Wales, education is the responsibility of:
  The Welsh Office Education Department,
  Cathays Park,
  Cardiff, CF1 3NQ.
  Tel. 0222 823360

In Scotland:
  The Scottish Education Department,
  New St Andrew's House,
  St James Centre,
  Edinburgh, EH1 3SY
  Tel. 031 556 8400

In Northern Ireland:
  The Northern Ireland Information Service,
  Stormont Castle,
  Belfast, BT4 3ST.

Each of these departments issues free comprehensive booklets about their work: very informative, useful guides.

Information about the DES is best obtained by writing to:
  DES,
  Publications Despatch Centre,
  Canons Park,
  Honeypot Lane,
  Stanmore,
  Middlesex, HA7 1AZ.

This is also the address to write to for HMI Reports, especially their periodic reviews which outline general national themes and trends; ask for their 'Education Observed' series. All this information is FREE; don't forget to mention you're a school governor. This is also the address to write to for details of the Assessment of Performance Unit (APU) which monitors children's academic performance over a wide range of subjects at different stages. The APU issues a variety of free occasional papers, leaflets, newsletters, discussion documents and summary reports.

HOME AND SCHOOL COUNCIL
81 Rustlings Road,
Sheffield, S11 7AB.

Seeks to improve communication between home and school; publishes useful, reasonably priced material.

NATIONAL ASSOCIATION OF GOVERNORS AND MANAGERS

Membership Secretary,
125 Beresford Road,
Birkenhead L43 2JD

Enrol now! For £5 membership fee you receive a comprehensive pack of information, regular newsletters, informed support and the chance to meet others locally and nationally. Help will also be given on starting your own NAGM branch locally. An excellent organisation.

NATIONAL CONFEDERATION OF PARENT TEACHER ASSOCIATIONS
43 Stonebridge Road,
Northfleet,
Gravesend,
Kent, DA11 9DS.

The support group for PTAs, well organised and with a high national profile – particularly evident during the teachers' dispute. Free advice, publications, and local groups.

NATIONAL ASSOCIATION FOR SUPPORT OF SMALL SCHOOLS
91 King Street,
Norwich, NR1 1PM.

Falling school rolls have meant that many schools, particularly rural ones, have felt vulnerable. This association can give useful advice.

Index